BENNY'S RUN ASHORE

BENNY'S RUN ASHORE

Harry Guest

ASHRIDGE PRESS

Published by:
Ashridge Press
41 Humberston Avenue, Humberston,
Nr Grimsby, Lincolnshire DN36 4SW

ISBN 1 901214 45 1

*I thank Julie Headley, Patrick Otter and Barry Herbert for their professional help,
guidance and encouragement. Gill for support and enthusiasm, and Margery for
always being there.
Enjoy life, it's there for living!*

Typesetting, design & production:
Country Books, Little Longstone, Derbyshire DE45 1NN

Cover origination:
GA Graphics, Stamford, Lincolnshire PE9 2RE

Printed & bound by:
MFP Design & Print, Stretford, Manchester M32 0JT

CHAPTER ONE

There was but the whisper of a breeze and the sea so calm the mill pond itself would have blushed with shame.

In the ghostly light of first dawn, His Majesty's destroyer Consort sliced her way almost silently through the waters off the west coast of Malaya, moving with phantom-like grace, a picture of sheer power and sleek beauty.

She had no need of speed for this was yet another of those mundane but essential routine patrols seeking out gun runners who sought to aid the terrorists in the jungles of Malaysia in 1948.

The shadowy figure wending its way from the bridge to the upper deck paused briefly to survey the peaceful scene before moving on to finally disappear through a hatchway leading to the crew's mess-decks up forward.

With practised ease the figure bobbed, ducked and warily weaved his way, skilfully avoiding contact with the hammocks slung overhead and with so little space in which to move any observer would realise this young seaman had performed this duty many many times.

Reaching a ladder in the bows, the seaman descended and repeated the function of dodging hammocks and their occupants. He was obliged to bend low, hindered by the legs and arms dangling from the hammocks.

He came to a halt at the foot of a hammock slung in a corner on the port side. Easing himself upright he took a hold of it, lightly, then gingerly shook it.

"Chef! Come on, it's nearly five o'clock." His whisper brought instant response for the hammock's occupant proved to be a light sleeper and at the first touch his eyes were open.

"I'm awake Smokey! I'm awake!" whispered Chef and as if to prove the point he stirred himself. Smokey, satisfied Chef really was awake, turned to depart knowing from experience that the ship's cook required no further calling.

Indeed, Smokey had hardly vanished from view before Chef had tossed aside the solitary blanket and in a swift movement was standing on the mess-deck. He was stark naked, a normal practice aboard since the sticky atmosphere below decks was stifling and there was no comfort to be had wearing clothes, however brief.

From habit and convenience Chef had placed his neatly folded underpants and white tropical shorts inside his 'mick' just above his pillow the night before. His shoes, tied together by their laces, were draped over the hammock's clews, one sock nestling in each.

He reached up, retrieved his pants and shorts and put them on, then, carefully, extricated his shoes and socks which he carried over to his locker, one of several running fore and aft, which doubled as additional seating. There he completed dressing before taking a pair of horn-rimmed spectacles from his own locker, giving them a perfunctory wipe on his shorts before putting them on, at the same time moving off in the general direction of the ladder leading up.

In no time at all he was out on deck gulping down the cooler, fresher morning air and after treating himself to a minute of pleasure at what he saw and felt around himself, he gave a contented grunt, stretched and made his way towards the ship's galley.

The ship's main galley was small but well planned and equally well equipped, situated between the forecastle structure and the funnel and taking the form of a cross. The port-starboard arm contained the large oil-fired range and ovens on the one side and the tiny officer's galley on the other, while the tail, running fore and aft, housed the sink and preparation tables to port and the dough and breadbins to starboard.

Chef glanced around his domain, satisfied himself all was in order and then from the top drawer in a set of three he took a small biscuit tin. From this he withdrew shaving kit, soap, toothpaste and toothbrush, fitted the plug into the sink, turned on the taps and humming softly but cheerily to himself commenced his morning ablutions.

This completed, he replaced the tin in the drawer and opened the bottom one, fumbling briefly before he unearthed a box of matches and a small matted clump of cotton waste. Crossing to the range he crouched to open up the valve allowing a strong current of air to hiss its way up and around the flues clearing out any residual fumes. He then closed the valve and opened the small door of the firehole into which he dropped the cotton waste. Now he turned on the oil valve allowing the fuel to run into the shallow pan and he watched until just enough had been soaked up by the ball of waste before turning off the valve.

Taking a match from the box he struck it and held it out until the tiny flame licked at the oil-soaked waste. After a hesitant flicker, the match went out.

"Sod it!" growled Chef fumbling for a second match. This time all went as planned and as the flames grew he closed the firehole door and turned on both air and oil fuel valves increasing or decreasing the flow until happy he had the correct mixture. The wrong mixture would result in dense black smoke belching from the galley smoke-stack and that would never do. It would be a dead giveaway, it being seen drifting up on the horizon long before the ship itself hove into view and would bring the skipper down on him like a ton of bricks.

He replaced the matches then washed his hands well to rid them of smell from the diesel fuel. He then surveyed the array of trays, dish-es, pots and pans spread before him on the lid of the large wooden doughbin.

It was the responsibility of each and every mess to supply their own breakfast requirement. It was Chef's duty to ensure it was cooked. The mixture of cookware lying before his gaze contained the hoped-for breakfasts of each mess. As he stood deliberating Smokey entered unheard.

"'Nother nice mornin', Chef," said Smokey at the same time unable to resist the temptation of poking his finger into one of the trays. He should have known better for the cook reacted like a coiled snake and Smokey whipped his hand away just in time to escape the rolling pin which thudded down.

"Keep y' thievin' 'ands off!" snarled Chef.

"Christ! You're a right mardy arse this mornin'," complained the unhappy seaman.

7

Chef tossed him an old fashioned look but said nothing, preferring to busy himself instead. "Pass me that tray of sausages."

Smokey reached out with his long arm and taking hold of the tray passed it to Chef as requested. Chef bunged it into an oven. "Yes sir, it's a smashin' mornin' an' no mistake," and as he spoke the seaman passed a tray of bacon.

"Just think," said the seaman gazing dreamily out to sea, "people pay thousands an' thousands of damned good money just to go on cruises an' 'ere we are gettin' it all for free."

This observation brought instant response from Chef. "Oh no we bloodywell ain't gerrin' it for free," he snapped. "We're workin' for it mate," adding with pointed sarcasm. "At least, some of us are."

Smokey pretended not to hear. "Just look at how calm an' peaceful it is. I can't imagine anybody gettin' seasick when it's like this, can you Chef?"

"Not so much seasick as sick of the sea," the cook's mood turned to one of thoughtful concern now. "Smokey, 'ave you 'eard 'ow long this blasted patrol is goin' to last?"

The seaman leaned round to face Chef. With feigned indifference he said, "I might 'ave."

"Well?"

Smokey was enjoying his moment. "According to the buzz I heard, mind you, it is only a buzz so perhaps I shouldn't say anything but I heard on the grapevine that we are going to Port Swettenham."

"Oh no! I don't bloody believe it." The news, true or not, had stopped Chef dead in his tracks. He stood there, shattered, praying that this Cockney character was joking.

But Smokey was not joking. "I 'eard the officer of the watch goin' on about it last night."

"What the 'ell do we want to go there for? Why that God forsaken 'ole? Why in God's name can't we go somewhere else? Somewhere where there's a bit of soddin' life?" Getting no response from his colleague he resigned himself to getting on with the chores.

As he divided his attention between stirring porridge, turning bacon and sausage in the oven, cracking eggs in the huge frying pan and checking eggs were on the boil, he let out the occasional expletive and moan.

"Port bloody Swettenham!" He checked the tank holding boiling water for tea and coffee making. It was almost empty. "Oh balls to it! Smokey, do me a favour will you? Top this water tank up for me will you? Otherwise there'll be no water for making tea."

"Yeah! Sure!"

"Wouldn't it be nice to go somewhere like the West Indies for a change," mused Chef having got used to the idea of Port Swettenham.

As the seaman filled the tank he asked where it was Chef would really like to go.

"I don't know. Anywhere really. Just as long as there's wine, women and song, where there's a bit of bloody life for a change. Honest to God, I'm really pissed off."

"Ain't we all," grinned Smokey. He had known his mate long enough to know he was in no way as despondent as he would have one believe.

"That's plenty. Don't put any more in otherwise it'll never boil in time."

"Bloody 'ell, I'll 'ave to shoot off." The mention of time had caused Smokey to glance at the clock. He hastily replaced the lid on the water tank and without further ado was gone.

Some four hours later found Chef lying on the bench seat outside the galley, basking in the warmth of the sun, completely relaxed in the knowledge that Jock, the Scottish chef, whose turn of duty it happened to be, was keeping an expert eye on things.

The smaller galley placed aft was Jock's true domain but he and Chef normally split the duties leaving the Petty Officer cook to concern himself with all the breadmaking.

The P.O. was happy to leave all the general cooking to his subordinates knowing they were quite competent. On the odd occasion he would perform duties for one or the other so enabling them to pop ashore. He himself seldom had the inclination to step ashore, boastfully claiming to have seen it all before. The truth lay nearer to the fact that he was something of a miser amassing every penny he could as some security for the future.

There were those, too, who insisted his diminutive wife was the instigator of his tightfistedness. Those who had met her spoke of how dominant she was, how her shrill voice set one's nerves on edge. They even went so far as to express feeling sorrow for their sinewy shipmate.

The tranquil scene was rudely shattered by the piercing blast of the bosun's pipe, pervading every department of the ship through her broadcasting system, commonly and correctly referred to as the S.R.E.

"Now what the 'ell's up?" growled Scouse, the burly, bearded stoker sitting on the bench at Chef's feet.

Over the S.R.E. came the sound of their skipper's voice. Loud and full of authority if not exactly distinct.

"Do you hear there! Do you hear there! This is your captain speaking." There was a pause perhaps allowing time for this fact to register, perhaps for dramatic effect but certainly now, all ears aboard HMS Consort were tuned in.

The skipper was heard to clear his throat and then he commenced. "During these last few days it has become painfully obvious that a great number of you are becoming apathetic towards your duties. I daresay that is understandable to some extent but it cannot be tolerated. Whilst appreciating the fact that we see little or no action, that all we er ... that all we er ... do ... is to cruise up and down ..."

"'E's lost 'is place," sniggered someone. He got a chorus of shushes for his trouble.

"... this is no excuse. This task we are undertaking is most vital and necessary. It is up to us to ensure no arms or ammunition reaches those terrorists via the sea and I am sure you are all aware of that. So! In order to bring a little discipline and interest back I have decided to undertake a spot of anti-submarine drill."

This was met with a loud sarcastic cheer.

"However ..." continued the captain "... that is not all ... I propose to take full advantage of the situation. Firstly we shall be dropping depth charges. This should refresh us all and put us back on our toes. Secondly, if all goes well, you could be refreshed another way ..." He paused and the huddled groups of listeners exchanged puzzled glances. "The dropping of depth charges should, hopefully, have the effect of scaring off any sharks and so I have given permission for hands to bathe."

These last words resulted in a spontaneous burst of cheering from all quarters. Faces beamed with joyful expectation. No one appeared bored now.

"Thirdly ..." still the captain went on "... I have arranged for a boat's crew to be available to pick up any fish that may be stunned by the charges, one never knows, it could possibly help out with the mess funds. Right. That is all."

The conclusion of this news brought forth another gratuitous cheer which was followed by a hive of noisy, boisterous activity as the crew departed in search of towels and swimming trunks, heedless of the fact that no mention of exactly when ëhands to batheí would be.

Chef turned to Scouse for reassurance before the big fellow hurried off.

"Do you think the depth-charges really will frighten away any sharks?" he asked.

"'Ow the fuck should I flamin' well know?"

"Alright, alright, no need for that," grinned Chef. "I just thought that a man with your vast knowledge would know all there was to know."

Chef had anticipated the sweeping backhander launched in his direction and leaned well out of harmís way. The outsize fist went whizzing past his nose to make painful contact with the bulkhead behind. "Aw shit!" bellowed the stoker jumping up to perform jiglike antics in an effort to ease the pain from his knuckles.

"Fuck off you little bastard!" roared the stoker making a quick grab at his tormentor but Chef was quicker and gone.

It was at this point that he bumped into Jock who was just coming out of the after-galley.

"I wuz just comin' lookin' f'uze Benny," he said, using his colleague's designated Christian name.

"Why? What's up?"

"Nothin', on'y if yuze want tae gae fae a swim ah'll tak' care o' things t'll y' get back."

"Aw thanks Jock mate. You're a real pal, honest. But can you manage both galleys, I mean, it's a lot to ask."

The expression on the Scot's face showed clearly what he felt about this remark. "Dinna be s'stupid mon. Y'didnae ask, I offered. Besides, are yuze f'gettin' ah've served on much bigger ships than this een?"

"Alright haggisface. Don't go gettin' a kink in your kilt. Anyway, tell you what, I'll bring you a nice big fat juicy fish back, alright?"

"Yuze jest bide y'time awhile laddie. Yuze jest let me get m'tot afor y'go. Once ah've got m'bubbly y'can dae as y'amind."

"Bloody 'ell Jock. They 'aven't even piped 'Up spirits' yet."

"Aye. I ken. An' they 'avnae piped 'ands tae bathe either so yuze jest 'old on a mintae."

Even as the Scot uttered the words the unique cry of the bosun's pipe whistled its proclamation. Tot time had arrived, the time when men from all sections of the ship not on duty and entitled to partake the Navy's beloved tradition of a daily issue of rum, sometimes called grog but likely bubbly, a more affectionate term, would make their separate ways to the various messdecks to imbibe.

Later, Jock returned to find Benny giving their P.O. a good start by knocking back the dough for him. The P.O. insisted on performing the actual kneading and baking himself, claiming that it not only relieved the monotony but also served to beget a fair degree of physical fitness. His staff, however, knew better. Truth was, he harboured a great pride in his breadmaking craft and justifiably so for Petty Officer Leonard Bancroft was acknowledged to be the best baker in the fleet.

Five minutes later Benny was savouring his own tot of rum. The messes were positively bustling with activity. Everyone seemed in a great hurry to finish off whatever chores they had, intent only on getting away for that refreshing swim.

"My God! This rum takes some lickin'," vowed Benny standing next in line. His senses savoured the strong aroma, issuing from the rum tub. He ran his tongue round his lips and smacked his mouth with deliberate exaggeration.

"Takes some licking? You are not supposed to lick it! You are supposed to drink the bleeding stuff!" snapped the rum bosun, clearly not amused.

"I hope you're not going for a swim by any chance, Chef!" The speaker was standing beside the rum tub, guardlike, and what a man. Pedlar Palmer stood five feet ten and measured almost a yard across his powerful shoulders. He was a gentle giant, gentle that is until roused but then, there were few who could call to mind the last time they had seen him lose his temper. Not unnaturally, he was greatly admired and much respected. Chef was a firm favourite of his, much smaller by comparison and Pedlar had, as it were, taken him under his wing.

Benny stood staring up at the big man askance. Was he sickening for something? Had he gone mental? "Am I going for a swim?" He glanced round at the grinning faces and began to suspect they were setting him up. "What kind of silly bloody question is that? Of course I'm going for a swim."

No one moved or spoke. They simply grinned and stared. "All right. What's so funny? Why shouldn't I go for a swim?" He stared up into Pedlar's face. "Come on! Why?"

With no change in his tone or stance the big chap smiled and said. "Why? I'll tell you why, my little cock sparrow. Because if you are going swimming you won't need your tot," and he placed a large fatherly arm around Chef.

"'Ave you flipped your lid or somethin'," he replied, pulling away.

"No I haven't. I'm telling you gospel Chef, going swimming on a tot and an empty stomach plays funny tricks."

"Bullshit! You just listen to me, you big sod, I've known you long enough now to know what's goin' on in that tiny mind of yours an' if you think you can kid me into givin' you my tot you've got another think comin'!"

"Aw Chef. You've got me all wrong. Honest."

Pedlar's pained expression and innocent tone created roars of laughter from the matelots around them. One, a short, plump, bald-headed rating, put his spoke in.

"Ol' Pedlar's right, Cookie. I got terrible cramp once when I went swimmin' after my tot."

"You twit! If you raised your eyebrows sharpish you'd get soddin' cramp. And don't call me Cookie either!"

This retort brought more howls of laughter from the others and several of them started to shout advice and guidance all at the same time.

"I'll tell you somethin', shall I, Pedlar?" Benny had raised his voice to be heard above the hubbub and he did a bit of finger prodding for emphasis. "You know only too well 'ow it breaks my 'eart to part with even a sniff of my tot, right?"

"Yeah, right."

"Right! An' you know that even when it's somebody's birthday or anniversary or when I've lost sippers in a bet, you know that even then it makes my poor 'eart bleed to part with the slightest drop."

"We all know that, Chef."

"Yeah! Well your 'eart can bleed now mate cos you ain't gettin' a single drop of my tot, so stuff that up your arse."

"Alright then. But just you remember this ..." Pedlar was doing the finger prodding bit now but with the difference of approximately one hundred pounds in weight, "...don't come running to me if you get into difficulties and drown."

"If I drown, you daft bastard, I won't be able to go runnin' to anybody."

And through all this humorous battle of words their audience grew. It was a commonplace situation between the two, so like a double comedy act.

"Right then! I hope you do drown and I'll tell you something for nothing. If you come anywhere near to me in the water I'll make sure you friggin' well drown!"

"Now Ped', you know you don't mean that."

"I know I bloody well do, and I'll tell you why. Nothing would give me greater pleasure than to bounce up and down on your skinny little chest, trying to pump the fuckin' water out. Alright. And as far as your tot is concerned. You can stick it up your arse."

Without further ado Chef calmly, deliberately and so dramatically, drank it down. Then, adding insult to injury he wiped the glass round with a finger which he licked and waved beneath the big one's nose.

"You lousy little swine!" Pedlar made a grab for his tormentor but he was yards too slow. "Let me get at him. I'll strangle the little bleeder," he snarled. Too late, for the ship's cook was far nimbler and all that Pedlar could do was to barge through the laughing throng after him.

Out on deck Chef saw that Consort was now moving forward at a fair old rate of knots. "Where's the fire?" he asked a seaman passing by.

"We're making a run to drop the depth charges," the seaman told him nodding sternwards by way of indication.

Chef turned his head just in time to see the first missiles hurtling through the air into the sea. They quickly exploded, throwing up tons of boiling water. The shattering roar shook the ship and for a split second Chef got the impression that the sea around them had been vibrated by an earthquake.

The mountainous splurge had hardly subsided before a second pair were on their way. The first pair had been fired simultaneously from either side of the stern but this time they rolled off the stern, guided by rails, again one from portside one from starboard, the ship's 'screws' propelling her rapidly forward out of harm's way.

Dotted here and there were a dozen or so crew members, all having sought the best vantage points without getting in the way of the duty watch or anyone involved in the task of releasing the deadly canisters.

Most men remain boys at heart and Benny more than most. A stimulating sensation coursed his veins as he waited for the detonation and just as he feared something must have gone wrong the sea erupted yet again.

"Fire!" bellowed the young officer in charge.

Two short, sharp reports cracked the air, echoing out into the distance and from either side near the stern more canisters were rocketed upwards and outwards, turning over and downwards after only a few feet, their short journey terminating with their unceremonious entry into the sea.

This time the explosions brought forth salt water, sand and seaweed, spewing violently forth, a certain indication of the detonation taking place right on the sea bed. There was the merest fraction of time elapse between the two charges.

Immediately after these two explosions, the officer in command of the situation signalled the bridge and at once Consort veered hard to starboard and cut her speed dramatically until she hove to as near the centre of the exercise as possible.

With the minimum delay the officer of the watch ordered the swinging out of the boom and the lowering of the rope ladder attached to it, all in readiness for 'hands to bathe'. This ladder would assist both the swimmers and the launch being dropped for safety and other factors, the skipper leaving nothing to chance.

While this went on, some matelots had already adorned themselves in swim trunks while others were keen to follow suit. More were scanning the water, eager to be the first to spot stunned fish or anything else that had fallen foul of the blasts.

The S.R.E. crackled into life. The bosun's pipe heralded the voice of the bosun himself, broadcasting the good tidings, 'hands to bathe on the port side'.

The duty officer surveyed the scene and barred the entry into the sea, waiting until most would-be bathers were assembled before addressing them. "Right you have thirty minutes only, got that? We want no heroics or schoolboy pranks and remember to keep your wits about you. Right! Off you go and don't forget, thirty minutes."

They needed no second bidding and the men swarmed past the officer to plunge, dive, jump and somersault from the ship's side, yelling, yodelling and cheering like ecstatic school boys.

Chef was not one of the early birds. He was hurrying back to the galley having forgotten to place his spectacles in a safe spot and made directly for the drawer in the galley in which he kept a few personal items.

"'Ey! Haggisface! Want me to bring you a nice Scotch salmon back?" he asked, opening the drawer and popping in his 'specs'.

"Ah'll gi' ye salmon y'Sassenach ye!" and catching Benny unawares he whacked him across the buttocks with the fish-slice he held.

"Ouch!" yelled Chef. "You lousy Scots git you, I'll ..." He stopped. Jock held the upper hand and he advanced, hand raised menacingly, threatening to repeat the swipe which already had weal marks glowing painfully on Benny's unprotected flesh.

"Now come on Jock. Cut it out, there's a good un. Come on else I'll be too late for a swim." In an attempt to thwart the Scot he faced him squarely, keeping his rear close to the set of drawers. He tried to sidle along but Jock was enjoying himself too much to give up so easily.

Instead of heeding poor Benny's plea Jock reached over and picked up a wicked looking carving knife, holding it menacingly he tossed the fish-slice away from him and out of Chef's reach. A sadistic grin spread across his face.

"Now laddie, 'ow would y'like y'wee cock-a-doodle cut off?"

"'Ey now, stop pissin' about!"

"If I cut y'wee cock off yuze would nae be able tae piss an' that's f'sure."

"Come on Jock, be a good un. The half hour's nearly over."

"Aye! But ye're nae goin' till y'say sorry."

"Sorry for what, for Christ's sake?"

Alex raised the knife and threatened to move in for the kill.

"Alright! I'm sorry," cried Benny feigning real terror but knowing the tricks Jock could get up to when he'd had more than his own share of rum.

The Scot stood back, laughing. "Ye'd best be off afore yon fish are all gone."

"Bollocks, you haggis faced bastard!" Chef snapped but not before he felt safe. He need not have worried for his words brought forth more laughter from Jock. He was still laughing when he watched Benny clamber over the guardrail to hesitate fleetingly before diving gracefully from view.

The sea was quite warm and felt wonderful to Benny after the clammy heat both below decks and in the galley.

"Oh boy, this is the life," he thought, swimming gently away from the ship. Suddenly his heart skipped a beat for he sensed he saw something silvery, glisten and shimmer down there just beneath him and ahead. So brief a glimpse he had, he at once thought it to be merely a product of his imagination.

But no. There it was again. Excitement took over from the initial shock when he realised it to be nothing more than an unfortunate fish, a victim of man's powers of destruction.

As it drifted nearer the surface, lying on its side, Benny was instantly reminded of a pet goldfish that had died years before. That too had no sense of balance and floundered about upside down in its globular prison until mercifully the end came.

Casting his fears aside Chef dived down until he grabbed the fish by its tail and hauled it to the surface.

It closely resembled the shape of a goldfish and the colour was similar but the size, now that was something else. It was all of eighteen inches long and of a rich hue, blending from reddish gold along the top through to harvest gold, then silver and finally to white along the belly.

Treading water, feeling sorry at its plight but elated that he had the good fortune to have stumbled across it, he felt a tingling sensation run along the bottom of his left foot.

Fear gripped him instantly. Without realising why, from instinct perhaps, he thrashed his arms and legs wildly, causing as much disturbance as he could, hoping in his panic to scare away the massive shark which he feared had dared to come so close.

Then, as quickly as fear had taken over, realisation came to him.

Fool, what else would it be but another fish?   He scanned the depths around him and there, sure enough, was a second helpless creature. Benny almost burst out laughing with relief.

Having chided himself he dived to retrieve this second fish. Suddenly there was another. Then another and another and another. He was beside himself with excitement now and would surely have danced for joy had he been on terra firma.

"Oh boy, oh boy!" he cried gleefully. "This'll shake the lads. Just wait till they see this little lot."

Why should he not applaud himself? Had he not outsmarted them by swimming towards the bows while most of them had settled for the stern end?

He was busy harvesting his crop, all, amazingly, of roughly the same size and colour and species. Surfacing yet again, a fish grasped in each hand, he herded them as closely together as he was able until he had a small shoal which he surveyed with some pride.

All this exertion and effort had played havoc with Chef's insides and he found himself with no option but to belch out loud. A noxious mixture of stomach juices laced with rancorous rum bubbled up to settle at the back of his throat, the tincture of rum stinging, bringing a tear to the eye.

"Damn and blast it!" he cursed. He recalled the words of Pedlar Palmer, decided discretion was best and considered how best to traverse the distance back to the safety of the ship. After all, there was this small matter of the fish.

He raised his head expecting Consort to be no more than yards away but no, she appeared to be miles off. "Oh my God, no!" he cried out aloud. Panic threatened to engulf him again yet somehow, strangely, some spark of reasoning stayed with him. He was not to know Consort had steamed off to check something.

Could it be a tidal current? Not likely since others would most probably have been caught up in it too. Yes, but had not the others been swimming nearer the stern?

"Christ! I should never 'ave 'ad that damned tot. If I get cramp now I've bloodywell 'ad it!"

Whether the thoughts of rum did it or not, who can say, but a second eruption took over his throat.

"Steady Benny lad. Steady. Just remember all they told you. Don't get your knickers in a twist. Do it like they said. Relax, that's it, take it nice and easy. Float, conserve all your energy. The minute they realise you are missing they'll come looking for you. But suppose they don't find you? Rubbish! Of course they'll find you."

It was then that he saw a head and arms moving through the water a mere twenty yards or so away. His heart jumped. His spirits soared. There, quite close to this first swimmer was another, then another, then a fourth, a fifth, there were swimmers all round the place, drifting and floating quite leisurely to and fro, as the mood took them.

Hardly believing his eyes he called out to them, joyfully, waving. The nearest waved and shouted back. Funny. Even the ship appeared to be getting nearer. Strange he had not noticed the other swimmers earlier. Had he perhaps been blinded by fear, he wondered, hating to admit he really had been scared.

Yet through it all he had, subconsciously, been a good shepherd to his flock of fish and he grinned broadly as this fact dawned. He grabbed the nearest fish and heaved it mightily in the general direction of Consort. He snatched up a second and repeated the process, then a third and so on and so on until every single fish had been hurled twenty odd feet closer to the ship.

He then swam after them, steadily, musing that perhaps his eyes had played tricks on him. Again he had cause to recall Pedlar Palmer's words of warning. Could he have been right? Was it the rum?

Chef acknowledged his shortsightedness yet found it hard to accept that his eyes were to blame for thinking the ship miles away and he was in mortal danger. Benny was not to know it at the time but later he would learn the truth of the matter and that there never had been any danger at all.

Having reached his haul of fish, now spreadeagled somewhat, he repeated the performance of hurling them in the direction of Consort. Again he swam after them and again he heaved them from him, his aim getting a trifle wild the wearier he got.

Finally the destroyer lay only feet from him. Just as well for Chef had totally spent himself with all the swimming, throwing and not to mention the constant vexation and discomfort of rum-induced indigestion.

Benny never quite knew how he managed to swim those last few feet. Indeed, he would not have made it if helping hands had not reached out mercifully.

A surge of relief overcame him now as he allowed his shipmates to take control of the fish he had brought, passing them along from hand to hand, along, up and over onto the deck. He himself collapsed in a heap on the deck.

Knackered or not, poor Chef found it necessary to move himself for the sun had heated the steel deck to a most uncomfortable degree. He scrambled upright and commenced the task of humping his catch galleywards.

Alex stood propping up the galley doorway. He had a totally blank expression on his face.

"'Ey Alex! Quick! Go an' get your camera an' take a picture of this little lot," suggested Benny. He held two of the fish aloft, striking a dramatic posture but the Scot did not so much as bat an eyelid.

"'Ow's this then 'aggisface. Cop a look at this lot!" persisted Chef.

"Y've got tae be jokin', supposin' yuze jest come an' hae a look at this wee lot," and as he spoke Jock's jerking thumb invited his chum to take a gander inside the galley.

Without a word, Benny ambled forward to peer beyond Jock at the interior of their work domain, allowing a moment to accustom his eyes to the darker aspect.

"Oh no!" Shattered by what he saw, he stood there, shaking his head. "I just do not believe it. Alex," he pleaded. "Tell me it's all a dirty rotten trick somebody is playin', please Alex tell me it's a mirage."

Jock said nothing. Did nothing but stare back at Benny that is, the look on his face said it all.

"But Jock ... I've never seen so many fish. Not in all my born days." They were strewn in every nook and cranny making the galley look like a corner of Billingsgate.

But Jock was far from finished. "By the way Benny lad, ah hope y've a very sharp knife 'andy, y'll be 'ere till the cows come 'ame, cleanin' an' guttin' that wee lot."

He flopped onto the galley step, cupping head in hands completely, totally, desolate. He barely felt the hot metal of the step, burning through his trunks.

"Och! Y'poor wee soul yuze. Come an' tell y'auld mate all aboot it then," scoffed the Scot as he placed a falsely comforting arm about Chef's shoulders, being totally unprepared for the reaction he got.

With amazing speed for one who was supposedly shattered, Benny leapt up, grabbed the nearest fish by its tail and belaboured the unfortunate Jock until one blow caught him full in the mouth causing him to spit and splutter with distaste. The force sent him reeling back into the galley where he landed with a squelch among the fish.

"Right y'Sassenach bastard ye, two can play at that game," and he grabbed a fish and launched an attack of his own. And so commenced a right royal battle. They stood there, toe to toe, attempting murder by fish flagellation.

Right into the centre of this farce strode none other than P.O. Bancroft. Not realising the danger he walked into the galley and straight into a mouthful of fish.

He performed an amazing about turn and tried to retreat as he yelled at them to cease fire, spitting out morsels left behind by the fish that struck him. Unfortunately he neither ducked nor retreated in time, for another flying fish sent his peaked cap sailing through the air to land in a large pan of potatoes boiling on the top of the range.

This brought hostilities to an abrupt conclusion. Shocked silence reigned.

The rich tan drained from the petty officer's face, leaving a countenance white with rage. This gave way to a blood-bursting purple and with eyes closed in an effort of self control, the P.O. concentrated intensely on retaining his dignity.

He opened his eyes. Benny and Jock were transfixed, mortified with humility. He glared down at them from his height of six feet, still not trusting himself to mouth one single syllable.

He continued to burn them up with his eyes. First Alex, then Chef, then Alex, then finally askance at what he could see of his cap bubbling away. Still without a word he held out a hand, potwards, his eyes returning to Benny, who was nearest the pot. The unhappy cook got the message and retrieved the steaming mess that was once his superior's titfer. He held it out for the P.O. to take, spilling water from it as he did so, ignoring the fact it was scalding his fingers.

The petty officer snatched it from him and from force of habit he almost put his cap on but remembered in time and instead hung it on one of the door latches.

"Right! What's it all about then?" he snarled.

The pair stood there, erect and motionless, naval discipline and training there for all to see. Neither spoke.

"Well?"

This time they both went to speak at once.

"We were just ..." started Benny.

"Having a we ..." began Alex.

"One at a time! You pathetic morons!"

"We were just lettin' a bit of steam off, Chief, that's all," explained Benny. Although only a petty officer, most crew members referred to him as Chief.

"Oh! I see. Just letting off steam?"

"Yes Chief."

"I see. An' that's all?"

"Yes Chief," they said together.

"I see! Then perhaps you would be good enough to tell me what in God's name all this lot is!" His voice had risen in volume as the sentence unfolded. A sweep of his hand indicated the mounds of fish.

"It's fish, Chief," said Benny all innocence.

"Fish?" roared the P.O.

"Yes Chief. Fish," confirmed Jock.

If the look on their superior's face was anything to go by they would have dropped dead. He rocked back and forth on his heels, the muscles of his face working overtime.

"Very funny indeed! I'm surprised you're not on the music halls." His voice was full of sarcasm and menace. "Whoís dumped all this lot in my galley?"

"I guess it's all mar fault Chief. I told the lads it would be a'right," confessed Jock.

"Oh! I see. You told them it would be okay did you? Well, fancy that. They didn't by any chance offer you any er ... inducement did they, eh?" His voice tinged with sarcastic innuendo.

"Och weel! One or two may 'ave offered sippers but ..."

"Sippers!" the P.O. exploded. They stared at him open mouthed. "And while you were negotiating your precious sippers, I don't suppose you gave a thought to the bread?"

"Bread, Chief?" asked the perplexed Scot.

"That's what I said, bread! You know, that stuff you make toast with. The stuff, the very same stuff and no other stuff that I have got to make from dough this very afternoon. The stuff I have to bung into the oven and bake until it is a nice crisp golden brown ... !" His voice had become a crescendo but his manner abruptly changed from threatening inferno to mild menace. He spoke so softly but with much intimidation and slow deliberation.

"You know what bread is, surely?"

"O' aye Chief, I do. It's jest that ah'd forgotten all aboot it."

"That, you little Scot clot!, is painfully obvious!"

"Perhaps we can all muckle in taegether Chief."

"Muckle in together? You mean knuckle in, you illiterate twit."

"I don't Chief, I mean muckle."

"Shut up! If I say you mean knuckle in, you mean knuckle in! What do you mean?"

"Knuckle in, Chief," agreed Alex but under his breath mumbled, "but I mean muckle in really."

Alex then tried another tack. "Och Chief, I could nae disappoint the lads wi' their wee fishes, now could I?"

"Bullshit! Couldn't disappoint the lads indeed! Couldn't disappoint yourself you mean. You never could resist the chance of extra grog and I thought you Scots were mad on whisky, not rum."

"Och we are, Chief, we are. But y'ken a wee drappie ony spirit disnae come amiss."

For what seemed an eternity, the P.O. stood there shaking his head ruefully until finally he heaved a mighty sigh of decision, throwing them off balance but happily so as it happened.

"Well, one thing's for sure," he resolved. "The bread has got to be baked and it won't get baked while this stinking lot's in the way, will it?"

"No Chief," they chorused, exchanging thankful glances.

"Right, then! First of all, get round to all the mess cooks and tell them to bring up every dish and tray, bucket, bowl, basin, anything, anything at all suitable to put this lot in and as soon as dinner is out of the way all three of us will need to get stuck in with this lot and the bread."

"Dinnae fret y'sel Chief, it's mar fault so ah'll get stuck intae it m'sel."

This remark caused the P.O. to finally succumb and he snatched up a fish, and as the Scot turned away to avoid the onslaught he belted him hard on the back of the neck with it.

"Don't talk like a stupid arsehole," he yelled. "What pissing time do you think we would be finished? The dough hasn't even been weighed off yet, or kneaded, or any damned thing else don't forget! Right! I want you both in here immediately after dinner and I can promise you you're going to work your balls off."

He moved to leave, reaching for his cap he put it on, forgetting all about its sorry state. It took his subordinates every bit of will power to keep them from roaring with laughter at the sight of him. Just as well for instead of departing he had stopped to turn and face Alex.

"And as for you, you great Scots ..." he decided against saying what he had in mind. "You just remember this! I shall want a fair share of any rum coming your way. Got that?"

Without waiting for Jock's answer, his answer would not have mattered anyway, he strode off.

The pair stared at each other, shrugged their shoulders signifying acceptance of defeat. While Benny prepared the midday meal as best he could, Alex went off to inform the mess cooks to bring all available receptacles to the galley if they wanted their fish cooking, threatening: "Nae trays, nae fish!"

CHAPTER TWO

As near twelve-thirty as makes no difference, Benny returned to the galley, having finished his dinner, or the little of it that he had fancied

He reviewed the spectacle before him, punting a couple of fish across the galley deck with his sandalled foot. The only purpose served by this act of depression was to add even further to it. One of them hit a table leg with sufficient enough force to start a small avalanche deckwards.

Shaking his head at the futility of it all he picked his way over to the sink and, placing the bung in the hole with one hand, he turned on the cold tap with the other.

Leaving the sink to fill to the desired level he sought a large bin which he dropped noisily into a handy spot.

"Christ!" he grumbled, staring around again at the mounds of fish and again shaking his head. "We'll be 'ere till bleedin' doomsday!"

Opening a drawer he took out a knife and as though blaming the unfortunate fishes he plucked one up and slit its belly open savagely and tossed the gutted carcase into an empty tray, its entrails into the waiting bin.

"You're just as bloody stupid," he growled, picking up a second fish. He put his nose close to the scaly creature which stared back at him with its lifeless eyes.

"Don't you realise all the trouble you are causing your poor old mum and dad?" he asked it, half expecting an answer. "Don't you realise they are probably searching all over the 'oggin' for you, worryin' to death about you."

He gazed about himself. "I don't know, though. Accordin' to this soddin' lot, your mum and dad will be 'ere. Still, one consolation, you'll all be gone together to that big fishy 'eaven in the sky. Now, 'old still, this is goin' to 'urt me more than it is you." With that, he gutted the second fish.

As his thoughts wandered, the sudden sound of splashing water stopped him dead.

"Oh shit!" he yelled springing frantically round to turn off the forgotten tap. Plunging his hand into the water he pulled out the plug and watched until the level was where he wanted in the first place, then returned to gutting the fish.

"Hello! Where's Haggis then?"

Chef looked up, not having seen or heard the P.O. enter. "No idea Chief, I ain't seen 'im," he said.

"Well, I hope for his sake he hasn't dropped off to sleep somewhere."

"Ye're a'right Chiefy, ah'm 'ere, ah'm 'ere," sniggered Jock having crept in behind the P.O.

"Well get round here where I can see you. And take that stupid grin off your face! These tiddlers are better looking."

Alex knew better than to argue. He reached into the drawer for a knife and joined Benny.

The petty officer himself selected a small knife and joined them and all three now, mindful of the urgency, toiled expeditiously.

"Jesus! Just look at this bleedin' blister!" cried Benny breaking the silence to display the painful postule in his palm.

"Och! Y'not the on'y one. Yuze jest look at mine," said Alex, not to be outdone.

"You'll have blisters on your arses before we're finished so just get on with it," ordered the P.O.

Once more they had filled the bin. "Come on then one of you! Get and empty it. And don't take so long this time."

The pair were only too thankful for a brief respite and both dived for the bin at once. Benny winked at Alex and they took a handle each, lifted the bin and struggled with it towards the exit.

"Go on then," said the Chief. "Perhaps you'll be quicker taking it between you."

They made aft, making for the gash chute, a funnel shaped chute secured over the stern of the ship.. Down this the crew disposed of every type of rubbish and waste.

Heaving the bin up to the chute they tipped it up and watched the contents slither seawards to enter with quite a splash. This done they plonked the bin down on the deck and settled their backsides, one each to a bollard.

The Scot lit a cigarette and gulped greedily at the smoke, not forgetting to keep one eye fixed on the galley door.

Benny, nursing his blister, also had an eye on the door. "I think we'd better make tracks 'Aggis." he said.

"Aye! I guess we 'ad at that."

"One thing, I think we've about broken the back of it."

"Aye! An' aboot broken ma back tae y'ken." Alex stubbed out the cigarette and they made their way galleyward.

In their short absence it seemed the P.O. had worked wonders. The fish they had cleaned and gutted now lay shipshape in their tins and trays. These in turn were stacked Bristol fashion and there was at long last, daylight to be seen. The mountain had become a molehill.

"It took you long enough to find the gash chute. I was beginning to hope you had both fallen over the side."

"We only stopped for a breather Chief," explained Benny doing his best to sound as debilitated as he felt.

Leonard Bancroft's voice was as cold as it was menacing. "Little breather, eh? Well I've got news for you. If you don't get mobile you will be taking your last breath, and that's a promise!"

Although they knew he did not really mean it, they hurried forward nonetheless, eager to oblige. Poor Benny. With a strangled oath he skated across the galley deck on a piece of fish, taking with him a heap of trays and fish.

Alex, left holding the empty bin, was powerless to help. He gazed in wide-eyed disbelief at his colleague sitting there, a tray of spilt fish adorning his soaked lap, a truly sorry but laughable sight.

Not a sound had come from their P.O. and Alex timidly glanced to see why.

The petty officer was standing with hands covering face and ears, hiding as much as he could and one got the impression that he was about to be struck by a bus from which there was absolutely no escape.

The cooks exchanged apprehensive glances, not daring to move.

At the precise moment Leonard Bancroft decided to remove his hands, a very strange and peculiar thing happened.

A large fish, lodged immediately above Benny's head, chose to dislodge itself and drop off. It may have been the gentle vibration of the ship. It could have been disturbed by Benny as he fell. Whatever the reason the fact remained that it landed with a most inconsiderate plop smack on top of Benny's head where it stayed, tail over one ear head over the other.

It broke the ice. First the P.O. and then Alex, began laughing. Initially a stifled giggle, it quickly became uncontrollable, roaring, bellyaching laughter, the noise bringing several matelots into the galley.

When at last the P.O. was able to pull himself together he stepped over to Benny and helped him to rise from the confusion.

"Well," he said. "I've seen a lot of funny things in my time but that took the biscuit, my God if it didn't."

"I know one thing," said Benny. "I shan't forget this bloody day in a 'urry, not even if I live to be ninety."

"Och mon! Jest yuze think o'the tales y'll be able tae tell your gran' children."

"Come on then lads," said the Chief. "We've all had our bit of fun, now let's see how quickly we can clear these last few up so I can make a start on the bread."

Alex swung back into action quite readily. The gaiety of the last few minutes having recharged his batteries but not so Benny.

"Come on then Stretton, let's be having you," ordered the P.O.

"Sorry Chief but I was just thinkin', we're on a loser really."

"Oh?"

"Yeah! Even if we do manage to gut all this lot there's no way we're going to cook them all, the fish fryer ain't nowhere near big enough an' they're bound to want chips fryin' as well."

"We'll cross that bridge when we come to it lad, in the meantime grab your knife and get stuck in."

Without a word the three pressed on now, working away steadily. The P.O. however, must have been chewing over Benny's words concerning the problem of cooking the fish.

"The only way to get round it is to steam the fish in the oven. We'll leave it in the trays as it is and see there's plenty of seasoned water covering them so they don't bake dry. When we've finished you can go round the messes and find out exactly how much they need now and the remainder can go in cold storage, okay?"

"Yes Chief. But supposin' they want it fried?"

"Then they're going to be unlucky Stretton lad. As long as we cook it for them that's all they have to worry about, right?"

Benny shrugged his shoulders. After all, who was he to argue?

Pausing in his labours he glanced about him. "There's only them few over there now Chief," he said.

"Yes, let's have them over here shall we," and as Benny reached for them Chief added pointedly. "You know Haggis, I'm really going to enjoy that rum tomorrow, damn me if I'm not."

That evening saw Benny sitting at the mess table with an over-loaded plateful of fish before him. His messmates were noisily gorging themselves, tucking into this manna from the sea but not he. Every now and then he would prod the food with the fork, totally indifferent.

"It's a funny thing," he said to no one in particular. "I was really looking forward to this when I caught it but now, urgh!" He shuddered and pulled a face full of repugnance.

He contemplated his plate and came to a determined decision, recalling all the fuss these fish had caused. The fear, the panic, the near exhaustion, all the extra work. And what about the blisters? But he had resolved firmly to see the situation through to the very end and to hell with it.

"I'm going to eat this fish," he loudly proclaimed. "Every last bit of the bastard!"

His declaration brought forth a thumping great cheer which echoed round the messdeck. Pedlar even had the gall to lay odds he would not manage it.

That did it. Bets were laid thick and fast. Oddly enough, having set the wheels in motion, Pedlar Palmer now laid odds that his little love-able pal would eat all the fish. No fool Pedlar. He had seen his chum in similar mood many times and on more than one such occasion had secretly admired such dogged determination and will power.

It was a struggle for Benny. Never really knowing how he managed to get through his plateful he stuffed the last morsel into his mouth and allowed himself the well merited luxury of a loud burp.

"You've left a bit there!" shouted one matelot, obviously one who had bet he would not do it.

To the accompaniment of more cheering, Chef picked up the plate and slowly licked it clean, thoroughly enjoying this playing to the gallery.

"As for you lot," he grinned. "You can all get stuffed!"

They laughed loud at this. He could say anything. Do anything. His sterling performance had earned their respect.

His hand was shaken heartily, his hair ruffled boisterously, his ribs tickled roughly and his back slapped painfully and he was chaired all around the messdecks.

Benny? Benny wanted to be violently sick!

CHAPTER THREE

The news reached Benny's ears at approximately ten thirty the next morning. The 'buzz' Smokey claimed to have heard, proved to be true.

H.M.S. Consort now steamed sedately for Port Swettenham. E.T.A. 6p.m. that evening.

The sea remained remarkably calm and the sky nursed only the odd cottonball cloud when Smokey sauntered up. Chef was busy polishing the brass tap outside the galley door.

"Heard the buzz yet Chef?"

"Mornin' Smokey. What buzz is that then?"

"That buzz I told you about yesterday. That one about us goin' to Port Swettenham. Well it's true. We are goin' there."

"Oh shit!"

"But that ain't all Chef! They reckon we'll be there for quite a few days."

"Aw no!" Chef stopped his polishing. "What in God's name do we want to go there for at all, never mind stoppin' there!"

"Don't ask me. It'll make a change though, won't it?"

"Yes! A change for the worse. Still..." he returned to the polishing. "There's nothin' we can do about it so I suppose it's no good moanin'."

He leaned back to study his handiwork then gave it another rub. "'Ere, Smokey, don't forget all the sippers we're due for this mornin'. We worked bleedin' 'ard on them fish. An' I've got the blisters to prove it," and he thrust the plaster-covered palm under Smokey's nose.

"Yeah! I know. But don't you worry mate. Everythin's under control. Everybody reckons what a great job you lot did yesterday. Don't worry, they won't let you down."

"Honest Smokey, if I never ever see another fish again it'll be too bloody soon."

"Aye! An' the same gaes f'me tae," said Jock by way of announcing his arrival on the scene.

"'Ey Jock, 'ave you 'eard we're goin' to Port Swettenham?" Chef asked him.

"Aye. I jest 'eard it the noo. There's nae much chance o'pickin' up a bit o'fanny at that God f'saken 'ole."

"Is that all you think about? You dirty old bastard," grinned Smokey.

"Oh, by the way 'Aggis. The Chief's been lookin' for you," said Benny.

"What does 'e want the noo?"

"'E's got a big tin of white paint, a big brush an' 'e said somethin' about paintin' the aft galley ready for the skipper's rounds on Saturday."

"Aw jings! It is nae lang since I did it mon."

"It's no good moanin' to me Jock. I'm only passin' the message on, that's all. 'E told me to tell you an' I've told you so that's me out."

"Aye well, I ken what 'e want's fine enough, an' it's nae paintin'," said Alex, his tone oozing implications unkind. "Anyways, let's get back tae this rum."

He turned to Smokey. "'Ow are yuze proposin' tae organise it?"

"Don't you worry yourself 'Aggis my ol' son. It's all been taken care of. You'll get every sipper you were promised. An' that's a promise."

"What's wi' all these promises? Is it because y'ken I dinnae trust yuze?"

"'Aggis." Smokey pretended to be deeply wounded. "You don't trust me? Me? Your old pal Smokey? 'Aggis. It 'urts to know you don't trust me, straight up it does."

"Mebbe, but no' 'alf as much as y'll be 'urt if y'dinnae come up wi'the rum. An' that's mar wee promise tae yuze." He jabbed Smokey hard in the ribs adding strength to the word 'promise'.

With perfect timing, the S.R.E crackled and the bosun's pipe was heard proclaiming it to be 'tot time'.

"Well, that's it chaps," cried Smokey. "I'd better get off and organise your sippers. See you in a bit."

Benny was leaning on the ship's rail, gazing into the distance. Alex joined him. "'E's a comical old sod is Smokey," said Benny casually.

"Aye, 'e is," Jock agreed.

"Do you know what 'e's done?"

"No, what?"

"'E's been round to all the rum bosuns an' got 'em to agree to arrange for all the sippers an' that, that anybody want's to give to us, to tip 'em back into the rum fannys and then save 'em all till we can go an' collect 'em when the coast's clear. I've told 'im, I 'ope they don't let the duty officer or anybody see 'em else that would put the kybosh on it. I reckon it's a good idea don't you 'Aggis?"

"Och! F'Christ's sake use y'loaf Benny! Can yuze honestly see all yon rum bosuns savin' it? Wi'oot 'elpin' themsels? Be y' age Chef f'God's sake."

"You know your trouble 'Aggis? You 'ave a very nasty suspicious mind."

"Aye, mebbe so but yuze jest wait an' see. O'aye, an' that's another thing. Dinnae f'get the Chiefy'll be wantin' 'is share tae."

"'E'll get it, don't you worry your shaggy little sporran." Alex remained a sceptic and grunted as much.

Benny faced up to his smaller shipmate. "Now look 'ere Jock. The crew really enjoyed that fish last night and they appreciated it an' all, not to mention the fact that it saved a good few bob on the mess funds, an' I'll stake my bottom dollar they'll all play the white man ... includin' the rum bosuns, an' you can think what you like," and with that he stomped off into the galley.

He was busying himself, bent over the ovens when Alex sauntered in. "D'yuze need an 'and?" he asked.

"You can pass me that tray of spuds if you like."

The Scot obliged. He was groping for the correct thing to say but Benny wisely saved him the trouble.

"Are you goin' to get your 'ead down after dinner Jock?" he asked.

"Och, I dunno. I really should write some letters y'ken, I 'avnae written 'ame since we left Singapore."

"Neither 'ave I mate."

"There's nothin' tae write aboot is there."

"Oh! What about yesterday for a start? You could write a bloody book on what happened yesterday."

"But that's only jest 'appened. I could nae write aboot it till it 'appened mon. Besides, dinnae talk tae me aboot yesterday."

Benny chuckled to himself and returned to his chores leaving the Scot to contemplate his blisters.

"Och well! Ah'm awa f'm'tot, be seein' yuze."

"Yeah, okay Alex. Don't forget to come back an' sort out the sippers."

"Aye. I wull," as if he would forget. Doubt still lingered but he said nothing more.

Benny watched him go then continued his labours, he made certain everything was coming along nicely and in order then strode off to collect his own rum ration.

He didn't get far. Barring his way at the door was a bearded seaman.

"Is the dinner ready yet Chef?" he asked. "I'm starving."

"It won't be long, Percy me old mate. Another ten minutes or so that's all?

"Great. I could eat a scabby bloody 'orse, shoes, tail and all," said Percy rubbing his hands together in eager anticipation. "I'll shoot off and get a couple of cloths then," he said, and off he shot.

Custom was to appoint some person, or persons, dependant upon the size of the mess, who was responsible for the rough preparation and the fetching and carrying of all meals, a rota system being worked with no one being exempt. They were also responsible for all aspects of cleaning up. Since most meals were direct from hot ovens or steaming pots, these 'cooks of the mess' as they were known found it necessary to bring along dry cloths with which to hold the food. This was the reason for Percy's errand.

"Hey Chef!" he had performed a brisk about-turn. "I almost forgot. We've got the bubbly ready for you down the mess and Curly said to ask you if you were coming down?"

"I can't just now Perce. I ain' even 'ad time to go for my own tot yet. Besides, I thought they were goin' to save it for us."

"Yes I know, but he was a bit worried in case the duty officer or anybody else comes round and spots it." He came up with an idea now. "Tell you what Chef, have you got a jug or bottle or something to put it in?"

Benny came up blank. "I don't know off 'and Perce, I'll 'ave to 'ave a look round."

"Leave it with me Chef. I'll come up with something," he said as he left.

Time passed and the mess-cooks had collected their meals and departed, leaving the galley almost deserted. On top of the range were arrayed a few plates of food being kept warm for members of the duty watch unable to leave their posts for the moment and Chef, perched on the edge of the galley step as he kept a wary eye on these meals.

Leaning on the ship's rail facing Chef were P.O. Bancroft and Alex. The three catering companions were in conference. The petty officer was in the chair.

"This is what we'll do. You two go and get the rum from the rating's messdecks while I go and get it from the chief's and P.O.'s. We'll smuggle it all back here and split it fair and square, three ways, okay?"

"Okay Chief," they echoed.

"But for God's sake don't go getting caught or we'll all end up walking the plank."

"You know us Chief," chirped Chef. "The smartest smugglers since smuggling was invented."

"Right then. I'll see both back here."

He strode off aft to be followed at a discreet distance by the Scot. Benny went up forward. Each of them carried a white enamelled jug which had been procured specifically for this purpose. The size of these jugs was such that should they be only half filled they would contain enough grog to sink over a dozen hard drinkers.

Chief was first to return, not having as many calls to make. He walked directly to the galley. Once inside he sought a suitable hiding place for the jug, strongly tempted to snatch a quick gulp of its contents to steady his nerves.

With the jug safely hidden he relaxed. Throughout the short escapade he had been fearful lest someone in authority should stumble across him and demand to know what was in the jug, even though there was little likelihood of this happening. After all, he was the head cook. He had every right to wander about with cooking and catering utensils. Just the same, he felt happier now he had hidden it.

"Bloody 'ell Chief," beamed Benny bouncing in and holding the jug he carried for the P.O. to inspect. "Just look at this lot."

"Hide it out of the way you idiot," snapped the Chief impatiently. He did however glance inside. "Hmm, there must be well over half a pint in there."

"'Alf a bloody pint? Come off it Chief. If there's not at least a pint in there I'll stand shaggin'."

He gazed around both to find a hiding place and to see how much his boss had gathered in. "'Ow much did you get Chief?"

"Put it behind here with mine," the P.O. told him, moving aside the heap of cleaning gear on top of the workbench beside the sink.

As he did the P.O.'s bidding, Chef leaned over to look inside the other's jug. His eyes lit up and he gasped. "Bloody 'ell, Chief. That's nearly as much as what I've got."

"Not bad is it," beamed Leonard Bancroft preening himself. "And don't forget mine is neaters, not two and one like yours."

Neat rum was issued to petty officers and chief petty officers but the lowerdeck ratings had theirs watered down. On the larger ships it would be two of water and one of rum. Smaller ships often were allowed one and one and even, on occasion, neat rum may be issued to all qualifying hands.

"Jings! I thought ah'd 'ad it back yonder," gasped Jock making a hasty entrance, chased by some imaginary monster.

P.O. Bancroft flew to the door fearing the worst. Pulling the Scot even further inside as he passed him he glanced fore and aft to satisfy himself the coast was clear then returned to question the panting cook. "Nobody saw you, did they?"

He had every right to be fearful. In the strictest sense, all issues of rum were to be drunk at the rum table at time of issue. All 'wets', 'sippers' and 'gulpers' were, quite simply, against all King's rules and regulations or, more correctly, Admiralty Fleet Orders.

However, human nature being what it is, eyes that became blind and could not see became strangely commonplace at tot times. And so it was that 'sippers', 'gulpers' and 'wets' were offered and taken on all such occasions as birthdays, anniversaries and a host of other shady excuses.

Should any soul have the great misfortune to get caught breaking the rules, then their prostitution of this fine and rare old naval traditional privilege would end pitiably for all involved. So P.O. Bancroft had every good reason to be anxious.

"Well, come on lad? If nobody saw you what the devil is wrong?" the P.O could not be patient.

"Naebody saw me, Chiefy, naebody saw me."

Both Chief and Benny were at a loss and the former was fast losing what composure remained.

Alex explained. "Ah'm oot o'breath y'ken because I ran round 'ere like the clappers an' ah'm shakin' because I slipped arse o'er tit an' verra nearly spilt the bloody lot, so I did."

The other two reached together for the jug instinctively, forgetting the obvious. If the rum was spilt, what could they hope to do about it now?

Alex heaved a mighty sigh of relief hugging the jug. "My God! The thought of all this runnin' o'er the ship's side nearly killed me!"

"If you had spilt it I'd have killed you!"

"Yeah! An' if Chief 'adn't killed you, I bloody well would 'ave."

"Yuze can both relax. I didnae spill a drop," and to illustrate he held forth the jug for them to take.

It was the Chief who took it. "Hmm!" Across his face spread a rare smile, one of the very pleased variety.

"The way I see it," he finally said, "we've got damned near enough to have one jug each."

"We 'avnae?" gasped a thrilled Scot.

"What say we each keep the jug we collected?" suggested the P.O.

"Suits me Chiefy," said Jock

However it obviously did not suit Benny.

"What's wrong with you?" asked Chief. "They're about equal."

"I didn't say they weren't equal, Chief."

"Well then?"

"It's just that your jug is full of neaters, Chief."

This revelation stung Jock to life. "Neaters? Aw Chiefy," he groaned, how could the P.O. do this to him?

"Alright, alright. Fair's fair I suppose. The best thing then is to mix it all up together."

"The trouble is, what can we mix it in?"

"Mix it all in one jug Chiefy."

"Don't talk so bloody stupid Jock. 'Ow in God's name can we get nearly three jugs into one?" asked Benny.

"Keep your voices down," hissed the P.O. "Now look. There is far too much here to drink in one session so why don't we put the neaters in a bottle for another day."

"I've got a better idea. Why don't we keep the two and one in bottles and drink the neaters now?"

"Because Stretton, my lad, the neat rum will keep, the two and one may not."

Benny grunted acceptance of this and silence reigned for a spell as the three contemplated the situation.

"Whatever we do we have got to be sensible," said the P.Q. "If we try to be clever and drink most of it today we shall all end up pissed as arseholes and then the fat would be in the fire."

The two begrudgingly agreed.

"Look," continued Chief "the obvious thing is to share the neaters tomorrow or later, no sense spoiling a good thing by being greedy is there?"

"No, I guess not Chief," agreed Chef. Jock simply shrugged.

"Of course not lad. Right then, pass me that bottle I put behind the bag of flour. I thought we might need one, that's why I put it there."

The petty officer gingerly fulfilled the task and finally stood erect, stretching his long, lean frame backwards to pacify the creaking in the small of his back.

"Ah well, that's one job done," he said screwing the top on the bottle. The three of them were so engrossed that they failed to hear the approach of the officer bearing down upon them.

"Everything alright Bancroft?"

The question hit them like a ton of bricks. Yet in spite of this devastating intrusion taking them completely off guard they still had the good sense to conceal the tell-tale jugs and bottle by turning and standing to attention, shoulder to shoulder, broadside on.

"Attention in the galley," roared P.O. Bancroft, at the same time saluting the owner of the voice.

It was a voice they knew only too well. It belonged to 'Jimmy the One', commonly referred to as 'Number One', the First Lieutenant, the Hon Willoughby Fitzroy-Smythe, Lieutenant Commander, D.S.O.

R.N.

"Sir!" yelled the P.O. concluded his salute, a blend of bluff and naval training holding him together.

"Stand easy," Number One's manner intimated a request rather than an order. "Sorry to barge in on you like this. I know how terribly busy you always are, what?"

"Sir!" said Chief having nothing else to think of to say.

The officer nodded to Alex. "Good afternoon Davidson. After galley alright, what?"

"Aye sair, it is thank y'sair."

"Fine. Good show. Good afternoon Stretton," turning his attention Bennywards. "And how are you, what?" Yes, he concluded always by saying "What?"

"I'm very well thank you sir!"

"Good. Fine. That's the spirit, what?"

He was quite obviously ill at ease but then, although they did not show it, so were the three members of his crew.

"Talking of er ... spirits ... I, er ... actually Chief I, er ..." Abruptly, and much to the consternation of the three, he changed the subject. Nose in the air sniffing, he observed "Strong smell of rum Bancroft, what?"

The three feared the worst. The First Lieutenant had rumbled them.

"Aye sir. It's the fumes sir ... comes up through the hatchway leading from the messdecks sir," he said, marvelling at his own brilliance. He secretly prayed that the officer was not playing cat and mouse with him.

The lieutenant glanced over his shoulder at the door through which he had entered. "Does it by jove? Can't say I noticed it as I came down from the wardroom."

He knows, the crafty swine, he knows, thought the P.O. So did the other two, all but trembling in their sandals.

With commendable nerve P.O. Bancroft said: "Ah no sir! That would be the wind sir. Not in the right direction." He sought support from the others. "We always get it when the wind's in this direction, don't we men?" He nudged them.

"Yes sir! Always get it sir!" confirmed Benny.

"Aye sair that's right enough sair," doubly confirming it.

Jimmy the One smiled. "Dear me, I say. You chaps will have to be jolly careful, be getting inebriated from the fumes, what?" He chortled at this.

The three joined in the weak attempt at laughter, still worried, still certain he was on to them.

"Hmmph! Yes, well. I er ... Bancroft!" He had blurted out the name with loud blunt deliberation and resolve. This was it for sure. Their time had come. "Bancroft," he repeated the name, softer now. "I, er ... about yesterday, what?"

"Yesterday, sir?"

"Yes, Bancroft. Yesterday," he coughed politely. "I er, I want you to realise this visit is all quite unofficial. Understood?"

A trio of "Sir!" said they understood but they did not understand. Not nearly.

"Thing is Bancroft, the captain and myself are agreed that you all three did a blessed good job yesterday. We accept that it not only helped out the, er, the mess funds, but also served to boost morale too and morale is so important, what?"

"Sir!"

"Yes, well, that being so, I have brought along a, er, small bottle of wine for you to share or do with what you will, what?"

Having finally got it off his chest he held out the bottle he had concealed in a deep pocket. He offered it to the P.O. but he was in a state of shock. So were the other two.

"Come along Bancroft! Take the blessed thing. What you did was all in the line of duty I know, but dash it all, you worked jolly hard, all of you. It's the one way we felt we could show our appreciation, what? Take it man!"

He thrust the bottle into the P.O.'s hands, forcefully. For a man who normally reflected a totally unemotional character, 'Jimmy' was, at this moment, almost floundering with embarrassment.

"Thank you very much sir! That's very kind of you indeed sir! Very kind indeed sir!"

"Yes, yes! Alright Bancroft" cutting the P.O. off. "No need for all that. No need at all."

Having dispensed with the gift he resumed his normal attitude. "You will remember all of you, this was really the captain's idea as much as mine and he wants it to be off the record, understand, what?"

40

"We'll thank him too when we see him sir!"

"You will not Bancroft. You will forget the whole incident. You too Stretton, you too Davidson. Not a word to anyone. Got that, what?"

"Sir!" they chorused.

"Fine! Fine!" the officer edged backwards, ready to leave yet still hesitating. "I take it then that I have your sworn oath as gentlemen. Not a word to anyone."

By now, Number One was framed in the doorway when he decided to say more.

"I do so prefer a happy ship as you all no doubt are aware and you chaps did us proud yesterday, what?" He smiled broadly, wagging an admonishing finger at them, mocking. "Don't drink the wretched stuff all in one go, what?"

Placing the finger he wagged across closed lips now, implying silence and secrecy, he gave a perfunctory salute and was gone.

"Jesus, that was ..."

The P.O.'s hastily raised hand commanded Benny to close his mouth at once. Walking stealthily over to the doorway he checked the coast was clear before closing the door as a precaution against further abrupt intrusions.

"Phew! That was fucking close!"

"Wael, I dinnae ken aboot yuze two but I think it calls fae a wee drink." Trust Jock to think of this. "I could drink a tap dry, so I could."

"Why drink a tap dry when we've got all this lot," grinned the P.O. as he wafted the bottle of wine temptingly beneath the Scot's nose. "Tell you what, we'll lock the bottles of 'neaters' and wine in this drawer and save them."

He took out a bunch of keys and unlocked his own personal drawer and placed the two bottles inside. Locking the drawer he reached up to lift down three cups from a shelf.

Benny rubbed his hands and winked knowingly at Alex who fingered his lips, eyes wide with avid aspiration.

The Scot grinned and returned the wink and also resolved to rub his hands miser fashion and there the pair stood, watching their boss measure out three equal portions of the 'two and one'.

"There we are then, lads," said he, raising a cup to his lips. "Cheers!"

Benny picked up a cup which he passed over to Alex then took the last cup for himself. "Cheers!" he said and helped himself to a great gulp.

Alex, never one to toy with his liqueur, downed his in one sweet swallow, closed his eyes to savour fully both taste and smell and not until appeased did he open his eyes to gaze smugly at the others and blissfully murmur, "Cheers!"

"You know what?" mused Benny. "I love the way bubbly makes my top lip go sort of numblike. You know, when it touches my lip when I'm drinkin' it?" He put it to the test by taking another gulp.

P.O. Bancroft sat himself down in the only chair available. He, along with the other two, feeling smug and content and relaxed.

Jock was slowly losing the glow of content. Having devoured his cup of grog in the one greedy gulp he now regretted the thought of the others having some left.

Chief had the best idea, concluded Benny, and parked himself atop the doughbin. Alex though, with some small difficulty on account of his size, struggled up to perch beside him.

They had barely emptied their cups, contemplating a refill, when the door slowly opened. Renewed panic hit them. The P.O. rushed to intercept whoever it might be as Benny and Alex cleared away the tell-tale cups and jugs.

For the second time that afternoon they found themselves confronted by an officer, this time, none other than the captain himself, Commander Richard 'Dickie Bird' Singer, D.S.O. R.N.

Not many in the fleet did not know or had not heard of 'Dickie Bird' Singer. Those who did make his acquaintance were not likely to forget him. A Canadian, he stood six foot six and weighed 15 stone plus. Not flab either but firm muscle and big bone. Entering the galley he was obliged to bend and stoop low.

"Attention in the galley," roared the P.O. for the second time. As much a warning as it was an order. Stamping smartly to attention himself he gave his skipper a brisk salute. "Sir!"

Unlike 'Number One', the skipper was a man of directness and decision. He had to be. He was always in command, of his ship, the situation and himself.

And so it was now. With absolutely no fuss or bother he placed a bottle of brandy into the hand of the P.O.

"There we are Chief, from the wardroom for services rendered."

The dumbstruck petty officer strived to sort out his senses; the captain, oblivious of the afternoon's events, held up a hand to stave off any forthcoming statement which might cause embarrassment.

"It's alright Chief, we want you to have it."

He cleverly changed the subject by gazing about the galley and without realising the implications said. "What are you all plotting then?"

This jerked the P.O. to life. "We are waiting sir!" he said, it being all he could think of for now.

"Waiting for what Chief?"

"Er, waiting for the er, waiting for the dough to rise sir," he blurted out, thankful for the inspiration but praying silently that the skipper would not ask to see this 'dough', it had been ready some time.

He cleverly forestalled this happening by drawing the captain's attention back to the brandy. "Thank you very much for the brandy sir, very kind of you but ..."

"No thanks needed Chief. You all did a fine job yesterday. Just use a little tact and keep it under your hats, alright." This was an order not a request.

"But sir ..." The P.O. was intent on telling him about the bottle 'Number One' had brought.

"No buts Chief. It costs the wardroom next to nothing anyway. Don't leave it lying about though, in fact," he smiled, "as long as it does not interfere with your breadmaking, why not relax and enjoy it now?"

"Yes sir, I think we will," and as the P.O. smiled back the skipper went, returning the salute with casual indifference.

"Oh my God!" wailed P.O. Bancroft as Benny closed the galley door.

"What's wrong Chief?" Benny asked.

"What's wrong lad? Can't you see what's wrong?"

"There cannae be anythin' wrong wi' gettin' a wee bottle o'brandy gied ye," said Jock.

"But don't you see?"

They stared back at him blankly, obviously, they did not see. He flopped down in the chair, a worried man.

"What happens when the skipper finds out that 'Jimmy' brought us a bottle as well?"

"Who's goin' to tell 'im?" asked Chef. "I certainly ain't."

"He'll be sure to tell him himself. He's bound to. If the skipper don't tell 'Jimmy', 'Jimmy's bound to tell the skipper."

"I dinnae see ony problem Chiefy," said Jock

"You wouldn't. You haven't got as much to lose as I have, my lad."

"Jock's right, all we have to do is keep our mouths shut an' if anybody wants to know why we didn't say anything, well, we were simply obeyin' orders and keepin' our promise, not to say a word. Remember?"

"Och! Look at it this way Chiefy, they gied it tae us tae drink so let's drink it. When we've drunk it they cannae tek it back."

"Good thinkin' 'Aggis."

The P.O. wasn't able to think. He had never been in quite such a spot as this, in spite of his boasting of sailing the seven seas. The fact that he had indulged himself in a cup full of rum, albeit watered, on top of his own tot, did not make for lucid thinking.

"Oh balls to it!" he decided. Tossing caution, and possibly rank, to the wind, he cried: "Come on lad's, let's all have a bloody good booze!"

To the others' delight he opened the bottle of brandy and poured what he felt sure was three equal amounts into the cups which had been hidden from sight behind Benny since the skipper's intrusion.

"There you are lads, get that down you. We've earned it so we'll drink it."

The P.O. dreamily sipping away, had a thought. "What a pity we can't lock the galley up from the inside," he said.

Benny frowned. "Why Chief?"

"If we could lock the galley from the inside, we could lock ourselves in and drink to our hearts content, out of sight of everybody."

"I 'ate to disillusion you Chief but ain't you forgettin' the bread?"

"Good God! The bread!"

The P.O. jumped up and reached for the doughbin lid, forcing them to scramble off it. He raised the lid and stared at the dough which had risen and threatened to push the lid off anyway.

"I forgot all about it. Well, there's only one thing for it. You two will have to give me a hand for a change. You can help me weigh it and mould it and put it in the tins and we can leave it and have a drink while it rises and the ovens are getting hot. I can manage the baking then," he told them.

They set to with a will and soon the job was done, thanks in no small way to the reward awaiting them.

"Right! That's the lot! Now all we have to do is wait till it's ready."

Singing "I'm forever blowing bubbles" Jock covered the tins with cloths, to keep them clean and warm.

With this chore out of the way they could return to the drink and this they promptly did. The cups were replenished with the little of what was left of the brandy and they started on the 'two and one'.

Naturally, with the sinking of the liquid spirits came the rising of the party spirits and soon the three cooks became three stentorian singers. Moral high. Singing flat.

They had drunk and sung the time away. They had drunk most of their senses away too. Yet through it all they retained their sense of duty and so the P.O. sent Benny off to check on the oven temperatures.

"I can't see it Chief," mumbled Benny trying to wipe the glass with the hand holding his drink. It spilt. His numbed brain ignored the fact.

"What do you mean, you can't see it?" asked Chief looking towards his cook with glazing eyes.

"All steamed up."

"What, yuze or the theb...thum..." Jock pulled his jumbled senses together as much he could and tried again. "Yuze or the thebble ... the themble ... aw shit. I cannae say thumblometer."

"The glass is steamed up Chief," said Benny, both he and Chief ignoring Alex.

"Let's have a look," and the P.O. struggled to his feet, moved over to the ovens and stupidly swung open one of the doors, bending down to do so.

A red-hot surge of air leapt out at him forcing him to fall back onto his backside in a most undignified manner.

"Fuck it!" he cried, closing the door again with some urgency. Benny who had also been compelled to collapse out of harm's way, began laughing.

Somewhere along the way they had forgotten about saving the wine and the 'neaters' and as they imbibed and sang away they were blissfully unaware of being watched.

At regular intervals the door leading to the officer's galley would be pulled quietly ajar. No more than a slit of an opening but enough for the eyes to watch them. These eyes missed nothing. They were the eyes of Phan Hoy Chiang, the officers' Chinese cook.

Phan Hoy kept very much to himself as a rule and would quite often work long hours in an effort to appease the whims of his officers, especially at cocktail parties, when special guests came aboard or during official visits.

It was quite evident from Phan Hoy's behaviour, if not from his inscrutable Chinese countenance, that he was most concerned by the crazy carrying on of his occidental shipmates.

Each time he gazed in to observe their worsening state, he would tut-tut-tut, shake his head almost off and mutter away to himself madly in his mother tongue.

The drink all but consumed, Alex decided to display his skill, or lack of it as it turned out, at sword dancing, the swords being two very long, extremely sharp carving knives.

He blamed the roll of the ship, the undulating surface of the deck, lack of practice, the wrong shoes, poor light, the knives, everything. He blamed everything but the booze for his ponderous, punitive prancing and the foolish way he persisted in falling over his own feet.

"Och tae 'ell wi' it mon." He sighed a sad sigh, sadly succumbing to sorry submission. "I wuz feart o'they knives. They're awfie sharp y'ken."

The P.O. rendered an old sea shanty for the others to enjoy. But after only the first line what started as a shanty became: "Roll me over in the clover." This they did enjoy.

Eventually this made way for 'Ten Green Bottles'. Unfortunate really because they only managed to get as far as the ninth bottle when P.O. Bancroft's will and wind wilted, he curled up on the deck and sank into saturated slumber.

Benny spotted this and he turned to inform Alex the trio had become a duet, when he caught a glimpse of Phan Hoy taking a glimpse at him.

"Oi! Phanny," he called, beckoning with limp arm. "Come an' 'ave a drink."

It just so happened that Phan Hoy loathed this or any other mispronouncing of his name and he now lost no time in telling Benny so.

"You no callee me fanny. You dlinkee too much allasame you callee me Phan Hoy, you un'erstan. Me name Phan Hoy no' fanny, al'light."

"Allighty allighty, come an' 'ave a bloody dlinkee, whatever your name issee."

The Chinaman would not. He was adamant. "No! Me not likee dlink. Me no' likes you dlinkee dlink. So solly allasame," and he clanged the door shut.

Benny, like the other two, was sitting on the deck, propped up by the bulkhead. He tried to rise and go after him. He rose only inches then fell back. Twice more he tried before giving up.

"Go wi'out then, you mardy arsed little sod!" he called.

Benny tried to focus his eyes on the Scot but those eyes slowly closed. Seconds before he sank into oblivion he spoke. "Oh shit!" he said then passed out. Alex? He was dead to the world.

They were not to see Phan Hoy Chiang enter their part of the galley. He flitted from one to the other with short shuffling steps, making sure they were really sparked out and then he did a strange and remarkable thing.

Going from one inert inebriate to the other again, he made them each as comfortable as his strength and conditions would allow.

He then began to tidy up all the mess. Hiding empty bottles and dirty cups and jugs and then he loaded the waiting bread tins into the ovens.

Later, when afternoon had become history and evening the present, Phan Hoy Chiang busied himself with both the crew's and the officer's cooking. He made sure there was ample hot water for teas and coffees and all else. He had completed the baking of the bread too.

He had performed seeming miracles without a hitch, though it must be said the sweatband around his balding forehead was a real necessity and his flimsy cotton vest clung to him, saturated as it was.

And the three ship's cooks? They slept on.

They knew nothing of Consort's steaming inland via the waterways lying between the islands and mainland. They had not heard the anchor drop at the appointed spot.

She now lay off the coast opposite the creek leading to Port Swettenham itself, a few miles inland, a tiny port but busy, with a depth of channel that could take even large ships and a channel wide enough to accommodate a goodly number of vessels.

It was fairly late and quite dark by the time Benny began to stir himself. He was the first of the three to awaken. His eyes refused to get it together. Painfully slowly, they did begin to focus and his jumbled wits sluggishly threaded themselves together until finally he managed to take some sort of stock of the situation.

He blinked. He screwed his eyes up tight. He opened them again, trying to ignore the red-hot needles stuck in his eyeballs somehow.

He opened them still wider when he saw it was the baked loaves staring back at him. He shook his head and focused again on the rich golden brown loaves stacked neat and tidy on top of the bread bin.

He had to be dreaming. He decided to pinch himself. But no. He was not dreaming, those loaves were real.

He reached out and grabbing a hold of the P.O.'s ankle he shook it wildly. "Oi! Chief, are you awake?"

Eventually the Chief managed a grunt. Not a very loud grunt but a grunt nonetheless. It served to spur Benny on.

"Chief! For God's sake!"

"For Christ's sake!" groaned the befuddled P.O. His manner warned whoever it was shaking him to stop forthwith.

"Why didn't you wake me up Chief?" persisted Benny.

"Wake you?" The stabbing light forced the squinting eye to retreat behind its filmy lid. Both lids remained clammed down tight while their owner continued talking quietly lest the noise of his own voice jar his throbbing head. "What do you mean?"

"So's I could have 'elped you with the bread."

"The bread?" Suddenly it registered. "Oh my God, the bread!" He now remembered the bread but forgot his hangover and shot up to a sitting position with a brusqueness that just was not on.

"Aw! Jesus!" he moaned wrapping his head in his hands in an effort at easing the pain. "I forgot all about the bread."

"Good grief Chief, you must 'ave been in a terrible state if you don't remember doin' the bread."

"Stretton son, I don't remember any damned thing!"

"Well, you've baked the bread Chief, whether you remember or not."

Resigned to the fact that his cook had flipped his lid, the P.O. turned his aching head to follow Benny's pointing finger.

When he saw the bread his eyes shot wide open. "Good God Almighty!" he gasped. "Who's done all that lot?"

"I thought you had Chief."

"I didn't do it! At least, I don't remember doing it."

"If you didn't do it, who did? I know I didn't do it."

As if by telepathy, they turned their attention to Alex. Yet even as they gazed down at his recumbent figure they doubted their thoughts.

"No Chief, not Alex, 'e couldn't 'ave managed if 'e'd been sober let alone the state 'e was in."

"But if we didn't bake it, he must have done. Let's wake him up and see."

"If 'e ' as done it, an' I honestly can't see ' ow 'e 'as, all I can say is 'e's made a marvellous job of it." Benny was holding one of the loaves, allowing fingers to caress, nose to smell and eyes to take in its appetising attributes.

"Never mind what it's like lad, wake him up and see if he did bake the damned things!"

Benny put the loaf down and starting gently at first, began to shake his Scots shipmate. Getting absolutely no response from the gentle stuff, he built up the volume until it became almost violent, doing his own headache no good.

"Come on you Scotch git, stir yourself," Chef shouted in his ear. But Jock snored on.

P.O. Bancroft reached and took hold of the breadbin lid for support and eased himself up. Finally he was erect if not upright.

"Jesus! What a head!" he groaned and sought refuge behind his hands. Making his unsteady way to the door, he opened it, gulped at the cool air, and gazed out into the darkness beyond to the distant lights of Swettenham.

"Come on 'Aggis, bloodywell stir yourself," urged Benny, persisting. The P.O. was trying to get his act together. He realised they were Port Swettenham's illuminations in the distance. Thing was, he did not remember getting here. He glanced down at his wristwatch.

"My God!" he gasped. "Did you know it has gone eleven o'clock lad?"

Benny stopped the shaking. "It never 'as?" he also gasped now.

He came back into the galley to stare down at Jock. "Well, he's got to be moved. He can't stay there all night."

"Come on Davidson, stir yourself, unless you want to find yourself on the quarterdeck." He tried the authoritative approach as he prodded him in the ribs. But Jock snored on.

Neither of them noticed that the door leading to the officer's galley had opened. Nor did they realise Phan Hoy Chiang stood watching them. To attract their attention he coughed discreetly and when they swung round startled he spoke.

"'Lo Chiefy. You likee me makee blead howso?"

Leonard Bancroft was flabbergasted. Benny dumbstruck.

"You?" they cried. "You?"

The tiny gentleman, grinning from ear to ear, bowed up and down as if attached to a spring, at the same time nodding merrily.

"Sure ting Chiefy, me make plenny good job for you, alligh?"

"Well I'll be a monkey's bloody uncle!" was all the Chief could find to say. He collapsed from the squatting position to sit like some rag doll, propped up by the bulkhead.

"Wassa marrer Chiefy? You no likee allasame?"

Chief twisted his head to look askance at him momentarily. Then he got to his feet, went to the neatly stacked bread and lifted a loaf up. He said not a word. Jock snored on.

Poker faced, the Chinaman watched. The P.O. squeezed and sniffed the loaf, got a knife and sliced it down the middle. Pulled a lump of soft bread from the centre, fondled and sniffed the lump.

Finally, the P.O. smiled and nodded. "Phan old son, you've done a cracking job. Thank you."

The poker face melted and with his characteristic shuffle Phan came right into the galley and pointed to the jugs and cups he had washed and dried and placed away tidily.

"Me makee plenny good job allound okay Chiefy?" he beamed proudly.

"You makee plenny good job allound alright Phan, I'll say you did."

"Merciful heavens! You chaps still working, what?" The sound of Number One's voice struck home with lightening force but the petty officer displayed remarkable self-control.

"Attention in the galley!" he yelled, aggravating his hangover no end. Jumping smartly to attention did not help he or Benny either.

Phan Hoy Chiang had slipped silently from sight. Jock snored on.

'Jimmy' returned the salute with his normal casual return at such times. At times of parades and such of course things were very prim and proper.

"We're just doing a bit of tidying up sir, that's all."

"Ah yes... Well I won't detain you Bancroft," clearing his throat. "I er, umph er, I've just been having a word with the captain, what?"

"Oh? Have you sir?"

His heart skipped a beat as he feared the worst. He exchanged a quick glance with Benny standing beside him. The pair forced themselves not to be intimidated but to put on a bold front.

"Yes Bancroft. He tells me he gave you a bottle of brandy, what?"

"Did he sir?" Implying the captain did no such thing.

"Yes Bancroft, he did. Tell me man, did you say anything to him, what?"

"I do believe I said thank you to..."

"Yes, yes!" cut in Number One irritably. "But did you tell him about the wine I gave you?"

"Wine sir? What wine was that sir?"

'Jimmy' smiled, pondered for a moment and then continued. "Fine! I merely wished to take a sounding Bancroft. One needs to know one's depth of water, what?"

"Of course sir!"

At the moment the officer moved to leave, Alex helped himself to a loud snore.

'Jimmy' had failed to notice the recumbent Scot who the other two had vainly tried to conceal with as much of themselves as they could. He thawed as quickly as he froze.

"My God Bancroft! Is he ill?"

"Er, no sir, not exactly sir!"

"Not exactly man?" he glared at the unhappy P.O. When next he spoke his whole manner had changed, his voice cold and menacing.

"Are you trying to be funny Bancroft?"

"Funny sir? No sir!"

"Then kindly tell me what you mean Bancroft by ... not exactly ill!"

"He's drunk sir!"

"What do you mean, drunk?"

"I mean he's drunk sir!"

"I know precisely what you mean Bancroft!" Having got over the immediate shock he regained some composure. He had also remembered the wine and brandy supplied by himself and the captain.

"How," he loosened his collar, cleared his throat and tried again. "...how the deuce did he get in that state, what?" The P.O.'s words struck home as he feared. The P.O. knew they would.

"Drinking the wine and brandy you and the captain gave us sir!"

"Surely Bancroft, surely he did not drink it all himself," he tugged at his collar again, clearly ill at ease. "You were supposed to share it, what?"

"Yes sir!"

"Did you share it?" getting agitated again.

"Yes sir, we did!"

"Then how come you two are not in his sorry state Bancroft, what?"

"There was his tot of rum too sir!"

"But dash it all Bancroft, both of you had rum issue too, what?"

"Yes sir, we did!"

"Then how is it he lies in a drunken stupor," he tossed a quick look at Jock lying there and shuddered with distaste, "...and you two are sober?"

"Well sir, it was like this, Stretton and myself had as much drink as Davidson but whereas we had a sleep this afternoon and slept it off sir, Davidson remained sober long enough to keep awake and bake the bread sir! He's probably only just given way to the drink sir!"

Benny struggled to contain himself. How did his guvnor think them up? His guvnor wondered that himself.

"Then you two were also ... drunk," he found the word distasteful.

"Oh no sir! We weren't exactly drunk sir! I would have said we were, well, merry sir!"

"Yes, I daresay you would Bancroft, I daresay you would. Tell me, did anyone else see you in this ... merry state, what?"

"Only Phan Hoy Chiang, as far as I'm aware sir!"

"Petty Officer Bancroft! You are a complete and utter fool!"

"Yes sir!"

"Good God man!" relenting again. "Don't you realise, we could all be hung, drawn and quartered."

"Sorry sir!"

"No good being sorry Bancroft. No good at all!" He turned his attention to Benny now. "And what about you Stretton, what have you to say."

"I can only say I'm sorry sir!"

"But damn it Stretton, it is not one iota of good being sorry if it ever leaks out that you three were ... drunk, or merry as a result of drinking drink supplied by myself and your captain ... from the wardroom. Totally out of order, they would throw the book at us damn it!"

He turned to Alex. "He is our prime consideration. He must not be seen by anyone until he has sobered himself, what?"

"We were just going to bed him down in here for the night when you came in sir!" lied the P.O. at it again with the quick thinking.

"Good idea Bancroft. Have you a camp bed, what?"

"We have one organised sir!" still lying.

The officer glanced at his watch. "Hmm! I shall have to be off. I shall explain to the duty officer that I have given Davidson permission to sleep in here tonight, and you too of course, what?"

"Me sir?"

"Yes Bancroft, you. You must stay with him naturally, in case he wanders off. Mustn't have that must we, what?"

"Of course not sir!"

"After all, it is up to you to see it does not leak out, otherwise I shall have your guts hanging from the yardarm, what? Goodnight to you both." And with a mere flick of a salute he was gone.

The P.O. saluted mechanically. Benny had attempted to stand to attention but failed miserably. Alex snored on.

"My God! What a carry on!" groaned the P.O. He went to the sink, turned on the cold water tap and stuck his head under it, allowing the refreshing water to pour itself all over it. He rubbed it over his face, opening and shutting his eyes in an effort to get the water onto his burning eyeballs.

He turned the tap off, grabbed a towel and rubbed himself dry, feeling much better for it.

"Come on lad, have a go, do you the world of good," he told Benny and he threw the towel to him.

Benny had sat himself down but decided perhaps it might be a good idea. "Yeah, I think I will Chief," he said.

"I'm not looking forward to sleeping in here lad. But I daren't do otherwise. If 'Jimmy' should pop his head in and I wasn't here he'd have me strung up lad."

"Well I 'ope you don't mind Chief but I think I'd prefer to stay in 'ere as well. Too bloody late to start wandering round the messdeck putting my 'ammock up."

The P.O. made the Scot as comfortable as he could and told Benny: "You'd better make yourself comfortable on the breadbin lad, it isn't long enough for me. I'll be okay on the floor down here."

They were soon settled down having left only the dim pilot light glowing. The doors were closed and they were soon feeling drowsy in the warm air. Alex? He still snored. Only now there were three of them.

CHAPTER FOUR

Benny dreamed of travelling on a lorry which bumped and banged into deep pot-holes every few yards, jolting his bones pitilessly as he lay huddled on the cold, steel floor. In spite of efforts to move he felt strangely paralysed, the fantasy of sleep became a nightmare until with one almighty jerk the lorry bounced him high and with savage abruptness he was awake.

He was sat bolt upright. His heart thumped and raced. He was wide awake. Alex stood over him, squinting through screwed up eyes, holding on to the bulkhead for support.

"Guid God alive mon, I thought y'wasnae goin' tae wake up ever aggen. Ah've been shakin' yuze somethin' shockin' f'ages mon."

Benny sat there on top of the breadbin. Silent, sleepy and sorry for himself.

"Jeez but mar head's sair!" whined Jock. "Serves you bleedin' right for wakin' me up," snarled Benny.

"It's gettin' dark so I thought ah'd better wake yuze so's we can sort oorsels oot."

"Gettin' dark?" Chef glanced at the clock as he tried to recollect exactly what was going on. He looked down at the sleeping Chief and it all came back to him.

"It ain't gettin' dark you dozeybugger, it's gettin' light."

"I don't believe it, I jest don't bloody believe it."

"Well you can take it from me mate, you've slept right through. Me an' the Chief both tried to wake you up but you were dead to the world. An' snore, Jesus, 'ow you can snore."

"Aye? Well yuze wunnae doin' sae bad y'sel jest now."

"Yeah? At least I didn't frighten the life out of 'Jimmy'."

"Och no! Ye're jokin'," he saw by Benny's face that he was not. "Oh my God! 'Ow did 'e come tae see me?"

Benny explained all about the previous night's developments and outcome and how they all three came to be sleeping in the galley. None of this did poor old Alex any good at all.

Funny, but seeing his shipmate so dejected got to Benny. Whereas he would normally torment and tease he now tried consoling him.

"Aw come on Alex ol' mate, there's nothin' to worry about. Honest. 'Jimmy' saw you admitted but 'e saw me an' Chief 'as well. Besides, 'e was a sight more concerned about somebody finding out they'd given us the wine an' brandy than 'e was about the state we were in."

The Scot was past caring.

"Why don't you bung your 'ead under the cold water tap an' freshen yourself up a bit?" suggested Benny.

Alex did not say anything but he did move to do as his shipmate said. He did something else too. He clumsily splashed some cold water smack into the face of the still sleeping petty officer. With a startled grunt and jerk he awoke.

"What the ...!" he began. "Oh it's you is it? You've finally returned from the grave?" He looked around and stood up. "Morning both!" he said, joining Alex at the sink to share in the dowsing.

All three of them sorted themselves out and were soon back in the routine of things. Still apprehensive however, each of them hoping no more would be said by Number One. Deep down, they knew it would.

Midway through the morning Benny was leaning on the guardrail immediately outside the galley, studying the scenery, when up strolled Smokey.

"Alright then Chef? Seen the notice board?" he asked.

"'Ello Smokey my ol' cock. No, I 'aven't seen the notice board, why?"

"There's somethin' on it that should just be up your street. The skipper's fixed it for some of us to go to Kuala Lumpur tomorrow."

"Honest?"

"Yeah. I don't know nothin' else, they've only just put the notice up."

"Find out what you can for me will you Smokey me ol' pal?

Sounds great don' it? I wonder who'll be goin'?"

"Dunno, I did 'ear somethin' about volunteers."

"I bloody well knew it! Volunteers! I might 'ave known there would 'ave to be a catch."

"There ain' a catch Chef, I think they just want about a dozen an' anybody that fancies it can put their names down. I suppose if they get too many names they'll pick 'em out the 'at."

Benny rubbed his hands together, excited by the prospect of such a trip.

"I wouldn't mind goin' Smokey. Anythin' to get away from this bloody ol' tub for a spell, besides, they reckon Kuala's a smashin' place. Wonder when it is?"

Smokey helped himself to a cigarette but did not offer his companion one. He knew he did not smoke and never had done. "Dunno," he said casually. "Tell you what Chef, I'm just off down the mess, I'll see what I can find out an' come an' let you know."

And as the Londoner went to seek more information Chef turned to lean with his back on the rail, lost in reverie.

Smokey returned much more quickly than Chef had anticipated, agog and bursting with news.

"Wait till I tell you Chef. You'll never believe it..."

He kept the cook waiting a little longer as he lit another cigarette.

"Come on! Come on!" begged Benny.

"I'd got it wrong, it ain' goin' to Kuala, well, they are but ..."

"Oh for Christ's sake Smokey, get a grip of your soddin' self."

"Some will be goin' to the R.A.F. base at Kuala Lumpur and some will be goin' to the Grenadier Guard's camp just outside."

"You what?" Benny found it hard to make head or tail of what was being said.

"Honest! An' them that go to the R.A.F. base will 'ave the chance to go up in a plane as well."

Benny leaned on the rails facing outboard. A smile spread across his face. "'Ow far would you say it is to Kuala Lumpur Smokey?"

"I'm no sure. Thirty, forty miles p'raps."

"Well, I'm goin' to put my name down, I'll 'ave to. find out if I can talk the Chief into lettin' me go."

Smokey blew smoke rings and decided his other tit-bit of news would now be appropriate.

"I bet you can't guess who is goin'," he teased.

"Who?" asked Benny not caring to guess but dying to know.

"Only your mucker."

"Don't tell me that jammy sod Pedlar is goin'?" but from Smokey's smirk he knew Pedlar was.

"An' ol' Ginger's goin', an' Larry 'Ope, an' Jimmy Newell an' all."

"The lucky bastards! An' 'ow long did you say it was for?"

"A week, ain' it Lofty?" seeking confirmation from the matelot who had strolled up to join them.

This newcomer stood a mere five foot two and that was stretching things. With typical naval humour, it was inevitable he was dubbed 'Lofty' even though, as a telegraphist, he would normally be referred to as 'Sparks'.

"What's a week?" Lofty wished to know having no conception of the chat going on before his arrival.

"That trip to Kuala Lumpur, ain' it right that some of us goin' to get a week in Kuala?"

Lofty gave Smokey a rueful glance and though small in stature he was never backwards in coming forward and so did not hesitate in putting Smokey to right. "Why don't you get your facts right you Cockney clot," he retorted

"I 'ave got my facts right, shortarse! I saw it on the noticeboard with my own eyes an'. . ."

"Smokey," patronising now, Lofty winked for Chef's benefit. "Smokey, if you had learnt to read properly you would have read that the ones going to the R.A.F. camp were only going for a day, right? Those who are going to the Grenadier camp will be stopping for a few days, right?

"A bloody week!" hissed Smokey.

"A few days," repeated Lofty, "and furthermore, they can, if they so desire, take part with one of the 'ferret' forces."

"Jeez! I'm glad I ain' goin' then if that's the bleedin' case!" Suddenly he didn't give a hoot how long the trip was to be.

"Why? Just think of all the excitement Smokey. My God! They may even get in on a piece of the action," and Benny's eyes lit up at the prospect.

"Yeah? Well I'll tell you Chef, you can all 'ave the action for me, I want to leave this bleedin' navy in one piece thank you very much."

Smokey was a National Serviceman and simply wished to get his service over and get out.

"'E's chicken Chef. Smokey's bloody chicken," scoffed Lofty

"Balls! I just don't fancy chasin' around no stinkin', rotten, lousy jungle lookin' f'soddin' terrorists who are hidin' there waitin' to jump up an' stick a bleedin' bayonet in your knackers!"

"Smokey, my old mate," Lofty placed a comforting hand on Smokey's arm, falsely soothing. "Where's that bulldog spirit? Where's your fighting spirit?"

"Now you just look 'ere shortarse," and Smokey's manner compelled Lofty to step back out of harm's way. "It was my bleedin' bulldog spirit that got me into this fuckin' outfit."

"You lyin' sod, you 'ad to join," Benny reminded him.

"I bleedin' didn', I could have gone down the coal mine!"

This statement had his tormentors gaping open mouthed then they burst out laughing. Smokey stomped off in disgust.

Benny poked his head into the galley to check everything was all okay and then strode off to have a look at the notice board for himself, leaving Lofty on the bench outside the galley where he remained until the P.O. cook arrived.

"'Ello there Lofty, 'ow you doin' then?" he greeted him as Lofty drew in his legs allowing easier passage.

"Fine ta!"

The P.O. entered the galley to re-emerge again having seen that none of his staff were in attendance. "Seen anything of Alex or Benny?"

"I haven't seen Alex, Chief, but Benny's just shot off to have a look at the notice board up by the canteen."

"Thanks!" And with that the petty officer sat himself down on the galley step. He and Lofty chatted idly until Benny turned up all smiles. The P.O. soon wiped the smiles away for with a grim expression he said, "I'm glad you're 'ere lad, I want both you and Alex, do you know where 'e is?"

"No Chief, I 'aven't seen 'im for ages."

"Well go and find 'im and tell 'im I want to see you both, alright?"

"I'll find 'im," said Benny and off he went to unearth his Scots mate. He did find him and ten minutes later the pair were in conference with the P.O. in the forward galley. They had listened intently to what he had to say.

"Well," he told them, "that's it in a nutshell. Personally I don't care which one of you goes, that is assuming either of you want to, I'll leave it up to you to sort out yourselves. Alright?"

"Cheers Chief!" acknowledged Benny.

"Jings mon, I wouldnae mind a wee trip in yon plane but I dinnae fancy yon jungle business," said Alex.

"Well then? What we goin' to do Alex? Toss a coin or what?" asked Benny.

"'Och laddie, yuze can go, ah'm a might tae auld f'that sort o'fun an' games."

"Now look Alex, you can't kid me. I know you really want to go, now don't you, speak the bloody truth," insisted Benny. Deep down he hoped the Scot did not want to go.

"I wouldnae mind goin' up in yon plane," condescended Alex.

"Tell you what," interrupted the petty officer, "I'll put two match-sticks in my hand, a long one and a short one. Whoever takes the long one can go, 'ow's that?"

"Yeah Chief, that's the best idea," agreed Benny. "What do you say Jock?"

"Aye. Suit y'sel," agreed the Scot only to immediately add a condition. That he take first pick.

"You can 'ave first pick 'Aggisface, of course you can," Benny told him.

They were ready to pull out a matchstick each from the Chief's out-stretched fists when Jock changed his mind.

"On second thoughts," he said, "yuze can go fust Benny, wi' ma luck ah'm bound tae pull oot the short een."

"Suit yourself you Scotch git," grinned Benny. He moved to take one of the matchsticks from the fists held out once more.

"Why don't we draw oor names oot the 'at?" asked Jock.

The P.O. threw the matchsticks away from him in disgust.

"Well, I'll be buggered," gasped a flabbergasted Benny.

"You don't trust a soul do you, you?" The petty officer decided to leave it at that.

"You can draw the names oot the 'at Chiefy."

"No thanks," the petty officer declined. "You'll still say it's fixed."

Benny had taken a sheet of notepaper from the drawer. Folding it in half he tore down the crease and handed the pieces to the P.O.

The P.O. wrote on them both, folded up the two pieces and looking round said: "All we want now is something to put them in."

Benny reached behind the door and lifted down a cap hanging there. "'Ere you are Chief, use this."

"Tell you what 'Aggis," suggested the Chief. "Phan is in 'is galley, go and ask 'im to come an' draw the name out."

"Aye Chiefy, yons a guid idea!" And off he went to collect Phan Hoy. He returned with the puzzled Chinaman and made to move behind Chief but clumsily caught the cap and it sprang away to land with a plop in the sink which was full of soapy water in which cloths were soaking.

The P.O. said nothing. He stood silent, one hand on hip, one hand across his eyes like a man deep in thought.

Benny said nothing either. He took out another sheet of paper and tore this in half to hold it, awaiting Chief's pleasure.

"Sorry aboot that Chiefy, jest one o'they things," mumbled Alex sadly.

The P.O. wrote the names down a second time as Phan Hoy was gazing from one to the other at a loss.

The cap was too wet to serve its intended purpose now and it was returned to hang from the door. Benny had unearthed a saucepan and the bits of paper were folded and dropped into it.

Holding the pan high the Chief called to Phan Hoy to take just one bit of paper out. Confused at first until they acted out what it was they wanted him to do, Phan Hoy beamed happily, no doubt feeling most important, and raised a hand to take a piece out. At the death Alex stopped proceedings.

"'Old on a wee minty Chief," he insisted. "I think we ought tae check yon bits o'paper first."

"What in God's name for?" snapped a most annoyed P.O.

"Well, yuze might 'ave put the same name on both pieces Chiefy y'ken."

"If I 'ave, it's your name so's I can get damned rid of you, you bloody great mistrusting sod you!"

"Och no Chiefy! You've got me wrong, it's jest that yuze could 'ave done it wi'oot realisin'."

"My name's not 'Aggis," sneered the P.O. He had taken and

unfolded the pieces of paper. "'Ere you shit-stirrin' bastard, satisfied?" Alex looked to see and reluctantly nodded that all was in order.

"I know one thing," continued the petty officer. "For somebody who said he didn't want to go you're kickin' up one 'ell of a damned stink."

He went to fold the pieces of paper but decided to double check. "Are you 'appy now then? Can we carry on now, laddie?"

"O'aye Chiefy," said a defeated Alex. Both he and Benny knew that when the word 'laddie' escaped his lips the end of the line had been reached.

"Right Phan. Take one out please," but Phan hesitated. Like Benny he was not happy to witness the reproach of their shipmate, even if he had brought it upon himself.

He gazed up at the saucepan held high above his head, shuffled his feet and shaking his head and arms tried to return to the officer's galley.

"Come on you dozey old twit," encouraged Chief waving the pan as some inducement.

"Look fanny," Instantly Benny realised his mistake. "Er Phan Hoy, I mean, sorry, all you have to do is like we've shown you, see? The minute you've done what we ask you can go back to your galley, you savvy?"

That seemed to do it. His face lit up with his full-moon smile. "Me savvy Chiefy, you wannee Phan Huy to makee magic allasame okay?"

"Look Phan Hoy," he decided to try pidgin English. "Me no wannee you make magic. No, me wannee you takee paper flom cup allasame me, you lookee see," and he demonstrated for the umpteenth time.

Realisation dawned at last. "Ah! Me savvy alligh Chiefy," and grinning through a mouthful of gold teeth at the P.O. whose arm was draped around his rounded shoulders, he did their bidding.

He passed the slip of paper to the Chief accompanied by cheers from the three and shuffled off hastily.

"Dozey ol' bugger," grinned Benny as he watched the petty officer unfold the paper slowly and tantalizingly. Before he could complete it Jock put his spoke in yet again.

"'Old on a wee minty Chiefy, 'old on afor yuze look at yon wee paper."

"Well? Now what?" asked the P.O.

"We didnae decide whether the name drawn oot would be the one goin' or the one stayin'."

"Oh my God!" blustered the petty officer also on the verge of laughter. "I've 'eard it all now! Anybody but a gormless bloody Scotsman called Alex Davidson would know full well the name drawn out would be the one goin', right?"

"Aye, weel, jest so long as we ken what we're doin' y'ken," said Jock calmly, not to be denied.

After delaying for one terse moment to gaze at Alex the P.O. returned to the nomination slip and he gaped at the name revealed. All he permitted himself was a loud, "Hmmm!"

"Aw come on Chief, play the white man," begged Benny.

"Aye Chiefy, whose name is on yon wee paper?" pleaded Alex.

"Well I don't know about you two but it's a bit of a disappointment for me," the P.O. sighed toying with their emotions.

They shook their heads looking at each other as they tried to fathom it out. "Why is it Chief?" asked Benny.

"I was 'oping I'd be gettin' rid of that trouble-making twit but I guess I'm unlucky," and as he spoke he passed the slip of paper over for them to peruse.

Benny let out a mighty yell. "Yippee! It's me." And he danced a jig crying out joyfully as he went. He flung open the door to the officer's galley shouting, "Good ol' Phan Hoy, you're a good un."

"Alright then lad, simmer down now and let's 'ave some work done shall we? You'll want to leave the place nice and clean and tidy for Jock and me before you shoot off in the morning, now won't you?" Odd the way his questions came out as orders.

"Yeah, okay Chief," said Benny simmering down in spite of himself. He turned to Alex who stood with a face as long as the Nile. "Sorry I beat you Alex," he said but the huge grin said otherwise. "You must admit though, it was all done fair and square."

"Aye, o'aye! It was a'fair an' square right enough," Alex conceded.

"Ah well, roll on tomorrow," chortled Benny bubbling over at the thought of the trip ahead. "I've got to go and sort some gear out I suppose. Trouble is," he was stirring it up again now, "I don't know 'ow you two will be able to manage without me."

The others chose to ignore this remark apart from dirty looks. "Come on Alex lad," said the P.O., "let's you and me take a walk to 'ave a look at the after galley." His friendly tone was meant to soften the blow.

"Aye," agreed Jock, "a guid idea Chiefy."

"See yuze," cried Jock and off he went dogging the heels of Petty Officer Bancroft.

As they sauntered along the upper deck Alex cast a cautious glance behind him, checking that Benny was way out of earshot. Satisfied all was safe he burst out laughing.

"'E's not watching is 'e?" asked an eager Chief not caring to turn round.

"No Chiefy, the coast's clear." Being assured the Chief himself looked round and then he joined in the laughter, disappearing into the after galley in a fit of merriment. Tears rolled down Alex's face and his Chief was close behind.

"Do you think young Stretton would say anything if he found out we had rigged it so 'e'd be the one to go?" and the remark brought more laughter.

"Och 'e'll never ken Chiefy," laughed Jock wiping tears away. "Besides, ah've brought yon wee bits o'paper wi'me so who's tae ken?" and he opened his hand to show the two pieces of paper.

There in bold block letters on each of them was the name 'Stretton'.

"Alex lad," observed P.O. Bancroft proudly. "You deserve a bloody Oscar for that performance."

"Aye Chiefy, mebbe, but y'didnae dae sae badly y'sel," and they fell about laughing all over again.

CHAPTER FIVE

Benny slept fitfully that night, he was far too full of anticipation. From early childhood he had always relished a challenge or the opportunity do something new. Joining the Royal Navy was all part of life's adventure to him and his ardour had not waned as he grew older. Life was still a great romance.

He viewed the prospect of flying or taking part in jungle operations with the Grenadiers as too good an opportunity to be missed. He did not intend to miss it either.

Poor Benny was not to know what really did lie ahead. He was to spend considerably longer ashore than his dreams could have foretold. Had he had a crystal ball, chances were he would not have made the descent down the rope ladder into the ship's launch waiting to whisk him and his fellow adventurers to Port Swettenham.

He sat in the launch absorbing it all. Last night's excited anticipation was stimulated by the banter bandied back and forth from all sides.

Chef found it hard to contain himself. Exchanging witticisms at every given opportunity helped to ease the tension considerably. All he wished for now was the speedy departure of the launch lest someone should cancel the whole adventure.

He gazed down at the small kit bag which contained his toiletries and a change of uniform clasped between his knees. He studied the spotless tropical shorts and shirt he wore and smiled. How long before the bright, gleaming white became dull, grubby grey he wondered, fully expecting the escapade to expedite the process. The sharp tones of authority rang out to disturb his reverie.

"Carry on coxs'n!" ordered the officer of the watch, his words echoing out across the early morning air.

The launch veered away from Consort and immediately a loud chorus of cheers, catcalls and jeers went up. Most of the cheers were from those off on the escapade. The catcalls and jeers naturally from those left behind. Arm waving and rude gestures completed the picture.

The gap between ship and launch grew steadily until finally the crew left lining the rails were no longer discernible and Consort herself seemed far off. The men in the boat automatically transferred their attention to the shore, craning their necks in an effort to peruse the nearing jetty and its surroundings.

"I ain't seen any crumpet yet," complained Pedlar Palmer as the launch gently nudged the timbered structure of the jetty and drew alongside, right at the foot of the steps.

The ship's officer, who had stood beneath the launch's canopy for the duration of the journey, stepped forward in readiness to step ashore and as the gunwale touched he stretched over to make his way up on to the jetty. With brisk strides he reached the waiting R.A.F. officer and saluted smartly.

The man from the air force, not to be outdone by the senior service, did his level best to stamp a foot through the jetty boards and knock himself senseless with his salute.

Luckily the timbers held and the two shook hands, exchanged names and greetings and generally sorted themselves out regarding what was going on. The naval representative then turned to address his men waiting eagerly below. "Right you men! Fall in on the jetty!"

The matelots surged forward in such a haste one would have thought their very lives depended on being the first to comply with the officer's command. In seconds they had fallen smartly in at the spot indicated.

Near the shore end of the jetty stood a large camouflaged lorry adorned with the R.A.F. insignia display on both front wings and tail board.

The men were standing at ease. The naval officer opened his briefcase, took out slips of paper and handed them to a leading seamen standing in line.

"Hand these round Jennings," he said, "one each." He watched and waited until Jennings had finished and then addressed them. He stood back to do this.

"Now, you will always remember that although you are going to be seconded to either the Royal Air Force or the Grenadier Guards, you will continue to conduct yourselves in a manner befitting the tradition of the Royal Navy. You will, at all times, show all due respect to both officers and N.C.O.s under whose charge you happen to be. Is that clearly understood?"

Grunts from the dozen matelots standing impatiently before him may have suggested they understood but the officer wanted more convincing.

"Is that understood?" he barked.

"Sir!" came a definite chorus now.

"Fine! I shall hand you over now, good luck and good hunting." He turned to the R.A.F. officer, shook his hand and saluting smartly strode off to make his way to the launch and Consort. He did not look back.

"What's 'e mean, good 'untin'?" some wag asked

"P'raps we're goin' after tigers," grinned Benny but all further wit was curtailed by the R.A.F. officer.

"Righty 'o chaps, everyone on the wagon," his words brought instant response and the matelots piled onto the lorry making plenty of noise about it too. As they clambered up the officer came behind them to watch.

"We've left the jolly old rear canvas rolled up for you so you can see where you are going," he said kindly. "Trouble is it is so dashed dusty along the way I'm afraid everywhere gets frightfully filthy."

They were almost settled down now but he had more to say. "I would just ask you to be as quiet as you can chaps. Terrorists you know. We normally would hide from view what we are carrying but dash it all, you want to see where you are going. Still, with any luck we will not come across any of the blighters. Better do it quietly though, one never knows."

"Any problems, bang on the cab," the officer told them and then he too went up front to climb into the cab, once there he stuck his head out of the window to call to them in subdued tones.

The merry matelots had each strived to find seats with suitable vantage points as the lorry pulled away but their efforts at watching the jungle pass by were marred by the jolting, bone-shaking antics of the vehicle as it clattered its way over what served as a road.

"I say chaps, wizard prang what!" chuckled Benny giving a good impression of the R.A.F. type up front, his shipmates grinned back at him, the mood was good.

"Oh boy, oh boy, Kuala Lumpur 'ere we come," said Pedlar. He would have rubbed his hands together at the prospect but he needed to hold on tight. The jarring did not stop his eyes lighting up though as he visualised the prospect of wine, women and song lying in wait.

If however the matelots had imagined Kuala Lumpur was to be the first stop they were in for disappointment. After a minute or so the lorry stopped among some army huts and buildings and watching curiously from scattered positions were army personnel and civilian workers.

The R.A.F. officer climbed down from the cab and came round to the lorry's rear. He was met by an army sergeant who had marched over towards the tail-board. They saluted each other and the sergeant took over.

"Right you sailor boys, follow me!" he barked as the driver, having also joined them, pulled out the securing pins and lowered the tail-board.

The matelots made a grab for their belongings but were stopped by the officer. "You won't want those chaps, you'll be back in a moment," he told them.

They clambered down to follow the sergeant who was already entering the huge hut beside the lorry. He pushed open a small door set in two massive ones behind which lay a loading bay.

The party followed the sergeant up half a dozen steps to the loading platform and on to another door to come to a halt at a form of serving hatch.

"Here you are Corps!" the sergeant called to the lance-corporal leaning on the hatch counter. "Get them fixed up, right!"

"'Ere we are then, who's first?" he called and promptly placed a Sten gun on the counter in front of him. A private hovering beside the corporal leaned over to place five magazines of ammunition beside the gun.

The stunned matelots never moved, apart from looking to each other for guidance and some explanation perhaps.

The sergeant soon changed all that. He reached out to grab both gun and magazines and then thrust them at the chest of the nearest matelot compelling him to take hold of them.

"You want one Sten and five mags each, got it? Not five Stens and one mag!" he snapped as Ginger copped the first lot. "Come on lad, move yourself!" he told him irritably. "When you have your Sten and mags get back to the lorry, got that? But not before you sign for them sailor boy!"

Simple request but not simple to perform. Struggling to hold on to the gun and magazines with one hand while writing with the other proved too much for Ginger and with a clatter first one and then another of the magazines fell to the floor.

"It's a good job we are not surrounded by terrorists," said the sergeant making no move to assist. Ginger dropped the gun and remaining mags beside the others and signed in comfort but this didn't please the sergeant at all.

"Pick them up!" he barked

"I am Sarge, I am," he grinned cheekily, "but I can't do everything at once."

This impertinence took the sergeant by surprise. His troops would not have dared to answer in such a manner. It did not help matters when the matelots cheered and laughed at Ginger's cheek.

"Silence!" he shouted. His colour had risen and he glared at them. "Now get this straight you lot! This game is for real. It is called life and death. Got that! And not only your own life and death but the life and death of your comrades, so I sincerely hope you navy boys know how to use a Sten otherwise God help you if you have to. You won't find it so funny then. That I promise you!"

The group felt rather foolish now as the big man glared at them with grim severity, plainly not a man to be trifled with.

"I ain't got a clue 'ow to use a Sten, Sarge," said Pedlar Palmer.

Benny decided he would rather not know than risk the sergeant's wrath. Besides, he had fired many other types of weapon, as would have all the others with him. It had been part of basic training. The Lanchester automatic rifles which they had on board were very similar to the Sten.

"Is there anyone else doesn't know the workings of a Sten?" asked the sergeant and the blank expressions he got were answer enough.

"Right! You had better gather round then and I'll do the best I can in what little time we have, to demonstrate. Let's hope to God it sinks in that's all I can say."

He took the Sten from Ginger. "This is how you load, right?" he grabbed a magazine and rammed it home expertly. "This little gadget here is for single shot firing or rapid shot firing. It will not fire at the moment because the bolt is being retained, so! To fire, knock the bolt over thus!" All the time demonstrating clearly. "And then, you squeeze the bloody trigger and pray. This is the trigger. Now, you do not waste time trying to fire this weapon from the shoulder, you fire it from the hip thus! The only time you bother firing from the shoulder is when you're firing singly and from a prone position, not likely in these circumstances. And please remember, be very careful, when cocked it will go off if you give it a good jar or drop it and you could end up blowing your own head off. Any questions?"

The sergeant obviously considered they had been instructed sufficiently for he handed the Sten back to Ginger, having first removed the magazine.

"No questions?" he asked again looking at them.

Pedlar Palmer could not resist the chance of a bit of leg pulling in spite of this formidable sergeant.

"Yes Sarge, I've got one, what do you do when the magazines empty?"

Clearing his throat, the sergeant faced Pedlar and spoke slowly and with a deliberation that implied. "I don't know how anyone can be so thick but please try to get the message." What he actually said was, "You simply change the mag!"

"Yes Sarge, I know that, but 'ow do you change it?" asked Pedlar.

The sergeant chewed at the inside of his cheek but uttered not one word. Instead he grabbed the gun back from Ginger and gave a silent demonstration on how to load and unload the magazine not once or twice but three times. During the whole procedure he never took his eyes from Pedlar's face and Pedlar feigned a very great, spellbound interest in it all.

Demonstration over Pedlar gave the sergeant a thumbs up sign and grinned happily. "Got it Sarge, thanks."

He handed the Sten back to Ginger. "Right then, if that is all you want to know we'll press on," he turned to the corporal at the hatch. As he did so Pedlar whispered in Benny's ear and winked.

Benny smiled, nodded and winked back. When he spoke his face was a picture of innocence.

"Excuse me Sergeant!" he called out. "But what do you do if the gun jams?"

"You do one of two things, Sonny Jim," snarled the sergeant, his face close to Benny's.

"What's that Sergeant?" asked Benny beginning to wonder if he should have listened to Pedlar.

"You either run like the clappers, or you bloody well pray!"

This brought laughter from the others but not the way Pedlar and Benny had intended.

Without waiting for any other questions the sergeant hurriedly continued the business of issuing guns and magazines, the matelots signing for them as they took them.

"I'm sorry we don't have pouches for you. You'll have to manage the best you can," the N.C.O. said. "Pity you don't have army uniform, that way you could have put the magazines in the pockets."

When they all had their Stens and magazines the sergeant led the way back to the lorry. "Well that's it then," he said and then surprised them by smiling and winking and wishing them all the best and a safe journey.

He stood beside the R.A.F. officer as they climbed into the lorry, finding it necessary to help each other by passing the guns back and forth until at last they were all seated.

"Righty 'o chaps, keep your guns handy, it is also vitally important that you keep your wits about you just to be on the safe side, don't want to be caught with our pants down do we?"

After this advice the officer and sergeant saluted each other and the former watched his driver secure the tail-board before they both went to the front of the lorry and climbed in. The big sergeant waved as the lorry pulled away in a circular movement to leave the army depot the way it had entered.

The road did not seem too bad to look at but looks were deceiving for the matelots continued to be jolted and jerked and jarred as the lorry pressed on.

"I 'ope we ain't got to suffer this lot for much longer," said Pedlar sounding as though he was shivering to death. He referred as much to the swirling choking dust as to the bone shaking.

The road beyond Port Swettenham was lined on either side with an amalgamation of dense and sparse jungle and the slim, sentinel like trees of small rubber plantations. This landscape was interposed by meagre clearings containing a varied assortment of huts and shacks, their cosmopolitan inhabitants, mainly of Chinese origin or Malay, together with a few Indians and Eurasians, who mingled content with an assortment of vociferous animals, domesticated here but really in keeping with farmyard or menagerie.

They journeyed on with few words spoken, content to hold on tight and gaze out at the passing countryside as it came into view from the rear of the lorry.

"'Ow about a sing-song then?" some thoughtless person suggested.

Immediately Benny gave full voice to 'Tipperary', proving equally thoughtless along with the rest who gleefully joined in.

No sooner had the singing started than it was finished. The R.A.F. officer shouting from the cab up front. All of which was rather strange when one considers the situation.

"Quiet please!" shouted the officer leaping from the cab as the lorry came to an abrupt halt.

"Shhh!" the matelots ordered each other fully thinking something terrible was wrong.

The officer, clearly most annoyed, glared up at them. "Now look here you chaps!" he snapped, feet astride, hands on hips. "I'm frightfully sorry but you really must stop that infernal noise. There is absolutely no point at all in advertising our presence any more than we are forced to, so, there will be no more singing. Got that?"

They mumbled a sheepish acceptance and apology and he hurried back to his seat up front. The lorry revved up and and they moved off once more.

"I've had enough of this bastard trip already," complained Ginger.

"Cheer up Ginger, it'll be alright when we get there," Benny said not at all daunted. It would take much more than this to demoralize him.

"Yeah! You give in too easy mate," Pedlar told Ginger. "Besides, it's for our own good when all's said an' done."

"All I can say is I'm bloody glad I'm in the 'Andrew'," Ginger said, 'Andrew' being a matelot's name for Royal Navy.

They travelled on. Sometimes chatting, often silent, at times giving their attention to some extra interest in the view as it passed by funnel-like to merge quickly into a contracting backcloth.

With avid interest Benny scanned the rubber plantations they passed, fascinated by the long neat rows of slender trees. He spotted workers tapping the bark for their precious rubber sap or emptying the coconut shell cups that had filled and excitedly pointed them out to whoever cared to look.

Suddenly a large notice board standing just inside the perimeter of one plantation caused Benny to gasp with astonishment; its warning short, sharp and most certainly to the point.

"Jesus!" he cried. "Just look at that bastard!" His tone and manner had the desired effect. Everyone clambering to the rear of the lorry to get a look.

"Christ!" Pedlar Palmer cried. "They don't piss about 'ere do they!"

Low whistles of amazement and other forceful expletives were uttered as the board's message hit them. No one doubted its precise, brutal and merciless warning, a stark warning proclaimed in big block letters of bright red on white background.

Leaving nothing to chance this warning was declared in three languages, English being one of them. The message read: WARNING! ALL TRESPASSERS WILL BE SHOT!

For emphasis, should such emphasis be necessary, a skull and crossbones painted in black was on a smaller board nailed to the same post.

Though they were not to know it at the time they were to see many such warning notices before reaching the end of their jaunt.

They were also to see large families of monkeys and baboons and exquisitely coloured birds and butterflies and whether they advertised their presence or not they gave out with a chorus of wolf whistles and catcalls on each occasion a young female happened to catch their eye.

Finally, the officer leaned out of the cab to inform them they were almost at Kuala Lumpur.

As with most townships, the buildings were well spread out at first but gradually they saw the beginnings of a fairly large metropolis. Benny remarked on how pretty most of the buildings looked with their minarets and pastel colours.

Kuala Lumpur itself was set in a fairly flat plain, the surrounding countryside rising gently. Whichever way Benny looked he saw lush greenery. Strangely, every tree, shrub, plant and bush appeared to be in full bloom and even his scant knowledge of things horticultural told him this was most unusual. He thought of home and how things blossomed and bloomed according to their season yet here, it all seemed to be happening at once. Perhaps it isn't really, he told himself.

They did not stop in Kuala but drove through and beyond until arriving at what was obviously another army camp. From the stature of the men on sentry duty at the gate Benny surmised they had arrived at the Grenadiers' camp. Set in a jungle the camp may have been but the disciplined smartness of the sentries proved as immaculate as ever.

The vehicle travelled just beyond the entrance and then reversed into it, the R.A.F. officer having climbed out to direct his driver.

Once again salute was exchanged for salute but what a difference in the delivery this time. The greeting by the R.A.F. officer was very spruce but that of his counterpart in the Grenadiers, that was something else again.

The tall young Guards lieutenant had rammed down first one foot and then the other, whipped up his arm and roared, "Shun!" with such force and determination and precision it left the Consort men wide eyed.

Formalities over, the man from the R.A.F. strode to the lorry rear. Seeing his approach Pedlar Palmer whispered loudly to his shipmates, "I'll lay you odds 'e starts off with that, 'Righty 'o chaps' routine."

"Righty 'o chaps," said the officer proving Pedlar correct. "Who among you is desirous of accepting the hospitality of His Majesty's Grenadiers?"

The matelots swopped uncertain glances but never moved or said anything, could it be the sight of all this brisk marching up and down had scared them off?

"Come along there, there's good chaps," the R.A.F. officer persisted.

"Yes chaps, don't be shy," said the young lieutenant standing beside the R.A.F. officer. What was it about the way he said this?

"Excuse me sir," asked a matelot named Mick. "but if we stay with your lot, do we get a chance to fly, sir?"

"'Fraid not old chap," chortled the chap from the R.A.F. before the lieutenant could answer for himself. "Only those who stay with us get the chance of a flight. Sorry and all that."

"Steady on there!" the Guards lieutenant found it amusing. "You sound as though you are canvassing for recruits."

He addressed the matelots. "This is the position men. The six of you who stay with us will remain until such time your captain asks for your return, probably about a week. The authorities have given full backing to the idea, it may be their idea even, full backing to the idea of inter-swapping the three armed services. In this way you will observe at first hand the part played by us and the part played by the R.A.F. in this fight against the terrorists. Six of our men and six R.A.F. chaps will be taking a look at the work carried out by your boat ..."

"Ship, sir!" Benny had corrected him before he could stop himself.

"I beg your pardon?"

"Consort is a ship sir," Benny informed him.

The two officers smiled at each other. "Yes, well, whatever, the thing is, it is felt in certain circles that this is a combined operation and so, they want us to combine as it were. Feel we may learn from one another," the lieutenant smiled broadly now as he added, "and I have learnt already that your boat is a ship have I not?"

"Now," continued the lieutenant, "if you attach yourself to us I cannot promise a flight but if you want excitement it may be possible to go out with a ferret force if there is one."

Benny did not hesitate. He never had been too keen on flying and he felt much more comfortable with the army officer.

"I'd like to stay with the Grenadiers sir, if I can," he told the lieutenant.

"Good! That's the spirit. Jump down then and bring your gear with you," the army officer said, full of encouragement, making Benny happy and proud.

He felt a bit of a fool however as he struggled with his kit, the Sten and the magazines. "Cherio you lot!" he called out as he climbed down.

Eyeing the ship's cook's five foot six inch frame beneath, rather than beside him, the lieutenant smiled and said, "Hmm! I must say you are a trifle on the small side."

"Yes, I maybe sir, but I'm not one to be trifled with," grinned the cook.

"Very well said indeed," and the officer laughed at this as did the others. "I'm sure we can look after you. Now, come along, who else?" he asked of the others.

"Stand back and let the rabbit see it's 'ole," cried Pedlar Palmer leaving his gear until he had jumped down before lifting it up. Having made a big show of it he stood beside Benny, winked and grinned.

Benny winked and grinned back. He would not admit it but he was a much happier soul now.

Whether a trip in an aircraft had any bearing on it or not the majority wanted to carry on to the air base in the lorry. It was bluntly explained to them that the party must be split six and six and if they did not sort it out for themselves then six would be detailed off. However, Benny was one of only four volunteers and, after some discussion, it was agreed that the remainder could continue to the R.A.F. camp.

Finally, as the big lorry trundled off with its contingent, the lieutenant turned to address his charges. His cultured tones were uncomplicated, he was well educated yet down to earth, young but able to command instant respect.

"I am the orderly officer," he told them now. "The first thing is to fix you all up with breakfast and then we can see about getting you kitted out, right?"

"Excuse me sir," Benny called after him as they marched off. The officer slowed down and swung round.

"Yes?"

"What puzzles me sir is why we were given these flippin' Stens an' that."

"Considered necessary. Would not do to travel without arms I'm afraid, these blighters soon get to know on the grapevine and would ambush quick as a flash. It may not stop them to know you are armed, but it may well serve as a deterrent."

They arrived at a hut outside which stood a truly huge man. The lieutenant called to him as they approached.

"Ser' Major!"

"Sir!" roared the man mountain. Benny could have sworn the

ground shook. He recalled all the terrible tales he had heard about army sergeant-majors and now suddenly, here he was face to face with one.

Again he was witnessing a smartness and bearing that had to be seen to be believed but this small party of matelots were to witness nothing other than the like during their stay. They were to learn that this was the Third Battalion Grenadier Guards, jungle or no jungle.

With the same double foot stamp and salute they had seen the lieutenant give earlier he stood waiting for his officer to continue. Though he wore jungle-green battledress there was no denying here was a man who would be a credit to any army anywhere in the world, every magnificent inch, professional soldier. Even Pedlar Palmer was a trifle envious and that in itself spoke volumes.

The orderly officer tapped the magazines tucked away in Benny's shirt. "Take them down to the armoury Ser' Major so that they may dispense with these and then take them along to 'A' Company's mess tent for breakfast."

"Mr Graham Sir!" roared the mountain. He looked down at the matelots, tweaking his well waxed moustache as he smiled knowingly and asked them firmly but politely to follow him.

All frivolity on the short walk was curtailed by the booming voice of the sergeant-major. "Come along then gentlemen! Come along!" he roared tapping his thigh impatiently with his baton. He waited until they caught up with him before turning to stride off.

They came to a halt at a door set in a brick building outside which stood a sentry, stern and solid.

"In here please gentlemen!" ordered the R.S.M. curtly. Ignoring the sentry he opened the door and stood back allowing them entrance. Inside they were met by row upon row of metal ammunition boxes in assorted sizes, stacked neatly in tiers on the floor. Lining the walls were racks full of rifles, Stens, Brens and pistols. At a long table three guardsmen in overalls worked away at bits and pieces strewn out before them, their denims sporting blotches of grease and oil.

They cleaned and polished with a will. The presence of the sergeant major may have had something to do with this.

The R.S.M. barked out an order. "Corp' Johnson! See these gentlemen's guns are put away safely while they go for breakfast!"

"Sir!" and the corporal made a space for the guns on the table. "Put them down here lads," he said to the lads from the sea.

Guns and magazines out of the way they tidied up their uniforms and followed the sergeant-major out of the building and on towards breakfast. He asked if they were hungry, the direct consensus of opinion a resounding "Yes!"

"You wouldn't chuckle Sergeant-Major," Benny said rubbing his stomach and doing his best to look starved to death. "I'm not kidding you but I could eat a side of bacon stuffed between two loaves and swilled down with a bucket of tea."

"Then you're due for disappointment," said the sergeant-major with a smile that said, "this is the army my lad, not Billy Butlin's."

"I could eat a bloody elephant with the trunk left on," said Pedlar. "An' its 'owdah an' all, as long as it was cooked prop'ly."

"'Owdah? Don't you mean doodah?" asked Benny with a chuckle.

Pedlar Palmer took a swipe at his shipmate who swiftly ducked out of harm's way. Or so he intended. In getting out of Pedlar's reach he bumped into and bounced off the fearsome frame of the sergeant-major who chose that precise moment to stop and face them.

"Sorry Sergeant-Major!" gasped Benny expecting the worst.

The huge N.C.O. gazed down at them as if in a quandary. He tweaked his waxed moustache, a habit it seemed, tapped his thigh with his cane.

"Hmph!" he snorted, whipping his cane smartly back under his armpit. "Well let me tell you gentlemen! It is as well you have hearty appetites because believe you me, you are going to need them while you are here!"

With that he wheeled round and marched off in the direction of 'A' Company's mess tent leaving them to follow.

As he progressed his booming voice informed them bluntly. "It may come as a surprise to you gentlemen to discover we do not live on the fat of the land here even if you do on your ship. We do not have the best of cooking facilities either gentlemen," he concluded brusquely.

They reached an extensive clearing edged by four or five big tents and looking back Benny saw the path they had taken stretched its way gently town the sloping field, reminding him of footpaths across the fields and farms back home. Even the furrows worn by the wheels of army lorries and light armoured vehicles and personnel carriers he could see parked in and around the transport sheds away to his right were reminiscent of home.

The transport sheds were of brick construction but in the main canvas and tenting provided the accommodation.

"We use that as our cinema, at least, when we get the chance," said the R.S.M. having seen Benny gaze at the largest transport shed. "We move all the wagons out of the way and if we want to sit down we take our own seat."

Benny had visions of a swarm of Grenadiers flocking into the transport shed armed with chairs, boxes, crates and all else, just as they did on Consort on film-show nights.

"We sometimes sit on the floor but anyway, we don't need to worry ourselves about that at the moment do we? Breakfast comes first and then as soon as you've eaten, gentlemen, we'll detail you off to your platoons."

The R.S.M. marched into one of the bigger tents and whether the matelots were intended to follow or not, they did.

"Peterson!" he barked. "Four mess kits! At the double!"

"Sir!" came the instant response. In a trice the guardsman had produced four complete mess kits which he placed upon the collapsible table in front of him.

"Sir!" he yelled again to show the order had been followed and completed. He also produced pen and requisite book which he opened and pushed forward for them to sign. This they each did in turn, signing and collecting a mess kit comprising two billycans, one fitting inside the other, a knife, fork, spoon and large tin mug.

When the last of them had his mess kit the R.S.M. turned and without a word marched out of the tent. Again the matelots were left slightly disconcerted but with a shrug of the shoulders Benny led the way after him.

They crossed the narrow path to where a group of guardsmen worked at a field kitchen.

"Corporal!" came the now familiar roar. "Breakfast for these gentlemen, and no special treats. They want to play soldiers, bless 'em, so soldiers is what they will be. Got that Corporal?"

"Sir!" the corporal had it.

The group of guardsmen laughed, highly amused. Not so the men of the sea. But then, they had not seen the sly wink passed over with the instructions.

"And Corporal..!"

"Sir!"

"When they have dined I want them in the orderly room!"

"Sir!" the corporal acknowledged.

"Well gentlemen, the best of British luck," and having spoken these words of irony, a glint of mischief in his eye, he smiled down at them, amused by their blank expressions.

"Gentlemen, you will need all the luck you can get before your stay with us is over," and with these words spreading dismay he marched off to the orderly room, laughing as he went.

The corporal stood scratching his head in disbelief. "Well I'll stand shaggin'," he said as much to himself as anyone. "'Wilky' of all people," he addressed his words to them now. "Do you know, all the time I've known the big ugly bastard, that is the first time I've ever seen him smile let alone laugh."

"I'm glad 'e finds us so bleedin' funny," said Pedlar cynically.

"You lot ought to be on the stage if you can make bastards like him laugh, my God if you hadn't." Having decided this, the corporal began to fill a billycan with beans and fried bread.

"Never mind the stage Corps, just let me get something down me quick before my stomach thinks my mouth's gone on strike," whined Barrett, impatiently holding out his billycan, perhaps hopeful of getting them both filled.

"Does anybody want porridge?" one of the army cooks wanted to know.

"Oh yes please!" said Benny eagerly moving across to where he presumed the porridge pot was.

Pedlar was more selective and asked what it was like before chancing it. They informed him it was not too bad this particular morning since a small amount of extra sugar had been added.

"In that case I'll try a drop," he said joining Benny at the porridge pot. "Our's don't come in drops mate," said the cook serving up the oats. "Our's is the thick stuff."

"It's bound to be better than the shit 'e dishes up," said Pedlar and as usual he left himself wide open to an attack from the one he tormented. With a swift stomp he brought the heel of his shoe crunching down on the instep of Pedlar.

"Vengeance is mine sayeth the Lord!" sneered Benny cocking a snook from a safe distance.

"Just you wait you little bleeder!" snarled Pedlar but all this served was to provide more amusement for those around him.

"You'll need to look after your feet if you stop with us for very long," warned the corporal with a grin.

A third guardsman had been filling their mugs from a huge tank by means of a tap set in the front at the bottom. "'Tain' exactly the Savoy but it's warm and wet," he told them as he passed the mugs over, "not a bad drop of stuff considerin'."

The words 'drop of stuff' hit Benny. "'Ey up Pedlar, guess what! I've just thought, we won't be gettin' our tot today will we?" Benny said sadly. Pedlar coughed and spluttered oats in all directions.

"Oh Christ yeah! No tot!" his despair was complete.

"Tot? What's all this about a tot then?" asked the corporal flicking remnants of Pedlar's porridge from himself by means of a cloth.

The matelots explained about the daily issue of rum. Pedlar was too busy coughing still.

"I shouldn't worry too much," the corporal told them. "You can get a good drink at the camp bar."

"I daresay you can, but it ain't the same as navy rum for fuck's sake," snapped Pedlar having got his voice back for the moment. "Besides soldier, we've got to pay for that."

Brian Barrett decided he wanted to sit down to finish his breakfast and asked if there were chairs. The corporal apologised for not having given it a thought and led them to a tent a few feet away. He informed them this was the mess tent and suggested they make themselves at home.

A flap on the tent had been rolled up and tied back creating a wide aperture that served as a doorway. Inside they saw chairs and tables, all of the fold-away type.

"Can we smoke in here?" asked Ginger. He looked about to see if anyone was smoking.

"We're not supposed to, it's up to you," said the young guardsman looking at the corporal, uncertain that he had said the right thing.

The corporal was spared by the intervention of Pedlar Palmer. "Look 'ere copper knob I've got to go wi'out my rum so you can go wi' out your pissin' fags. Besides, it's no good comin' to live wi' this lot if you ain't goin' to go by the rules, right!"

Ginger knew better than to back-chat him. Benny could get away with it but no one else.

Benny gazed out at the tents beyond, puzzled by the absence of inhabitants. He noticed only the odd soldier moving about or performing some task. He asked the young Grenadier where everybody was and was informed that a large number were on patrols while others were performing all kinds of duties, those on night guards would probably be sleeping and those off duty were no doubt shopping or sightseeing around Kuala Lumpur.

Ginger and Brian were also gazing through the flap watching the army cooks as they busied themselves preparing the next meal. Pedlar was still dining.

"Smashing cup of tea ain' it," observed Ginger finishing off his third mugfull. Brian agreed by nodding his head as he got up and went off to get himself another one.

"I enjoyed my breakfast as well," Brian said returning. "Didn't you?"

"Yes I damned well did, makes you wonder how they manage it in these conditions don't it?" mused Ginger.

"Yeah Ginge, but you've got to remember they're used to it, they do it all the time."

"I know they do but they still make a darned good job of it though, at least I think they do anyway."

"You're right Ginger, they do make a good job of it an' I know what I'm talking about, I 'ad to work on field kitchens as part of my trainin'," said Benny having also joined the little group.

The corporal who had busied himself elsewhere, came up to them and asked them to put back the chairs and told them where the water was to wash up their mess-kits. He also suggested that the R.S.M. may be getting anxious at the length of time they were taking.

As they went off in search of the orderly tent Benny asked the corporal what position in camp the sergeant-major held, saying he got the impression he was an important man.

"Oh he is important! He most certainly is! He's more important than the officers in a way," explained the corporal. "You see he is a regimental sergeant-major, not just a company sergeant-major, wields a lot of power does old Wilky, you would be surprised. He's not such a bad old bastard really I suppose, bloody good professional old Wilky."

When they reached the orderly tent the R.S.M. was talking to a baby-faced lieutenant and the corporal having discharged his duty, saluted and departed.

"You survived our grub then?" grinned the R.S.M. his baton beating a tattoo on his thigh again. "Right then! Any questions before we proceed further gentlemen?"

Benny had a question. "It isn't really important sergeant-major but I was wondering, why is most of the camp housed in tents and yet there seems to be quite a few brick buildings?"

Instead of ridicule, something he half expected, the R.S.M. treated the question with the same seriousness with which it had been asked.

"It's like this my lad," he said whipping the baton up under his armpit. "The Japanese had a camp here during the last big war and the transport sheds and gatehouse are all that is left which remain habitable. The other structures are derelict and would take far too much money to put in order. In any case, with any luck we shan't be here all that long so why bother?"

"'E's just being a nosey little sod!" said Pedlar Palmer meaning to torment Benny.

Unfortunately for Pedlar the R.S.M. knew nothing of their friendly feud and his words met with ice-cold glare. Obviously, neither he nor his officer considered the remark a worthy one.

"An inquisitive mind is a mind which acquires knowledge," the officer said making his feelings plain.

"Pardon me sir, we must press on," the R.S.M. said more in keeping with an order than a request.

"Yes, of course Ser'Major. When we have kitted them out and allocated platoons they can be left to their platoon commanders I think."

"Indeed they can sir!" agreed the R.S.M. and having returned his salute the officer turned and entered the inner sanctum of the orderly tent.

Once more the party strode out along the pathways between tents like a broody hen and her anxious chicks. This time they stopped outside the tent adjoining the one from which they had received their mess kits.

Inside, it did not take a master sleuth to realise that here was the clothing store for everywhere the matelots looked they saw masses of uniforms and accessories.

"Blenkinsop!" roared the RSM. "Sir!" The answer, muffled and distant, came from somewhere in the rear of the tent. Then emerged a figure, fearful.

"Blenkinsop, you nasty little National Serviceman you. You've been sleeping again, haven't you?" Once again the baton was tapping his massive thigh.

"Me sir? No sir, not me sir!" stammered the unfortunate guardsman.

"Son, do not lie to me, too long in the tooth. Blenkinsop, if you persist in sleeping when you should be working it is only fair that you work when you should be sleeping, get my meaning Blenkinsop?"

"Sir!"

"Good! Now, at the double and I do mean at the double, four sets of uniforms these gentlemen for the use of, move!"

And how poor Blenkinsop moved. He sped from rack to shelf to bundle to rack only to drop items in his over eagerness and hastily retrieving them. All the time he had an eye on his glowering superior.

Watching his performance Benny whispered to Pedlar, "Jesus! No wonder 'e's tired if that's 'ow 'e 'as to work."

The R.S.M., who through it all had never taken his eyes from Blenkinsop, stopped his rocking and glared as the guardsman laid four sets of jungle green uniforms on the table in front. Then he erupted.

"What have we forgotten then, Blenkinsop?"

"Sir?"

"Blenkinsop..." said the R.S.M. with sarcastic condemnation. "I do believe we have forgotten to take the measurements of these gentlemen!"

"But I just thought the smallest sizes we had would do sir!"

"You just thought? You Blenkinsop are not able to think, you are never awake long enough to think."

The R.S.M. leaned right forward to place his hands on the table and his face up close to Blenkinsop's, their noses almost brushing each other.

The guardsman's eyes reflected the dread of impending doom he saw mirrored so uncomfortably close to his own. For fully half a minute Wilky's eyes burned into the other's before the R.S.M. stood back, then with his cane pointed to Pedlar Palmer.

"Does that gentleman look as if he takes the smallest size?" he asked.

Blenkinsop swallowed, and struggled vainly to don a surprised smile. "Oh, that one, I didn't see that one sir!"

"You didn't see him? The biggest of the bloody lot and you say you didn't see him? I know what it is Blenkinsop, if you're not sleepwalking you must have sleeping sickness and I have an excellent cure for sleeping sickness lad. This evening, instead of propping up the bar in the N.A.A.F.I. tent, you can come and keep me company. You and I shall indulge in a little walking, up and down the parade ground. You horrible dose of sleeping sickness you!"

Deeming the matter of no further interest he closed it abruptly and acted as if it had never happened. He swivelled round to speak to Pedlar. "I'll wager you are about an eighteen neck sailor?"

"Well, eighteen an' alf to be exact," Pedlar told him and then added a respectful, "Sergeant Major." These last few minutes had convinced even he that it would be foolish to tangle with R.S.M. Wilkins.

Grenadier Blenkinsop required no prompting now and swiftly exchanged the shirts for ones more in keeping with Pedlar's bull-like neck.

"What waist, about a forty?" he asked Pedlar.

Pedlar nodded. "Yeah! Somewhere around that mark, give or take an inch!"

"Hmm!" The R.S.M. was eyeing Pedlar up and down. "Hmm!" he murmured again. "Don't just stand there man! Get him fixed up!"

Ten minutes or so later the group struggled out of the tent laden with army uniforms and kit. Now, in addition to their own naval and personal gear, they toted jungle green shirts and trousers, gaiters, webbing, one pair of ordinary boots, one pair of calf-length, lace-up jungle boots with sturdy thick rubber soles and canvas uppers, long socks, bush hat and the mess kits handed to them earlier.

They were now passing between neat rows of smaller tents, all of uniform size and all facing the same way. Here and there a guardsman was to be seen busying himself with cleaning or polishing or writing or lazing. Benny noticed that none of them appeared to be under six foot. There may have been but in any case they were all of a size to be expected. After all, he reminded himself, this was the Grenadier Guards.

At the end of each tidy row was placed a small notice-board telling the observer which platoon happened to be housed therein.

Coming to a halt at the end of one such row the R.S.M. gave vent to his ear splitting roar. "'B Platoon Commander ... at the double!"

A muffled "Sir!" echoed from within the first tent and instantly a corporal emerged to stamp smartly to attention and snap "Sir!" once more.

"Brought you a new recruit Corporal," the R.S.M. told him. He turned to the matelots and asked which of them would like to join 'B' Platoon. They looked at each other hesitantly. Ginger happened to be standing nearest and it came as no great surprise when he felt his hand on his shoulder and heard his words inviting him to be the one joining 'B' Platoon.

"Do we 'ave to split up, Sir?" asked Benny deciding it may carry a bit more weight to add the 'sir'.

"Sorry son, the position is this, if any of you happen to be with a platoon going out on ferret duty it would be hard enough and dangerous enough trying to cope with one inexperienced body, taking along two or more green-behind-the-ears, would be tantamount to suicide. A training stint yes, no problem, wouldn't matter a toss then but out here ..." He shook his head and turned his nose up at the thought. "Could cost a lot of lives I'm afraid."

Ginger moved forward to volunteer himself. "It don't matter to me one way or the other Sarge," he said.

The big man swallowed hard at being referred to simply as 'Sarge' but on the point of utterance changed his mind. "Good man," said the R.S.M. condescending. His arm went around Ginger's shoulders as he half shepherded him towards the corporal. "There you are then Higgins, your new Grenadier ... and the best of British!"

The corporal smiled, amused. "Thank you sir!" he said leading Ginger off and lending a helping hand as the matelot dropped something on the way. They disappeared inside the first tent and the party moved on to the next row.

The notice-board at the end of the next row proclaimed it to be 'C' Platoon and the R.S.M.'s great roar beckoned the commander. This time it was a sergeant who emerged, seemingly wise to their coming.

"Sir!" he cried stamping to attention.

Benny took an instant liking to this sergeant who reminded him of an American film star and, almost without realising it, he had stepped forward to volunteer himself for 'C' Platoon.

"Hmm!" murmured the R.S.M. twirling his moustache and grinning. "Seems our young friend can't wait to join your platoon Sergeant Riley."

The sergeant agreed, a friendly smile invading his handsome face. "It certainly looks that way Sar'Major," he said.

From the way these two addressed each other it was evident at once that here was deep understanding and respect on both sides. Both wore medal ribbons and not just campaign ones either.

Benny reasoned they would be about the same age too, around the forty mark he reckoned. Served in this same battalion for a long time no doubt and although Benny was not to know it at the time he was to learn his assumptions were sound.

"Well then young feller-me-lad, you may not know it but you have picked the best bloody sergeant in the whole British army," R.S.M. Wilkins told him and his beaming face had the others believing him.

Sergeant Riley laughed. "Take no notice of him son, he's only saying it because it's true," and his humour had the others laughing too.

Reaching out the sergeant helped himself to the biggest part of Benny's load saying, "Come on then, follow me if you're joining us," and with that he strode off for his tent while Benny struggled gladly along behind him trying to keep up.

"Follow me gentlemen," said the R.S.M. leading the way for the remaining matelots as they went off to find their platoons

Inside the fourth tent of row 'C' the sergeant had dropped the articles he carried on to an empty camp bed. It was a large wooden framed one, much higher off the ground than the ones normally seen. There were four beds in the tent and still ample room to walk about.

"Just dump your gear down their old son and we'll go and complete the formalities," the sergeant said kindly.

These were attended to in Sergeant Riley's tent, the first in the row. He said, "Sit down old son," sitting and motioning to a folding stool standing beside his small desk.

Benny did not mind being called 'old son' by this man, in fact he rather enjoyed it, it seemed to endorse the affinity between them. He parked himself on the stool as the sergeant withdrew a sheath of papers from a drawer in the desk.

"Right, let's have a look at what we've got here then shall we?" He studied the papers briefly and continued. "When we've done all the necessary we'll go a tour round the camp so's you'll know where you are and everything is."

"Okay, Sarge."

"Right, we'll fill this lot in first old son and then go for dinner then take it from there, now, what's your name?

Benny carefully gave details of his full name and his home address in Nuneaton, Warwickshire, all of which were faithfully recorded by Sergeant Riley, along with his birth date in July, 1927. Recorded, too, was the fact that he was not married. His mother was recorded as his next of kin, his service unit as H.M.S. Consort and religion as C. of E.

"Good, now all we want to know is whether or not you want to volunteer to go out on ferret force if we go out on one while you're with us?"

"You bet I do," Benny's face was alive with enthusiasm. "It's somethin' I'm really lookin' forward to," he said truthfully.

"Right old son! We'll see what we can do shall we?" the sergeant said. "Just sign this form on the dotted line for me then."

Benny signed the form and the sergeant placed it back with the others and returned them all to the drawer. "Between you and me there is a good chance we shall be going out," said the sergeant leaning forward resting his forearms on his knees. "It's our turn next, but I must warn it isn't any picnic, the flaming jungle's bad enough on its own without having to worry about bloody reds taking pot shots at you."

"Yeah! I can just imagine Sarge, be a good job when it's all over won't it?" said Benny. "'Ow long do these ferret force whatsits take then?"

"Huh! There's never any telling, sometimes a couple of days, sometimes a couple of weeks, there are so many things can happen," the sergeant told him as he stood up to smarten up his tunic. "I can tell you one thing, if you do come with us you'll be with us until we all come back, you won't be able to hop on a bus and make your own way back," he grinned broadly as he said this.

"And if your skipper or anybody wants you they'll have to bloody well wait, won't they old son," said the sergeant grinning even more.

"Yeah!" chuckled Benny finding the thought highly amusing. "You know what Sarge?" said the ship's cook beaming, "I reckon I'm goin' to enjoy this little trip ashore wi' you lot, honest, I've been looking for somethin' like this to 'appen for a long time. You wouldn't believe 'ow bloody monotonous it gets goin' up an' down the coastline, day in an' day out."

"I understand what you're saying but you know, and this is no disrespect to you, trying to sort these bloody terrorists out is a very serious business." The sergeant had discarded the humour now, his manner had become grave.

"One stupid move, one word spoken too loudly, or a cough or sneeze, or one person trying to be clever could all end up with disastrous results, the whole platoon could finish up getting wiped out ... "

"It's alright Sarge," said Benny interrupting, clearly seeing what the guardsman was getting at. "I know what you're tryin' to say but I won't let you down I promise. I know I act stupid at times but I'm not really."

"Seriously old son," the sergeant said. "I didn't think you would let me down. Not for one minute. If I did you wouldn't be getting the chance if it crops up."

Benny decided it was time he answered the call of nature. "'Ey up Sarge, where's the 'eads round here?"

"Where's the what?" Sergeant Riley screwed up his face at this. "What the devil's the heads?"

It dawned on Benny that he was no longer mixing with naval personnel. "Sorry Sarge, I'm forgettin', I meant the lavatory, toilet, bogs or whatever it is you call it."

"Latrines? Kharsi? Call it what you like, it all means the same thing," and the sergeant grinned.

He moved to the opening and Benny joined him. "I might as well come with you," the sergeant decided leading off.

They had walked to the end of the row of tents to a small clearing and the N.C.O. pointed to a small corrugated-iron structure similar to the type often seen on building sites and allotments. It stood on sloping ground a hundred yards or so from all tents. There was no roof.

The sergeant went into one side, Benny the other, the parting words of the sergeant planting odd suspicions in his mind. "There you are then old son," he said. "It's all your's."

Dirty sacking served as door and partitions and Benny lifted this to one side intent on entering. He did not. He stopped dead in his tracks. He was shocked rigid and filled with instant nausea for there in the ground had been dug a deep hole over which a short, stout, tree branch rested on two stumps, one each side of the hole serving as a most rudimentary seat.

It was the sight and the stench that hit him. With the lack of flushing facilities, this stench was sickening in the extreme. Benny struggled in vain to hold his breath, his face contorted as the fumes permeated the air on all sides. To add to this a myriad of flies buzzed noisily.

Benny had forgotten all about his need to urinate. He was far too busy wrestling against the overpowering feeling that he was going to vomit.

The sergeant was talking to a guardsman when Benny staggered out holding his nose. They laughed at poor Benny's plight. "What's the matter old son?" asked the sergeant enjoying it. "You don't look too well."

The two soldiers laughed again as Benny whipped his hand to mouth and retched. He was play-acting for their benefit but he really did feel sick.

The sergeant decided enough was enough and concluded the chat he had been having with the guardsman. "Right then, tell him I'll be along as soon as I've sorted sailor boy out, okay?"

The sergeant apologised for having to leave him when they reached the tent. "The company commander wants to see me so what I suggest is that you change your gear while you're waiting for me, I shouldn't be too long and then we'll see about some dinner, okay old son?"

With a mere hint of a wave the sergeant went to see his platoon commander and Benny ducked under the tent flap.

He contemplated the heap of jungle green and then his own tropical white uniform. It had long ago ceased to be spotless. He had been so engrossed in the day's events he had not given it a thought. He did now and the thought did nothing for his morale.

"Bloody 'ell," he gasped. He attempted a perfunctory dusting down but conceded defeat and began to disrobe. He tossedthe grubby clothes on the floor with careless indifference, then from the jumble of jungle green flung on the bed he sorted out a pair of trousers and pulled them on, at least he attempted to. They may well have been the smallest size they had but they were still at least five or six inches too long for Benny's twenty-nine inch inside leg.

He picked up the jacket that served as either a shirt or tunic and held it out at arm's length to study it. But he was interrupted by the falling down of his trousers, which, having not been fastened, he had striven to support by holding his legs tightly together. Here they remained while he donned the jacket.

"Hmm!" he murmered shaking his head. The garment fitted quite nicely ... around the body. Unfortunately his wrists and hands were lost from view, enveloped in several inches of excess material.

He stood there pondering, looking and feeling a proper circus clown. The sound of approaching voices decided him. He would remove them forthwith.

Benny was far too slow for as he struggled to find his way out of the lengthy sleeves and the problems they created, two guardsmen entered. They stopped in their tracks as soon as they spotted Benny. They gaped, not believing their eyes.

Benny grinned sheepishly. "It doesn't fit," he said fully expecting them to burst out laughing. "Or at least," he went on, "it only fits where it touches!"

But they did not laugh. There was however a twinkle reflected in their eyes now, hinting at friendly humour and they smiled as they moved to introduce themselves. They had to wait for Benny to disentangle his hands from the long sleeves before they could shake hands however.

"Hi!" said the one nearest to him shooting out his hand. "My name's Bert and this here's Moggy. His name is Maurice but we always call him Moggy."

"Pleased to meet you," said Benny shaking Bert's hand as it dwarfed his own. "They call me Benny."

"Hello Benny," said Moggy. He had big bony hands that were matched by the rest of his frame and as with all these many other big men Benny had met during the last few hours, he gave the sailor a feeling of inadequacy.

"Pleased to meet you Maurice," he said.

"Aw, call me Moggy, everybody else does," said the guardman, "and may I say welcome to our humble abode."

"Thanks! I must admit though, I don't 'alf feel out of place 'ere."

"'Ow do you mean?" asked Bert.

"Well, a little sod like me amongst all you big buggers," Benny told them. He grinned, "there's one thing about it, if you're all as big as the ones I've met up to now the terrorists should see you comin'."

They laughed and Bert asked, "Where abouts do you come from Benny?"

"Back in England you mean?" Bert nodded and Benny told him, "I come from Coventry," thinking it a waste of time to say Nuneaton since he probably never heard of it.

"I thought so," smiled Bert pleased with himself. "I thought when I 'eard your accent you didn't come too far away from me."

"Where do you come from then?" asked Benny, his interest awakened.

"From Daventry," and Bert paused to let it sink in before adding, "an' Moggy 'ere comes from Matlock, mind you," he said with a devilish grin, "I don't think he knows much about the bath part of it, if you get my meanin' Benny?"

Benny considered it time to get away from this line of chat, he had seen it get out of hand before. "Is this your tent then?" he asked them.

"Yeah! There's four of us in here as a rule but the other two have gone to your ship on that exchange caper," explained Moggy.

Benny chuckled to himself at the thought of these tall guardsmen having to bob and duck as they moved about on Consort. He knew from experience how many hazardous obstructions there were to clout unwary skulls.

"'Ow many went on all together?" Benny wanted to know.

"Only six," Bert told him. "I don't know 'ow many Brylcream wallahs went though, do you Moggy?"

"Six I think, same as us," said Moggy. "Lord above know's what it's all about cos I don't," and as he spoke he sat down on his bed, reached down under it and pulled out a small box which contained shoe brushes, cloths and polish.

He drew out a pair of black boots, picked one up and studied it, his hand inside it. Benny waited for him to start polishing the boot at the same time wondering why for the shoe positively sparkled. The toe cap was like lacquered gloss. He marvelled at it and was about to remark so when Moggy dropped his forearms onto his knees and looked at Bert, pensive.

"I wonder how poor old Bill is?" he asked his fellow guardsman.

"Not too good last I 'eard," Bert said, his tone saddened.

Benny wondered who old Bill was and what could be wrong with him but Bert, reading his thoughts perhaps, put him in the picture. "'E was one that should 'ave gone on your ship Benny," he said. "Poor old sod got wounded though an' ended up in 'ospital instead."

"Wounded?" Benny's ears were flapping now. "'Ow did that 'appen then, terrorists?"

"Oh ar! It was the bastard terrorists alright!" Bert said, his face told its own tale about how he felt over this. "Walked smack into a fuckin' ambush we did, made me bleedin' sweat I don't mind admittin'."

"We were lucky not to get wiped out," Moggy said adding his little bit with equal grimness.

Between them, first one taking up the story then the other taking over, they went on to explain how a party of twenty five Grenadiers had gone out on a routine patrol only to find themselves in the middle of a large group of 'reds'. They had obviously been tipped off by informers and were lying in wait. Three of the guardsmen had been wounded, one severely, but the patrol had given a very good account of themselves, killing two, wounding at least five and taking one prisoner before the rest fled.

They explained that it was rare to come in contact and even rarer to kill, wound or take any prisoners since they were extremely adept at jungle warfare.

The guardsmen had spit and polished their boots, stopping only to put their few words in as they felt the need, either to confirm or correct or add, and Benny watched fascinated as they polished away.

He had buttoned up the jacket and put on the army boots. The amazing thing was they had boots to fit his feet if not uniform to fit his body.

His companions rendered help and advice leaving their 'bulling' to tuck him up here, roll up his sleeves and neatly fold the excess trouser leg so that the long gaiters concealed the overlong material.

Now Benny did not present so comical a figure. He picked up a boot to gaze at the dazzling toe. "'Ow the bloody 'ell do you get a shine like that?" he asked.

"Easy when you know 'ow," grinned Moggy. "You burn 'em, polish 'em, spit on 'em, rub 'em with a toothbrush or comb, spit on 'em, polish 'em, rub 'em with a toothbrush or comb, spit on 'em, add a more polish, spit on 'em, rub 'em ..."

"Alright! Alright!" laughed Benny interrupting Bert's marathon explanation. "I get the message, an' I take your word for it, it's hard bloody work!"

"Let's just say it's all part of the bullshit routine we 'ave to put up with," said Bert "Our boots are only a small part of it."

"We have to get everything shining and polished and blancoed. You ought to see the performance sometimes, buttons, everything," Moggy told Benny who now realised that he had no longer cause for complaint regarding the amount of spitting and polishing he had to do on board.

"What do you mean by 'burn 'em'?" he asked visualising roaring flames licking round the boots.

They explained that different people had different methods but that the basic idea was to heat the toe cap with a candle or match or lighter and then to rub hard and smooth with the back of a comb or handle of a toothbrush. They were on the point of demonstrating when a bugle summoned them to dinner.

"That's it, grub up!" declared Bert reaching for his mess tins which lay beneath the foot of his bed. Then, striding for the tent exit he called, "Come on then sailor boy, grab your tackle if you want any grub."

Benny hesitated, unsure. "I'm sure the sergeant said somethin' about comin' back to show me where ..." A familiar voice cut him short.

"Talking about me old son?" asked the sergeant having loomed up to bar the exit of all three. "Good, now you two are here you can take young Benny to dinner and show him the ropes, okay? I'm tied up with Captain Gregory just now."

"You can call me Chef if you like Sarge, if it's any easier," Benny told him. "I ain't a proud chap."

The guardsmen had accepted the responsibility of having Benny under their wing and the sergeant strode briskly off leaving them to make their way towards the mess tent.

"Come on then, pull your fingers out," cried Bert eating up the ground with great strides. "We're on parade at thirteen thirty hours remember Moggy!"

Benny found himself jogging as he tried to keep up with them. He reflected the difference between dining aboard ship and out here in the middle of the jungle and this in turn reminded him of his tot.

"I know one thing chaps," he called after them, "I'm goin' to miss my rum ration."

"Yeah!" said Moggy over his shoulder. "I suppose there'll be quite a few things you'll miss."

"Including bloody dinner if you don't get a move on," shouted Bert intent only on getting to the field kitchens and food.

Guardsmen were coming together from all directions now, all funnelling towards the field kitchen spread a few yards from the mess tents. Bert yelled to one just ahead of themselves.

"'Ey Alan, come and meet Benny!"

The soldier half turned, saw who it was calling him and paused waiting for them to catch up. "Bloody 'ell! Scrapin' the bottom of the barrel now ain' they?" grinned Alan eyeing the matelot up and down in some disbelief. Benny, used to far worse than this, merely smiled back.

"You ignorant bleeder!" snapped Bert. "For your information mate, Benny just 'appens to be one of the navy lads who've come to stay with us, 'e's standin' in for Joe. Right?"

Alan beamed down at Benny, reached out a hand and said, "Pleased to meet you Benny mate, anybody's got to be better than Joe, even from the bottom of the barrel."

"This here's Tim by the way," he added, jerking a thumb in the direction of a newcomer.

"'Ello Tim," and Benny thrust forward a hand in greeting.

"Hello, pleased to meet you," smiled Tim, his round boyish face marred by pimples and spots of adolescence, "and what part of the world do you come from when you're at home?" he asked cheerily.

"'E comes from Coventry, well near Coventry," Bert told him before Chef had chance to say so himself. They had now joined the queue filtering along.

"Coventry?" Alan gasped. "Bloody hell! I went out with a girl from there, she was cracker as well," his vivid expression conjured up a

95

picture of rare beauty for them.

"Where do you two come from?" Chef asked. Alan told him he came from Leeds and Tim from Blackburn.

"Bloody foreigners," sneered Bert and this did bring a physical response from Alan. He waded in throwing playful punches and Bert did his best to knock his head off with his mess tins. They both stopped dead however when the R.S.M.'s voice blasted their ear drums from six feet.

"Silence! You 'orrible lot!" He had been standing just inside the mess tent and came out to see what the hubbub was about. "If we have a pantomime I'll put you down as fairies but we are not going to have a pantomime are we?"

"No sir!" said Alan trying to give an impression of innocence.

"No gentlemen we are not, but we are going to have din-dins if we are good boys," he leaned forward from the hips swaying from one to the other as he growled at them.

He had allowed the rest to file past to the field kitchens as he chastised these two. "Right! Go and get your din-dins but remember, any pratting about and I'll have you pratting about on the parade ground! Got that?"

More jostling and banter came further down the line but the instant the R.S.M. was spotted it stopped, like magic. The line of troops walked past him strangely subdued and most orderly, they reached the field kitchen to be served by the cooks and then made for the mess-tents to sit and dine.

Benny and the others were edging forward and were about to be served. Bert nudged him saying, "Get your cans ready." He glanced round and saw the men about him had put knife, fork and spoon into a breast pocket for convenience and carried one billycan in each hand. Their mugs were clutched in either one or two fingers.

Suddenly it was Benny's turn. He held forth his utensils and with a 'slop', 'slurp' and 'plop' the regimental cooks had dumped his share of the rations into the proffered tins. Into one billycan went the main course and into the other went the sweet. While this had been happening a cook had grabbed the mug from his fingers and filled it with tea. He hooked it back into his fingers, all without a word, before reaching for the next in line.

Following Bert and company into the mess tent Benny studied

what he now carried with mixed emotions. He remarked that he would not like to carry it far.

"Don't you worry sailor boy, you wouldn't get far," said Bert sitting down.

"Why's that then?" asked the ship's cook putting his food on the table, struggling not to spill his tea.

"Why?" cried Moggy since Bert had a mouthful of sausage. "With this greedy lot of bastards about? Huh!" he grunted and left the rest to Benny's imagination. Besides, he too had a mouthful of his own to contend with now.

"Get it down you Benny lad," said Bert through a mixture of tea and food.

"If you don't want it sailor, pass it over here," Alan said stuffing food down at a rate of knots.

Benny wasn't really listening. He was watching with some amusement the way these guardsmen ate like ravenous wolves, swilling the food down with great gulps of tea. He tucked into his own slowly.

Bert, Moggy and Alan, with apologies for having to shoot off, were on their way out while Benny was still on his main course. They had arranged for Tim, who was off duty, to look after Benny and he had said he would take him on a tour of the camp.

Benny had explained that he felt the sergeant intended to do this but maybe he was still tied up with Captain Gregory.

"I'm glad you're not leaving me on my own," he told Tim as they washed up their utensils in the huge tanks provided. "I'd get lost in this bloody great maze of tents."

He found himself dreaming of life on Consort and thought how very different life was here with these guardsmen. Still, he told himself, it was all part of the exercise. Besides, how else could one of the services really appreciate or understand the part played by the other two in this struggle to beat the terrorists? It occurred to him that no matter how clear a picture he painted, his shipmates would never truly realise what it was actually like in these conditions. But, he was forced to admit, to him it was both enjoyable and exciting. Poor Benny, he was not to know what lay around the corner, was he?

Tim suggested they take their mess kits to the tent before embarking on any tour and when they arrived they found Bert sitting on his bed puffing away at a cigarette. He was leaning back on the folded blankets and pillows relaxing and day-dreaming.

"I thought you were on duty?" Tim said surprised.

"I was but it's been changed, I'm not on till later tonight now," Bert said giving no hint as to whether he bothered or not. He spoke to Benny next. "Sit y'self down for five minutes sailor, let your dinner settle," he said.

Tim excused himself to take his mess kit to his tent and Benny put away his own before plopping down on his camp bed as if exhausted. Funny thing, he felt it.

"Want a smoke?" asked Bert. "No ta! Thank's all the same," said Benny lying back to rest his head on his hands. "I don't smoke."

"You what!" gasped Bert sitting upright with surprise. "Don't smoke?" he said lying back now that he accepted the fact. "God's truth, I thought all you matelots smoked. Did you 'ear that Timmo?" he asked Tim who had returned to sit himself on Moggy's bed.

"'E's pulling your leg mate," said Tim. "What do you do with all them duty free fags then?" Tim wished to know hoping to catch the ship's cook out.

"Ah! That would be tellin'," grinned Benny and with a wink implied that he did very nicely thank you very much and then he changed the topic of conversation.

"I see your boots shine the same as Bert's an' Moggy's," he said with an admiring gaze at Tim's footwear. Tim raised a leg to glance at his boot. He twisted his ankle back and forth studying his shining footwear and grunted, non-committal.

"I was sayin' to them," persisted Benny. "It beats me 'ow you manage to get a shine like that."

"Bullshit!" said Tim turning at the same time to ask Bert for a cigarette. "Smoke your bloody own you cheeky sod!" snapped Bert. "Bullshit, Benny," said Tim as he lit up the cigarette and took up the chat where he had left off. "That's all it is."

"Maybe," Benny said still admiring the boot Tim was gazing idly at again, perhaps seeing it in a different light now he had a smoke. "But I still think it's marvellous."

"Huh!" scoffed Tim. "You wouldn't think it was so marvellous if you had to bull the bleeding things!"

"It ain't so bad really," Bert condescended, lighting up another cigarette. "At least it's better than whitewashin' coal."

"Whitewashin' coal," spluttered Benny. "You're jokin'!"

"I ain't," Bert insisted. He turned to Tim for confirmation. "I ain't jokin' am I?"

"It's right Benny," confirmed Tim, "honest to God, you wouldn't believe all the bullshitting that goes on in this mob."

"You bloody matelots don't know 'ow well off you are," said Bert looking fairly well off himself nonetheless.

"'Ey!" cried the ship's cook not taking this lying down. "You 'old your 'orses a minute! How dare they? It ain't all milk an' 'oney in the 'Andrew' let me tell you!"

"The 'Andrew'?" asked Bert pulling a puzzled face.

"Yeah, the navy. There's one thing," he persisted determined to set the record straight. "You don't get seasick on terra firma, now do you?"

"No! But you can get your bloody arse shot off," grinned Bert cheekily. "Well, you can say what you like, bullshit or no bullshit, I wish I could get half as good a shine on my shoes," Benny told them and he meant every word.

"Well Benny," said Tim finishing his cigarette and getting up from the bed. "It's time we made a move."

"Yeah, okay comin'," said Benny, getting to his feet and attempting to sort out his oversize uniform as best he could.

Tim's guided tour proved most illuminating and it took much longer than the ship's cook had imagined it would. He had had no conception of just how large an area a battalion of troops required.

He had been introduced to, and welcomed by, countless dozens of Grenadier Guardsmen as they strolled up and down and around. One thing above all else however was to be embedded in his mind forever and that, the sight of these guardsmen performing marching miracles.

Tim had stopped to point out what he said was a kind of Changing of the Guard taking place on the large clearing that served as a parade ground. Benny was transfixed with wonder.

He witnessed the unbelievable spectacle of men marching and counter-marching with a precision that took the breath away and this on a makeshift parade ground that was little more than a rough clearing set in the heart of the Malayan jungle.

The ship's cook felt his heart swelling with pride. If only his shipmates were here to witness it with him. If only they could see him now, serving with the Third Battalion Grenadier Guards. Well? He was, wasn't he?

CHAPTER SIX

Bert sat on the ground cross legged, using the bed and a small case as a desk as they all wrote home. He stared towards the roof of the tent, head to one side seeking inspiration. After writing nothing more than 'Dear Mum and Dad' he had come to a full stop. What could he tell them? Nothing exciting or interesting ever happened out here. Well it did he supposed but he couldn't tell them.

Bert and Moggy had supplied Benny with paper, pen and envelope and he sat on the bed, a folded blanket and pillow resting on his knees served as his writing-top. Benny had pages to relate. Sadly however our ship's cook found he could not relate pages. The other's told him that the censor had a keen eye, thick black pen and staunch determination to see no news which might be of information to the enemy got through. Benny was now stuck for something to write about.

Moggy sat on his bed leaning back against his blankets and pillow. He used a large hardback novel to support his notepaper. He seemed to have something to write about but he had paused in his scribing to chew at the end of his pen.

"How do you spell Utopia?" he asked no one in particular. He studied the two unsuccessful attempts he had already made as he waited for help but no one in particular was listening.

"It's U.T.O.P.I.A.," Benny said rattling off the letters quickly knowing Moggy would not remember them.

"What the 'ell do you want to spell Utopia for?" asked Bert as Benny spelt and Moggy wrote.

"Mind your own bleeding business," he was told for his trouble.

Moggy, happy now that he had his word spelt, buried his nose in his letter intent on getting on with it.

Bert had winked mischievously at Benny. He was intent too. Intent on Moggy not getting on with his letter. "What did you want Utopia for?" he asked trying to sound sincere. "Are you writing poetry or somethin'?"

"Don't talk so bloody wet!" snapped Moggy. "Do I look like a poet for God's sake?"

"Yeah! Come to think about it, just let your 'air grow down to your shoulder dearie," said Bert putting on an effeminate tone and manner. "I'm sure you'd make a very good poet!"

Any response was cut short by the unnanounced arrival of Sergeant Riley.

"By your beds!" he ordered and the response was immediate. Benny stood up too not sure if it affected him or not.

He looked at Benny and smiled a friendly smile and the ship's cook had a feeling he had something important to say concerning himself. He had. His news set Benny's heart thumping.

"Gentlemen," said the sergeant. "We have an early morning ahead of us. Intelligence have informed us that communist guerrillas have been located a few miles away and we are to go and ferret them out, okay?"

"Okay Sarge!" the trio beamed. Benny sensed now that in spite of a moan or two the guardsmen were just as keen as he to get on with the job of sorting out these troublesome terrorists.

"What are you getting excited about sailor boy?" asked the sergeant and Benny's face fell flat. "Nobody has said anything about you going."

"But Sarge, you said ..." he was shattered as he turned to his guardsmen colleagues. "'E said I could go didn't 'e?" he pleaded but they merely shrugged their shoulders implying it was all news to them. Benny had not seen the winks.

The torment in Benny's eyes melted his teasing and along with Moggy and Bert, he laughed. "It's alright old son," and as he spoke he ruffled Benny's hair like a father would. "We've already got permission for you to come if you want to."

"If I want to? You know I do," he reached forward to snatch up the hand of the sergeant and shake it as if his life had just been saved.

The instant he had gone Benny started to do a highland fling but Bert caught him by the shoulders to stop him. "I don't want to be a wet blanket but if I were you I would save all the celebrations until I got back."

Benny had the sensation of cold water trickling down his back. Was Bert implying there was a good chance he would not be coming back?

"Oh bloody 'ell," gasped Bert remembering something. "I've just thought, that's put paid to that little drinking session we were goin' to 'ave tonight."

Benny was not worrying about drinking sessions. His mind was full only of tomorrow and its promises. It hit him suddenly. No one had yet mentioned the time they would be getting up in the morning. He was assured they would find out.

"It would be as well Benny if you finished off your letters so's they could be posted," suggested Moggy being helpful. "You never know how long it will be before you can get to write again, if you ever do get to write again," he added being most unhelpful now.

"I finished mine just as the sergeant came in," he told the others. "It only want's postin'."

"I've finished mine as well," Moggy said ferreting around his stationery. "Damned trouble is I can't find my stamps."

"Blimey!" gasped Benny slapping his forehead for being such an idiot. "I never thought about a stamp."

Without a word but wearing an old fashioned look Bert opened his wallet of stationery and took from it a stamp which he held out for Benny to take.

"Oh thank's Bert mate, you're a real pal you are," he took the stamp, licked it and stuck it on the envelope he held. "'Ow much do I owe you?"

"It tells you on the bloody stamp," grinned Bert cheekily. "'Ave I got to do all your thinkin' for you or what?"

"Sorry," chuckled Benny too happy with life to retort otherwise. He felt down into his pockets looking for change and the sound of money chinking caused Bert to explain that anything likely to make any unnecessary noise like keys or money should be left behind or placed in safe keeping since the slightest sound could betray their presence in the jungle, as could strong after shave and such.

Benny thought of his fellow matelots who he had not seen since they were all split up earlier that morning and wondered if he would see them at the N.A.A.F.I. Knowing Pedlar and Ginger, they were sure to be there.

"Do you know," he said reflective. "I 'aven't seen any of my shipmates since we got 'ere, funny ain' it?"

"I saw a couple of 'em gettin' on the wagon goin' into Kuala before dinner. P'raps they've gone shoppin' or somethin'," Bert said casually.

"Wonder who that was then?" wondered Benny. "I was thinkin' if we might see any of 'em at the bar," he said still wondering who it was that had gone into Kuala Lumpur.

"Well," said Bert having come to a decision. "I don't know about you pair but I'm off for a pint."

They both rose to tidy up and join him in his walk to the N.A.A.F.I. dropping their letters in the post box on the way.

Inside the tent they ordered three pints. Benny, showing willing, pulled a Malayan ten dollar note from his money belt. Their eyes lit up when they saw this.

"'Oly bloody mackerel!" cried Bert. "Just look at what old money bags 'as got!"

"Christ!" cried Moggy. "Keep that lot safe else it will soon disappear," he said.

The beer was warm. Warm and not by choice. Benny sipped at it and pulled a face. "Urgh!" he cried putting his glass down on the table. His companions laughed and took great gulps of theirs.

Music from Radio Malaya was being broadcast from two loudspeakers at the end of the tent. Benny gazed about and saw Alan and Tim approaching their table and then suddenly he was a much happier man for behind them came his old pal Pedlar Palmer and Ginger.

He beckoned them as he got to his feet and made for the bar intending to get them a drink but he was too late. "It's alright Chef," Pedlar called to him. He jerked a thumb barwards. "Brian's gettin' 'em in."

He looked in the direction the thumb pointed and saw Brian Barrett was being served. "Come an' sit with us over 'ere," he invited. "Where the 'ell 'ave you been all day?"

"We've been out gettin' stores would you believe," Pedlar informed him going on to ask where he himself had been. Benny performed the introductions and related the day's events and news. Before he could say anything about tomorrow however he caught the looks coming his way from Moggy and Bert and realised he was meant to say nothing.

During the evening one or two more of 'C' platoon joined them and were introduced and as the beer went down the spirits crept up. They were in the middle of a good old sing song when Sergeant Riley made his entrance. The merriment came to a halt as one by one they realised he was in their midst.

Bert was first to speak. "Only 'avin' a couple Sarge," he said. "I'm as dry as a bone, honest."

"That's alright soldier," smiled the sergeant. "Just as long as you don't get up in the morning with a hangover — and late! I've only come to remind you to get your suppers tonight gentlemen, we won't be having breakfast in the morning because we have a very early start."

Bert had stated they were only having two pints. Foolish statement really since Pedlar and company were in their midst. There was the added consideration of the next day's programme. Pedlar had finally got the story out of them after the sergeant had dropped by to warn them of the need to rise very early. He had poured scorn and ridicule over Benny for being so stupid to go but the ship's cook knew he was secretly envious.

The two pints became three and then four and no doubt with the speed they were drinking would soon have become 'one over the eight' but for timely intervention of supper time.

They collected their mess kits and sauntered down to the field kitchen. When Benny approached the cluster of army ovens and cooking facilities he thought the beer was playing tricks with his eyes but no, he was seeing what he saw, not any illusion or mirage.

"Them natives over there," said Benny indicating to Bert where they were by use of head and eyes. "Over there look, moving around the field kitchens, look at 'em!" He stared at them with amusement and wonder.

"Oh, them Dyaks you mean," Bert spoke with admiration. "they're a Godsend Benny, a real Godsend," he said, explaining they were an aboriginal race of headhunters from Borneo who were attached to them and helping fight the 'reds'.

"Don't you let appearances fool you, they are bloody deadly I might tell you. You ask Moggy 'ere, 'e'll tell you the same."

"It's right sailor," and Moggy's expression tallied with that of Bert's. "Mind you, it's only natural when you think about it, they've been born and bred in jungles which are probably much worse than these so it's only common sense they should be some of the best jungle fighters in the world."

"Yeah!" agreed Benny holding out his mess tins and mug for the cooks to fill. As they strolled to the mess tent with their meal Bert and Moggy explained how these colourful Dyaks served several useful purposes from tracking to actually fighting. They would go out in the dark of night in search of their prey and when they caught up with them, usually as they slept, they would decapitate them.

"They are 'ead 'unters when all's said an' done," Bert reminded him.

"From the way they're behaving it look's as if they're off again tonight somewhere," observed Moggy thoughtfully.

"I can't get over 'ow small they are," said Benny. He found it hard to conceive from their features and apparently friendly manner that these self same men could be bloodthirsty killers. Their hair was thick, slick and jet black, cut in the style of roof thatching, a thick fringe over their eyes.

"They look just like a bunch of cheeky schoolkids don't they?" he said as much to himself as the others. "Who'd think they were cold blooded head hunters?"

They finished dining and pottered over to the tanks holding the washing-up water. As they washed out their utensils Benny gave Bert a nudge and pointed to where one Dyak stood beside one of the cooks. Each and every time the cook moved, so did the Dyak. He was literally getting under the feet of the tall Grenadier.

As Benny watched it amused him. It amused Bert. It amused Moggy. It most certainly did not amuse the guardsman. Alan and Tim and the three other matelots, joined them to stand and watch with amusement. So too did others.

"What do you think's goin' on?" asked Benny hoping someone would tell him.

"He's after Ginger's scalp," Bert said, as if it were the most natural thing in the world.

Suddenly Benny wondered if it was amusing after all. He stared into Bert's face. "You're kiddin'," he said but knew he was not.

"I ain't, honest mate," Bert told him. "You see the colour of his 'air? Red ain' it?" No doubt about it, Benny had to agree. "Well," continued Bert, "I don't know 'ow true it is but they reckon they've never seen red haired people before and to get a red 'aired scalp would be a treasure beyond price see."

"Surely to God 'e wouldn't 'ave the audacity to scalp 'im," cried Benny wondering if the red haired Guardsman was aware of the danger. "Would 'e Bert?" he asked all but pleading.

"No, stupid," grinned Moggy. "All he want's probably is just a lock of his hair."

They remained watching and every now and again the cook would glare down at the grinning Dyak and swear at him, at the same time pushing him away. This served to encourage the little man. He would grin all the more, hold out his hands like a beggar might and nod his head vigorously.

The unhappy cook swore some more but was stopped by the intervention of Sergeant Riley. "Alright Hartopp! That's enough!" the sergeant told him firmly.

The guardsman turned to him pleading. "But Sarge," he cried. "The little bleeder is driving me up the pissing wall!"

"Well soldier," the sergeant said still calm and controlled. "You know the answer as well as I do!"

"Give him some of my hair?" gasped the cook staring at the sergeant madly for daring to suggest such a thing. "Never!" said the adamant cook.

"Well, it's your funeral," said the sergeant and Benny wondered if the N.C.O. had chosen these words deliberately. "Just you remember though Hartopp, he may get tired of waiting!"

Hartopp got the meaning but was unsure what to say or do now. He glanced at the grinning Dyak who still hovered at his feet, then at the sergeant.

"Just think about it lad," the sergeant went on. "If he gets tired of waiting for a lock of your gorgeous hair, well ..."

Those around witnessing the proceedings could plainly see what was afoot and Benny whispered to those near him. "'E's a bloody good actor ain' 'e." Only Hartopp was unaware he was being set up.

And now Sergeant Riley played his ace. "We won't be able to help you," he said almost apologetic. "He will just sneak up in the night and that will be that and who knows," he deliberated, knowing he had won the game, "he may not be able to stop himself, centuries of inborn instinct may take over and he won't be able to settle for just a lock of hair. How do you think we would feel having to write home to your parents telling them we had to bury their son's headless ..."

"Alright!" yelled Hartopp. He had heard from the others in the past about the exploits of these Dyaks and really believed there was something in what the sergeant said.

He looked for a sharp knife, found one and passed it to the sergeant. Benny could not help but feel for the young guardsman yet at the same time had to admit he was enjoying himself.

"Only a small bit Sarge," begged the cook.

The sergeant turned to his audience and gave them a cheeky wink. Then, with all due ceremony, he took hold of a clump of hair and carefully cut it off, his action bringing uproarious applause.

The little Dyak, having guessed what was happening, held his hand out with agitated animation while at the same time mumbling excitedly. The sergeant went to hand over the lock of hair but the Dyak could restrain himself no longer. He reached up and snatched it from the sergeant's grasp and immediately shot off to show his fellow tribesmen his prize, the cheers of the troops following him.

His fellows mobbed him and the free-for-all did not stop until each had a few strands of hair for himself. It would be bound in some way and attached to the thongs around their waists, in some cases joining the small pieces of conserved scalp already hanging there. What tales they would have to tell when they got back home to Borneo, Benny told himself.

Ginger caressed the affected spot lovingly. "I should have bloody-well known better," he moaned. "Fancy cutting off a damned great fistful like that Sarge, you must have cut half my hair off."

"Would you rather have lost it all Hartopp?" asked the N.C.O.

The cook knew that was the end of the matter and still caressing his hair went back about his chores.

That night Benny thought he would never get to sleep. He and his two army buddies had exchanged small talk, stories and jokes for what seemed ages. He listened to their heavy breathing now and envied them. He just could not get to sleep.

Quite apart from his mind working overtime chewing over the future and its promises there was the added drawback of weird animal noises emanating from the surrounding jungle. Just when he thought sleep would never come, he slept although the animals he had heard in his waking hours now invaded his dreams.

CHAPTER SEVEN

It was dark when Benny woke. Sergeant Riley had shaken him by the shoulder gently as he said softly, "Time to make a move sailor old son."

"Right Sarge," Benny told him and, satisfied, the sergeant moved silently on, even as he did so Benny was getting dressed.

Benny saw in the dim light that Bert and Moggy were already up. Moggy, who had been busy getting dressed, stifled a laugh, unable to contain himself. "Just where the hell do you think you're going?" he asked in a whisper.

"Why?" Benny asked. "Just take a look at yourself for God's sake," Moggy suggested. "Have a look at this idiot, Bert."

Bert too struggled to keep his laughter quiet. "Well," he cried softly. "What a bloody fine soldier you look!"

Benny did look. He did not believe it. How he had come to dress the way he had he would never know but he did know he had to sort himself out quickly. His tunic shirt was on inside out. He had laced up the jungle boots leaving his trouser leg on the outside and the broad webbing belt was around his waist but not around his trousers.

"You need all your jungle gear on Benny mate," Bert told him. "We may be in it for a few days so make sure you get it right. Try and get it as comfortable as you can, no lumps or twists that are soon going to cause you problems."

Benny struggled some more and, with the help of his mates, he was finally ready and not a moment too soon for the sergeant stuck his head under the tent flap to call softly but firmly. "Hurry up. We're moving out!" and his head disappeared.

"Got everythin' Benny?" Bert asked making a mental note of his own requirements. "Boots laced all the way up to keep the leeches out?"

"Leeches?" Benny asked as they made their way out. "What bloody leeches?"

Moggy turned the lamp out and followed behind. "Oh you'll soon find out what leeches are," he said.

The lorry was parked near the transport sheds. At the tailboard stood a young second lieutenant, revolver nestling in the holster at his side. Sergeant Riley stood near the rear handing out guns and magazines and emergency ration packs. The corporal gave out packs of sandwiches.

The young officer smiled warmly when he saw Benny approach. "Aha," he said, "and you, I take it, will be our guest?"

"Yes sir!" said Benny smiling back and adding, "I was 'opin' it didn't show." The officer said nothing to this but did broaden his smile.

"His name is Stretton sir!" Sergeant Riley informed him as he held out a Sten for the ship's cook. This was followed by four magazines, emergency rations and, finally, sandwiches. Thus laden Benny clambered up, helped by guardsmen seated near the rear. He had stuffed the magazines into the breast pouches provided and the rations into the haversack. He sat down and with both hands free to hold the Sten he felt better and much more relaxed although the cumbersome kit did not make for comfort.

Once they were all on Sergeant Riley checked the tailboard and then helped release the rolled up canvas which fell to shut out what little light there was.

The engine burst into life and Benny's jungle jaunt had begun. He couldn't see his fellow passengers except when a match was struck to light a cigarette. He may not be able to see them but he could plainly hear them coughing and making all the other noises associated with the first cigarettes of the morning.

One other thing Benny clearly felt was the tenseness which engulfed the lorry. Even Benny, born chatterbox though he was, had nothing he wished to say at this moment.

He could see through the chinks that it was almost daylight now and was just wondering how much farther they had to travel when the lorry ground to a stop, jerking its human cargo to life.

Benny could hear foreign tongues cackling away near the front of the vehicle. Sergeant Riley held a finger to his lips commanding total silence but he need not have bothered for they sat tense and expectant. They had gone through it all before. Benny felt sure that those outside would hear the thumping of his heart for thump it did.

The voices were whispering still and suddenly Benny realised that one almost inaudible whisper was coming from inside the lorry. He peered hard and saw that up front sat a slightly built man wearing civilian clothes. He saw that although this man wore European attire and a Panama hat he was Chinese. It was he who was whispering, holding his head close to the side of the lorry his mouth touching the canvas covering.

Benny then heard the conversation repeated in English for the benefit of the officer. He was dying to ask what was going on but had already disciplined himself to remaining silent. This for Benny would be no mean achievement.

Suddenly the lorry was on the move again and, unable to resist, Benny turned in an effort to peer through the gaps in the canvas and saw they were passing through a village where even at this hour people were milling about.

Soon Sergeant Riley spoke to them. "You may relax a little now gentlemen but keep it quiet please!" His voice was soft but it was a definite order nonetheless.

As if by magic the tension eased. Benny was puzzled by the way things were developing. Why could they relax now when they were probably nearer the enemy? Why all the whispering? And who was the Chinaman up front and what was he doing on the lorry?

He turned to Bert sitting beside him. "Jesus Bert! I wish they'd open the back up," he made a show of fanning away the troublesome smoke. "This smoke's bloody killin' me," he fanned some more. "God! What would I give for a breath of fresh air!"

"We daren't 'ave the back rolled up Benny," Bert quietly explained. "We don't want them to see us or 'ow many of us there are and secondly, and this is vital really, there is no way that bloke up front," he jerked a thumb to indicate the civilian, "wants to be seen."

"What's old Charlie Chan doin' up there?" asked Benny unable to resist the wit.

"Funny you should call 'im that Benny," Bert smiled. "That's what 'e is really, a sort of detective. 'E works for our intelligence, interpreter as well 'e is," Bert's tone was one of admiration. "You can take it from me Benny mate, 'e's a very shrewd operator that one, very clever bloke."

"What was 'e doin' back there?" Benny asked. "'E was talkin' to another intelligence agent probably, your guess is as good as mine but whoever it was they were most likely puttin' 'im wise to all the latest moves and goin's on."

"Just like the films ain' it," he stared at the oriental trying to make up his mind whether or not he looked like a red-under-the-bed. "Bloody 'ell," he said finally, "talk about fun an' games!"

"But this is not fun and games," came the sobering words from Sergeant Riley sitting on the other side of him. "This is all for real old son, and you would do well to remember that!" They came to a second halt ten minutes later and once again the sergeant bade them be silent. They heard the cab door open and then the canvas at the rear was pulled aside.

"Right men! Out you get!" it was the young second lieutenant. The troops pushed the cover to one side as they clambered out, well versed in the procedure.

Benny found it more difficult to climb down since his legs and arms were so much shorter than those of the guardsmen but when he finally did stand down he saw they had stopped in a small clearing at the foot of hilly terrain.

He was surprised. Although the latter few miles had been a rougher ride he had not guessed the vehicle had left the road at all.

As the Grenadiers disembarked they automatically formed two ranks, two rows of Guardsmen and one ship's cook. The driver, checking all was in order, wished them luck, saluted the officer and climbed back into his cab to drive the lorry back to camp. The mysterious Chinaman was still on board, still hidden from view.

The officer watched solemnly until they were out off sight before turning to his men, the sergeant, the corporal and twelve other ranks including Benny.

"Right men!" the officer said in a voice just loud enough for them to hear. "This is the position we find ourselves in," he paused to smile. "If our information is reliable, and I must say that up to the present it has been and of course we have no choice but to act on it, we are after a group of at least thirty 'reds' and we know they are in this area since 'D' platoon stumbled across them yesterday.

"After a brief skirmish the enemy took off but not before 'D' platoon had wounded at least one and taken two prisoners. One guardsman was slightly wounded in the shoulder. This skirmish took place about five miles north of here and while we push north 'A' platoon will be coming in from the west and 'B' platoon from the east and hopefully we should catch them in the middle."

The guardsmen were obviously pleased with his news for a murmur of approval swept through the ranks.

"Alright! Remember I said hopefully men," he said dampening the wave of excitement. "We all of us know just how tricky it is trying to nab these beggars, and an area of jungle such as we have to cover poses a multitude of problems." He paused to glance at his watch. "We all know only too well — just how cunning these devils are. We are aware that the skirmish may be a red-herring and that 'D' platoon could fall into an ambush or the like but intelligence do not think so. Well men, that's the picture, with any luck we may get a crack at the blighters first. Right Sergeant, carry on."

Leaving the sergeant to take charge now he marched off along the overgrown pathway ahead.

"You know the drill men, off you go then," and one by one the guardsmen followed their officer. They left a few yards distance between each one for fear of ambush or attack.

"Right old son," said the sergeant to Benny. "You had better stay nearer the rear, okay!" His warm and friendly smile was meant to reassure the sailor. "Just keep your eyes and ears open and watch what we do, and whatever happens old son, for God's sake keep your head, okay?"

"I won't let you down Sarge, you'll see," but Benny's heart was thumping and he suddenly felt unsure. He wondered if any of his shipmates were with the other platoons. Would he cope if he had to use his Sten gun? Would it jam? He recalled his childhood and the games of cowboys and indians he had played. Never had any problems with those make-believe weapons. Like the sergeant had pointed out though, this was for real!

The sergeant had winked when he told him he would not let him down and now he was with Gregory. "As for you Gregory," Sergeant Riley growled. "You had better make sure those eyes in your arse are in perfect working order, or else!"

The reason for his remark was obvious and Benny, although seeing the humour was left in no doubt as to the earnest intent of Sergeant Riley's words to the soldier bringing up the rear, the one very often first to be attacked and very often a quick silent death that those in front did not see or hear. "Yes," thought Benny thankful to be three from the rear, "he has every need to have eyes in his backside."

The line moved on steadily, making good progress. The sergeant had moved up to lead now and the corporal was in front of Benny. No one spoke except by sign language and they travelled like this for something like half a mile as the crow flies. In reality it was more like two. The path had long since ceased to exist, the lieutenant using a compass that was strapped to his wrist like a wristwatch. The compass was vital, the dense undergrowth blotting out any view beyond a few feet and they were forced to make their way, first one way and then another, always as the undergrowth dictated.

Benny had noticed some of the guardsmen carrying machetes but these were not brought into use, he reasoned correctly that the noise would be heard some distance off. All the time animals and birds could be heard calling and whistling but Benny saw none. He shivered at the strange atmosphere.

After an hour the jungle became thicker and they were compelled to use machetes but, always with the fear of discovery in the users' minds, they were used only when necessary and with the minimum noise.

Sometimes they worked their way upwards, climbing and slipping on the wet undergrowth. Other times they were going downhill then it became difficult to maintain one's balance. They progressed along valleys, crossed streams and rivulets dancing and glistening over and around pebbles and stones in careless abandon.

Once or twice they stumbled across clearings and these they crossed with extreme awareness and caution, intent on presenting the smallest target to any unseen enemy who may be lying in wait.

As the sun rose higher so did the heat increase until it became humid and intense and the guardsmen freely perspired. Benny had travelled extensively aboard ships of the Royal Navy but never had he experienced anything like this.

There was nothing to be seen but thick, lush greenery. Even the sky itself was screened by this thick foliage, almost like a translucent, laceworked umbrella.

The noise of animals was commonplace now as baboons, monkeys, apes and heaven knew what else cried out their warnings to each other. Large, beautifully coloured butterflies flitted about, the slender beams of sunlight reflecting their beauty and indifference. Birds now rendered a loud yet rich chorus of song and insects buzzed their busy way around them.

Benny whispered softly to Bert just up ahead. "I can't see us lasting long in this bloody lot, can you?"

Bert's reply was blunt: "We've got no choice!" He smiled and added: "You'll be alright, you'd be surprised the tricks we've been taught to survive in this lot."

"Yeah!" said Moggy who followed Benny and had been listening. "Just watch this for a start," he invited and with his machete he sliced through a thick stem of grass resembling sugar cane leaving about four feet of it standing. He pressed his thumb firmly over the top of this stem and wrapping his fingers round it, held it as he sliced through it once more leaving him holding a length of stem about eighteen inches long.

Benny watched spellbound as Moggy raised the stem so that the bottom end was just above his open mouth. He removed his thumb from the top and Benny saw a clear liquid flow out to be swallowed down Moggy's gaping gullet.

They had both stopped during this demonstration and the soldier following on behind Moggy hissed an angry warning and waved them on their way.

Benny cursed, annoyed with himself for his stupid behaviour which could jeopardise everything. He cursed even more when he realised Bert was out of sight. Feeling genuine concern at being cut off he put a spurt on.

His fear was unfounded for as soon as he turned the next protruding thicket he crashed into Bert who immediately raised a hand commanding silence.

The ship's cook signalled as much to the following Moggy and then turned back to see why Bert had stopped. The sergeant and his officer were crouched together up front studying a large clearing. The other guardsmen were squatting and waiting, eyes darting everywhere, Stens at the ready. Benny's heart stepped up its beat.

At first he was sure they had unearthed terrorists but no, they were merely surveying the surroundings and checking maps and compass to get their bearings. The officer and sergeant were able to see landmarks in the distance now there was a unobstructed view and satisfied they beckoned the men to them.

When they were all present the officer addressed them. "Sergeant Riley and myself are going to check the clearing, spread out and cover us. Should be no problem but," he shrugged his shoulders and drew his revolver, "you never know." All proved to be well and the two returned, obviously more relaxed than when they went.

"We're going to camp here for a spell," the sergeant told them having gathered them around him. "It's as safe as we can expect to find and situated in a way that makes it difficult for anyone to sneak up on us. Should that happen anyway, there are plenty of holes and hills for us to take cover."

He detailed Gregory and Brown to take the first half-hour guard duty, telling them that was long enough in the heat.

Gregory and Brown took up positions some distance from their comrades, one on either side of the clearing. They had been told they could sit down if they wished but had been warned of the dangers of falling asleep. Sid Gregory and Alf Brown did sit down and Benny did not blame them, especially if their feet and legs felt like his.

He saw that the others were stretching out on the grass and copied them. It felt very, good, even if he found it difficult in view of the load he toted. He closed his eyes thinking to rest them as he relaxed. He fell sound asleep.

CHAPTER EIGHT

Benny's fortywinks were cut to no more than thirty for he woke to find Sergeant Riley shaking him gently.

"Come on son, you'd better get yourself something to eat," the sergeant told him. Benny eased himself up and the N.C.O. moved on.

He ran a dry tongue over his lips and pulled a face. He was parched. He could feel the perspiration running down his face, neck and back.

Benny gazed around as he helped himself to a drink from the water bottle attached to his belt. He then fumbled in the haversack for the sandwiches and began tucking in hungrily. He saw most of the others were also eating.

"You'd better save some sailor," said Bert. "You never know 'ow long it's goin' to be before we get the next lot!"

"Yeah!" he sighed. "I suppose you're right," but added, "mind you Bert, the bread's goin' dry now, 'ardly seems worth savin'."

"Oh you'll eat it alright mate."

Something about the way Bert said this persuaded the ship's cook to return the remainder of the sandwiches to the haversack.

He saw that the first guards on lookout had been changed and wondered how long he had slept. "'E still looks pretty fresh," he said staring at the young lieutenant.

"Who, old Fenny?" mused Bert observing the officer with casual indifference. "'E's not a bad sort really, 'e ain't been out 'ere all that long."

"What did you call 'im? " Benny found this amusing.

Bert grinned back. "Yeah! Fenny! 'Is name's Fenton-Dowell really but we call 'im Fenny, what else could we call 'im wi' a name like that?"

"I love the way 'e talks," decided Benny gazing at the officer idly. "It's proper 'igh fallutin' ain' it?"

"That's because 'e's a member of the aristocracy," condescended the guardsman pulling at a grass stalk to chew. "Baronet or knight or per'aps it's 'is dad who's a lord or somethin', I don' know," he excused his lack of really knowing by extending the field. "Anyway, we've got no end of royalty an' blue-blooded nobs in our mob," he informed the sailor.

"Yeah? We've got loads of blue nobs in the navy mate," sneered Benny mocking. "Especially when we sail round the North Pole!"

At this point the sergeant whistled softly and beckoned his troops to rally round him. He and the officer had been sitting talking quietly but now decisions had been made.

"We're moving out," he told them. "Remember, give yourselves plenty of space between each one and from now on be prepared for anything, do not fire unless you have to," he took time out to let his eyes pass over them making certain they understood fully their position. "Shooting the odd straggler or lookout is bloody pointless if it warns the rest of them off."

He paused again. "Any questions?" he asked solemnly, expecting them to be too well versed to need ask anything. They had no questions so he continued.

"Right! Brown!" he called looking straight at him. "Up front with Lieutenant Fenton-Dowell ... and convince yourself you have been blessed with forty pairs of eyes," he glared at Brown daring him to convince himself otherwise. "Because if so much as one leaf stirs without you seeing it ..." He left the rest unsaid but Brown got the message.

The sergeant waved him off with nothing more than a pointing finger on the end of a flicking wrist. Brown strode off to where the officer waited and leading the line of trekkers they made their way onward into the darkness.

On and on they trudged. The thick undergrowth odious now with so much rotting vegetation underfoot. It was a lonely, awesome plod. At least ten or twelve yards separated each man now, each holding his Sten at his hip ready for action.

This time the unhappy Benny found himself last but one of the line, the doubtful privilege of bringing up the rear falling to Bert.

There was this constant feeling that hidden eyes watched every step and this sensation stretched the nerves to the limit. Benny felt most uncomfortable and thanked God he was not Bert.

They scrambled down the banks of a swiftly flowing stream and wading through clambered up the opposite side, forced to use one hand to steady themselves.

The undergrowth grew more sparing now and Benny saw several of the troops up ahead of him between the trees and brush. A snapping twig right behind him had him leaping round in alarm. It was Bert. The relief at seeing him balanced out the fear he had felt.

"Sorry sailor," apologised the guardsman accepting it would have been his own fault. "I just decided I was too bleedin' far behind you!" He was playing it safe having no intention of being stabbed or clobbered, out of sight and sound of his comrades.

They continued in silence. The going was easier now with room between the smaller trees and shrubbery affording almost normal walking and the immediate landscape might easily have passed for an English wood.

Just when Benny thought nothing would ever happen, it did. With no warning Bert launched himself through the air to barge forcibly into Benny and send him crashing sideways to the ground, having spat out the words, "For Christ's sake watch out!"

Without realising he was doing it the ship's cook released the safety catch of the Sten and looked in vain for the unseen enemy. He saw no one.

Bert was dusting himself down casually. Benny gazed up at him and shook his head in shocked disbelief. Getting slowly to his feet he wanted to know what the devil the guardsman was playing at. Bert said nothing but giving his companion a glare that said he must keep his wits about him, pointed to a branch spreading itself just above them.

The ship's cook raised his eyes to stare at what appeared to be an outsize rugby football. It hung from the branch over the track they walked along and Benny, intent on peering through the trees and brush, had failed to see it. He would almost certainly have caught it with his head.

"Jeeezus you were lucky!" sighed Bert with relief. "We both were," he nodded at this large sphere.

Benny stared at it wondering what all the fuss was about, he saw now for himself. A huge hornet buzzed its way up to it and effected an entrance. Then another. One came out to zoom off, coming too close to Benny's nose for comfort.

"God Almighty!" choked Benny. "Just look at the size of them big bastards. I see now why you shoved me out the way!"

The sailor had reason to be thankful on two counts. Firstly the Bert's intervention had probably saved their lives and secondly he was glad it had not been terrorists that were the cause of the sudden push. His flesh still crept at the thought of either.

They had made up the lost ground and felt safer for doing so, neither having the desire to get lost or caught on their own. The thin line of troops moved on tirelessly. They weaved and bobbed their way along. Up and down hillocks, on high ground, along small valleys. Quite suddenly they were on a wide path which went around the hill they climbed. On one side could be seen an overgrown wall. It leaned back into the slight slope as though holding it back. As Benny studied what he could of it beneath the veil of greenery he concluded that it had been there a long, long time. The path itself bore no trace of having been used for years and like the wall was covered with a thick carpet of moss and weed.

The path moved away from the hillside now and moved to the left of it. On either side tall trees sought the sun and the undergrowth grew thicker. As ever the strong, pungent aroma of rotting vegetation filled their nostrils.

Benny spotted the long wooden pipe as it lay partly hidden by the grasses on the verge of the path. Without thinking he darted forward and disentangled it. The thin tube was at least ten feet long and not knowing what it was he turned to Bert to ask his opinion.

He got a shock to see that Bert was crouched in the longer grass on the outside of the path. He had his safety catch off and held the gun ready as he very carefully studied their surroundings for tell-tale signs. Not a muscle moved in his grim face.

With barely discernable movements of his hand he instructed Benny to get down low. The ship's cook needed no further telling and dropping the pipe, he dived for the undergrowth and released the safety catch on his Sten.

The only sound was the loud, incessant barking and baying of baboons and the screaming of the monkeys. Benny saw his unearthing of the pipe had nothing to do with Bert's sudden move. All the guardsmen up ahead were crouched in equal readiness.

He saw too that Sergeant Riley was crouching his way back along the line stopping at each man in turn to whisper something. If he had not been so keen to pick up the long pipe he would have witnessed the warning signals passed along. He cursed himself. Lack of training and of common sense could have let all of them down.

When he reached Benny he explained, "We've spotted a thin spiral of smoke just ahead and we're cutting in to surround it and see what it's all about. Watch the men in front of you and copy them, we move alternately one to left, one to right. If the man in front moves left, you go right, got that?"

"Got it Sarge," hissed Benny hoping he had.

"Good," continued the N.C.O. "We've gone through all this many times so follow what we do. We may charge in, we may lie in wait, we won't know till we get close enough to assess the situation. If we get close enough, you must trust your instincts now. From here on in you're on your own old son."

"Don't worry about me Sarge," he said quietly confident. "I'll be okay!"

"Sure you will," and the sergeant's friendly grin returned as he patted Benny on the shoulder and moved back to Bert.

If the sergeant had been sociable Bert certainly was not for as soon the N.C.O. had gone Bert crept up to the sailor and tore him a strip off. "Do you realise you could have dropped us all in the shit prancing about like that?" he growled.

"Yeah! I know Bert an' I'm sorry," Benny genuinely was and accepted the ticking off.

"An' what about this bastard?" snarled Bert glaring. He reached over and fully released the safety catch on Benny's Sten. The catch the sailor thought he had released. In his haste he had only half released it. "I've seen it 'appen all too bloody often, you squeeze the trigger an' nothin' appens an' by the time you realise the safety catch ain' off properly, it's too bleedin' late, you're fuckin' dead!"

Benny said nothing. What could he say? He knew Bert spoke the truth and it was for all their good.

"What was it you went prattin' about after?" asked Bert.

Benny had completely forgotten the pipe. He glanced round and saw it lying in the middle of the path a few feet away. "It's like a sugar cane ain' it?" he reckoned.

"That, Benny baby, is a blow-pipe," Bert told him with the air of a man fully conversant with such things. "It's what the Sakai use."

"The Sakai?" he strained his eyes to make sure the others were still awaiting orders to move. "They're the nomadic aboriginals of Malaya. Not all that many of 'em left now, just like a tribe of gypsies they are, wandering all over the jungle." He continued as Benny listened eagerly, never one to miss so interesting a subject. "You've got to be very lucky indeed to ever come across 'em."

"Do you reckon they still use blow-pipes?" Benny wished to know.

"Of course they do you dozey bugger!" chuckled Bert. "They ain't changed their ways since time began, still the same as they were centuries ago."

Benny had an idea. "Do you think they'd mind if I pinched this one for a souvenir?"

Bert stared at him in utter disbelief. "Don't talk so bloody pisspotical!" he jeered. "You can't cart that damned thing all over the jungle with you for God's sake!"

Bert didn't wait for areply. Instead he had seen the sergeant beckon them forward. Whoever had been scouting out the area had completed the task and they were now making preparations to investigate the smoke.

They stood together now near a narrow gap in the dense undergrowth. It was a path of sorts going to the right and anyone could easily pass by without knowing of its existence.

Gathered together in a closely knit group the sergeant pointed through the trees to the thin spiral of smoke. Benny marvelled that anyone should have seen it at all and considered whoever it was must have most remarkable powers of observation.

It was at this point that the sergeant noticed the blow-pipe. "Where in God's name are you going with that thing?" he demanded to know.

"I was 'oping to take it 'ome to show my gran'children one day," explained Benny preferring to study the rough carvings on the blow-pipe than the stern lines on the sergeant's face.

"Why not take an elephant?" suggested the sergeant cynically. "You could at least ride the flaming thing home!" The lieutenant standing behind his N.C.O. was smiling with amused understanding. The sergeant shook his head and got back to matters of more import than a native blow-pipe.

"Right then," the sergeant concluded. "Double check your bolts everyone, all set? Right! Let's go!"

The sergeant himself led the way with astonishing fleetness of foot that belied his bulk. He darted along in a crouched position followed by the officer and the men. They kept close up together as ordered, swiftly running, leaping, jumping as the brush and terrain dictated.

Up ahead the officer lay on his stomach now, guiding his men first one way then the other. He waved Benny to his right. He saw Moggy just ahead, crouched on one knee scanning the undergrowth, watchful and fully alert. Benny remembered his orders and dropped on one knee, not really sure where to look or for what he nevertheless did his best to keep the flag flying on behalf of the Royal Navy if nothing else.

The instant he was able to take stock of his surroundings he was astounded. The landscape reminded him of a gigantic basin and he struggled to find words to describe this wonderful scene. He gazed down the slopes over the top of the trees that grew right down to the bottom, the lush foliage spread like some gorgeous carpet, woven in a multitude of brilliant colours. He marvelled at the majesty of the trees growing on the opposite side, reaching up their branches like some mighty choir clad in so many rich and splendid gowns of every shade and hue of green and brown. No artist could ever hope to capture such colourful splendour.

He was jolted back to reality. Moggy had thrown a small twig to catch his attention, he was signalling that they were ready to move in. He was the only person Benny could see and so he had to rely on him for instructions.

Moggy signalled they were moving into the centre and Benny, keeping his own line of approach, forced his way through the thick undergrowth as quickly as conditions would allow to converge with his comrades on the agreed spot. He held his finger on the trigger as he ran and got quite a shock when he found himself in a small clearing gazing at the source of the smoke. He had not realised just how close they had been to it all the time.

The wispy column of smoke came from a tiny fire set near the middle of the clearing. On either side of it were two tiny thatched huts built on stilts.

Grenadiers ran back and forth, leaping up the frail ladders to search the interiors, probing every likely, and unlikely, hiding place in their search for arms and ammunition, or anything that would indicate the presence of terrorists while other members of the platoon kept a watch on the jungle.

He saw the toddler first. He had been hiding somewhere amid the buildings. Then he saw the young woman. He could not believe his eyes. She was so beautiful as she swayed gracefully towards the fire, she clutched a baby to her naked breast. Her expression betrayed no feeling or emotion. Benny had travelled many countries but never had he seen such classic and perfect features, her breasts were firm and proud.

Unable to stop himself he uttered a loud "Wow!" She was far prettier than pretty. Much more than the term beautiful implied, the colour of rich milk coffee.

Although she wore nothing more than a leather thong, she looked so relaxed and calm as the soldiers conducted their search. She seemed not to notice the appreciative eyes drinking in her charms.

Benny felt his heart thumping away as he sought words to describe her. He felt certain he had to be in the Garden of Eden. "You can tempt me with an apple anytime my darlin'," he murmured to himself wanting to take her home along with the blow-pipe. The blow-pipe? What the hell had he done with it? He hadn't a clue and suddenly he didn't care.

Bert came up to him and interrupted his train of thought. "Well bugger me," he gasped staring at the woman. "You know just now when we were talkin' about the Sakai?"

"Yeah!"

"Well, she is a Sakai. This is a Sakai site."

"Bloody 'ell!" gasped the ship's cook. "If all the women are like this one I reckon I'll stop 'ere an' live wi' 'em."

"You won't unearth anything feasting your beady eyes on her!" snapped the corporal.

125

Bert knowing he had dropped a clanger, kept his mouth shut now. The N.C.O. winked at Benny obviously putting it down to his being led astray by the one who should know far better at such times.

"Get up there and give it a good going over, now!" barked the corporal pointing up the ladder leading into one of the small huts.

"You'd better go with him in case he loses the way," the corporal told Benny and Benny trailed after his tent-mate close enough to hear him mutter an oath.

The frail-looking ladder was actually quite well made, the rungs secured by a hardy raffia-type of grass. Even so, Benny waited until Bert had stepped off it before risking it.

The hut's floor of roughly hewn boards was covered in places by mats of reeds obviously woven neatly by the inhabitants. Benny saw stout bamboo canes were interlinked with the floor boards and the gaps between revealed the earth below.

They poked about among ingeniously arranged shelves attached by reeds to the bamboo uprights of the hut. Benny picked up a wooden cylindrical container. It was about six or seven inches deep with an opening the size of a small cup, in it were a score or so of what could only be described as miniature arrows. He was in the act of withdrawing one of these when Bert reached out to hold his arm and stop him.

"Don't touch the point for Christ's sake!" he cried out almost frantic with concern. "Them are poisonous darts what they use for the blow-pipes!"

After a further search Bert told him: "We'd better be gettin' off mate," and then he noticed that the woman had stood beside the ladder watching their every move. Could it be, he asked himself, that she was afraid they might unearth something? "'Ey up Benny, that woman ain't took 'er eyes off us for a second," he told him.

"She fancies me, that's why," grinned Benny caressing the two inch long feathered flights of the darts. The arrowhead tips were embedded in a block of cork. "Just look at this," he persisted holding out the darts and pointing to the cork. "It's bloody brilliant 'ow they think of everythin', don't they?"

"I thought she might be 'angin' about to see if we found anythin'," Bert told him waiting to see what he thought about it.

Benny told him what he thought about it. "More likely she's

watchin' to see we don't pinch anythin'." He shrugged as he thought about it. "Mind you, it don't look as if they've got much to pinch does it?"

Moggy had been making a fuss of the toddler, patting him on the head and handing him a piece of chewing-gum, he said, "There you are, have yourself a good chew." With a big toothy grin the boy shot off to hide behind a pile of wood.

Moggy then took a packet of toffees from a pocket, walked to the woman and, using sign language and pidgin English, offered her them. She stepped back, watching him with an air of mistrust.

"There's nothing wrong with them my love," he promised doing his best to win her over. "Look, I'll show you," he said taking out a toffee. He went to great pains removing its wrapper and holding out his hands to show there was nothing up his sleeve, he held the wrapper in one hand the toffee in the other. With a smile, he tossed the wrapper away and opened his mouth wide popped in the toffee.

"Scrumptious!" he told her grinning and at the same time rubbed his stomach and smacked his lips. "Hmmmm!" he held out the bag once more for her to take."Plenny good yum yum, okay, you likee?"

She may not have understood a single word but she most certainly got the message. There was quite a group of Grenadiers watching now, smiling and encouraging her to take the sweets. For the first time the flicker of a smile occupied her exquisite features and she took the sweets offered with timid demureness. Benny felt sure she was blushing but who could tell?

Immediately she held the bag in her hand a tiny grass monkey sprang from somewhere on the roof and leapt up onto her shoulder where it sat holding out a furry hand begging a toffee. This brought a laugh which, in turn, brought the officer and sergeant.

"For God's sake!" hissed the sergeant. His troops were instantly silent. But even the sergeant and his officer allowed themselves a smile when they saw the monkey making no bones about what he wanted.

"Let's move out then!" ordered the N.C.O. leading the way. He went off using a path opposite to the way they had entered, and as they were leaving Benny, being at the rear end, watched the woman handing sweets to her child who now clung to her thigh and the monkey who clung round her neck. Benny turned and waved as she stood watching their departure placidly. His heart leapt when suddenly, at the very moment he'd given up hope, she smiled and raised her hand to say farewell. Without knowing why he blew her a kiss then turned to hurry away.

The Grenadiers had discovered only two paths in the undergrowth around the huts, the one they had entered by and the one they now took. They were in single file but moving with much more purpose as if there was a sense of urgency.

Struggling through the brush trying to keep up Benny called softly to Bert asking what the rush was for.

"It's Sarge," explained the Grenadier. He caught up as much as he dare to put the sailor in the picture. "'E's got an instinct and its told 'im the 'reds' have been in them 'uts we've just left. Now they couldn't 'ave left along the way we came so they must 'ave left along this way. The burnin' question is, 'ow long ago an' 'ow far are they in front?"

It dawned on Benny now that he had not seen any menfolk around the Sakai clearing and he asked Bert about this.

"They ain't daft Benny mate, they'd know we were comin' well in advance an' the menfolk would clear off out of the way, they'd take all the other women an' kids wi' 'em, leavin' just that one an' the babies just to make it look right see?"

"'Ow would they know we were comin'?"

"Christ Benny! The jungle is their way of life," he was panting a little now with the effort of talking and hurrying at the same time. "They know every call the animals make an' all the animals have their own warnin' cries, the animals would warn each other, an' that would warn them, see?"

They hurried on. After something like twenty minutes the undergrowth thinned leaving tall slender trees thinly spread out standing like lonely sentinels. No word had been spoken yet the Grenadiers were running now, fanning out in all directions knowing exactly what they were about. Benny made an effort to copy them but just as he crouched and ran he saw flames leaping up from a hut as they ran forward to encircle it.

The flames had barely started yet in seconds they had grown from licking to roaring and throwing out billowing clouds of dense smoke and intense heat, threatened to engulf the whole area.

The hut was a copy of the ones they had recently left behind and, watching it collapse, throwing up an abundance of shooting sparks, Benny knew it was another Sakai home.

The guardsmen were crouched low in a circle around the hut, facing out, watching intently the surrounding jungle. The officer and Sergeant Riley were hurrying to and fro as near to the fast disappearing hut as they dare, trying to see if anyone had been trapped in the inferno. There was nothing they could do but stand back and watch the whole burning mass finally cave in to finish in a white hot mound.

The near-silence was shattered when Gregory angrily spat out an oath through tightly clenched teeth. "The lousy rotten bastards!" he cursed.

His outburst broke the spell and the officer ordered his sergeant to call the men together.

"Right lads, spread out across the clearing and move forward at the double, go!" Without hesitation the guardsmen fanned out across the glade and sped off through the trees, ready for any emergency. Benny was near the centre of the line doing his darndest to imitate his bigger comrades.

They ran along the glade but were forced to a halt as they reached its end. A tall impenetrable thicket barred all further progress. The glade, only eighty to ninety feet wide but quite long, proved to be entirely surrounded by this thicket. Benny did not know about the others but he felt rather foolish having run into this dead end.

"Well Sergeant," said the officer with some deliberation. "No one has passed through this little lot," nodding at the wall built by nature.

"No sir!" agreed Sergeant Riley. "We know they didn't go out the way we came either sir!"

"Gregory," called the officer still thinking deeply. "Tell me, why did you curse like that back there?"

"I couldn't help it sir! I was so flaming mad at them lousy rotten terrorists sir!" he said "Begging your pardon sir!"

"So you think they are 'reds' too Gregory?" said the officer ignoring his mild apology. "Why should you think that?"

"They would have turfed out the Sakai sir, and taken over the hut for themselves. The look-outs would have warned them we were coming so they got the wind up and hopped it sir! They set fire to the hut to let us think the Sakai had done it themselves sir! Trying to kid us there are no 'reds' round these parts, sir!"

"But it could have been the Sakai," suggested the officer not believing it was. "They do burn down their dwellings when they move on!"

"Yes sir! I know that sir! But that's just it sir!" Gregory was not to be swayed from his beliefs. "If these Sakai had burnt their home down because we were coming, why didn't the others? And that's not all sir! If they were moving on why didn't they take their pots and pans and things? Sir!"

The officer gazed at his guardsman pleased that he had not gone about his duties with eyes closed and had reasoned things out so well. Without taking his eyes from Gregory he asked the sergeant's opinion.

"Gregory is right sir, I think he's got it all worked out very nicely sir!"

"So do I," beamed the officer. "Well done Gregory, we shall make something of you yet." He became serious now and got down to the matter in hand. "Right Sergeant. There has to be a way through this damned bush and they cannot be all that far ahead of us. Take half a dozen men with you and look for an opening down that side, I'll take the rest down this side," he indicated his right. If you find an opening stand by it until we work our way around to you," he added.

He motioned the sergeant to lead off and as this group hurried off down the left hand side of the glade searching the thicket for an outlet, the officer led the remainder down the right.

Both parties continued the hurried scanning for an outlet they knew had to be in the dense thicket somewhere. It was the officer who found it. He motioned for the men with him to get down and wait for the rest. When the sergeant did complete the circle to get back to his officer he shook his head.

"Nothing sir!" he said confidently.

"Good." The news was just what the doctor ordered. "Then we know they had to go this way!" Without a word more the officer made his way into the well concealed gap and the others followed.

Progress was much slower now for they had to force their way through the thicket sticking out across the makeshift path. They did not have to suffer this for long however. With startling abruptness the dense growth ended and they found themselves on a much wider path running across the one they had just trod.

The expression on the officer's face reflected his disappointment. He stood shaking his head, glancing first one way then the other. "Damn!" he cursed.

They all knew the reason for his oath. A moment ago it was thought they had the enemy on the run. They still had him on the run. Now they had a problem. Which direction were they running now?

The young lieutenant displayed to them that he had not received his commission for nothing. "Right Sergeant, take someone with you and scout about down that way. Corporal!"

"Sir!"

"You come with me, the rest of you keep low and quiet until we get back!"

"Right Sergeant Riley, give yourself five minutes," and having issued his orders he hurried off to the right followed by the corporal. The sergeant beckoned to Moggy and they went scurrying off to the left. This time it was Sergeant Riley who unearthed the way the enemy had taken. He sent Moggy off to find and tell the officer, who first satisfied himself there were no signs of anyone making their escape along the path he checked before rejoining his sergeant.

The sergeant pointed to signs which were a clear giveaway to person or persons having passed this way very recently. Even as the grim faced sergeant pointed to these signs a clump of trodden down grass sprang upright. "You see sir? This has to be the way and I don't think it's a false trail sir, either."

"Hmmm!" mused the officer stroking his chin "I don't think it is Sergeant."

The N.C.O. pointed to broken twigs and sunken spots where human feet had pressed into the moist earth. In places they were clearly defined. "It hasn't been long ago either sir!" he decided with conviction. More blades of grass snatched themselves upright as if confirming this.

It was plain to see the sergeant's excitement now he sensed the 'reds' were so close. Even Benny felt the tense but eager undercurrent now the scent of the 'hunt' was in their nostrils. Even Benny could see the broken bracken and foliage.

Second Lieutenant Fenton-Dowell's face was illuminated like a scientist making some startling discovery after searching years for it. "We shall catch these beggars yet, Sergeant!" he beamed. If Sergeant Riley had not barred his way he would surely have rushed off headlong after them regardless of the consequences.

But the sergeant did bar his progress. He did it for a good reason too. "Beg pardon sir. No disrespect or anything but ..." he paused but decided it had to be said. "Permission to go first sir!"

The young officer proudly drew himself up to his full height before he spoke. "Sergeant! I am fully aware that you are well versed in this type of warfare and may seek to protect me since I am not," he stared back at his N.C.O. poker-faced, giving nothing away. "But unlike you I have no dependants or wife to consider, besides we are wasting precious time," he smiled now.

The sergeant retired gracefully. "If that's how you want it sir!" and he stepped aside allowing the officer to pass.

"That is the way I want it Sergeant." He addressed them all now. "Keep your wits about you and if we make contact try to take them alive, got that?"

They mumbled that they had and the officer turned to stride off after the unknown. Once more the green-clad file moved snake-like through the Malaysian jungle, its clammy, steamy heat inducing perspiration that soaked into their uniforms, never letting up.

The path narrowed again but still allowed fairly easy progress even though the undergrowth had become dense. The branches overhead were lower and heavy with leaves. It was darker and gloomy and Benny felt distinctly uneasy.

He suddenly went very cold and shivered, some sixth sense warned him of danger. He knew that hidden eyes watched him. Fear gripped him. He knew he must not panic but it was one hell of a struggle not to. Instinctively he crouched lower, his finger feeling the trigger of the Sten. The sweat that a moment or so ago had been the result of clammy heat had been replaced by the cold sweat of fear of the unknown.

Benny would never know what it was possessed him to look down at the spot, but he did and there it was, a wickedly evil, yellow skinned face, its slanting eyes burning with fierce hatred directly into his own.

Sheer instinct took control and almost without realising what he was doing, Benny poked the nose of his Sten under the nose of the face and with a jerk motioned the owner to get up and step out, or else!

As the 'red' moved slowly he spat out a mouthful of Chinese and even as Bert yelled a warning Benny knew there was someone coming at him from behind. He whipped round just as a charging terrorist was about to ram a long-bladed knife into his back. Benny reacted like lightening.

All in one hectic movement he arched back and as the man flew past, already committed, he swung back to belt him hard on the back of the skull with the butt of his Sten. There was the sickening sound of bone splintering.

Before he had chance to recover he saw the other 'red' coming at him from the corner of his eye. Frantically he tried to dodge the blade. He felt the impact and sensed the steel penetrate but felt no pain. The blow had knocked him face down, almost on top of the man with the cracked skull and he waited for the end.

The end he waited for did not come. Instead he heard a sickening thud and a short grunt of pain. Something fell across the back of his legs.

"Benny? Are you alright?" it felt so good to hear the voice of Bert whispering anxiously as he bent over him.

"Yeah!" he grunted twisting round to look at the guardsman. Now he felt a pain.

"Fuckin' 'ell Benny mate, that was too close for comfort," said Bert lifting the 'red' from Benny's legs like he would a sack of potatoes.

"Is 'e dead?" Benny asked getting to his feet.

"No! I didn't 'it 'im 'ard enough." Bert assured him. "Mind you, the bastard's goin' to 'ave a bloody good 'eadache for a long time." He stared down at the unconscious figure. "Jesus Christ, I never want to go through that again."

"Neither do I mate," grinned Benny but the grin lied.

"I'm bloody serious," insisted the sorry guardsman. "I'd never 'ave dared show my face if anythin' 'ad 'appened to you. For one awful minute I thought the little bastard 'ad stabbed you."

"'E did," Benny told him trying to play it down.

"'Ey?" gasped Bert shocked. "Where?"

"Round 'ere somewhere," Benny said turning his back and point-

133

ing.

"Oh my God!" stammered the guardsman. "Christ you were lucky!" his tone changed from the anxious to the relieved.

"You mean I could be dead," said Benny

"You might 'ave been as well if the blade 'adn't gone through this thick webbin'," and Bert caught hold of the webbing to show him. Benny cried out in pain. "Sorry, I didn't real ... Jeeezus ... you ain' 'alf lost some blood. Why didn't you say?"

"Cos I didn't bloodywell know," grinned Benny at the stupidity of it all. "'E stabbed me round the back an' my eyes are round the front."

Grunts from the 'red' lying at his feet stopped him short. "'Ello! Old 'Chinky Chops' is comin' to," he said.

The terrorist groaned and started to stir. Blood trickled from the wound caused by Bert. "Make one false move you slant-eyed bastard an' they'll be able to use you to strain the tea," Bert growled through clenched teeth, his Sten aimed right between the eyes.

The 'red' simply sat there, resting his head on his hands, it seemed all the fight had left him.

"I wonder why they jumped you?" Bert wondered now.

"They didn't jump me," explained the ship's cook. "I knew somebody was there and I was keepin' 'im covered while I made 'im come out."

"I thought it was funny," Bert was happier now he understood. "They usually wait to nobble the last one, Jeeezus!" All at once he was not happy. "God Almighty Benny, do you realise that you saved my life. If you 'adn't discovered 'em they would've clobbered me. You wouldn't 'ave been able to get back in time to 'elp me even if you'd 'eard anythin'."

Benny was embarrassed by all this. "Look mate, you saved my life probably when you belted this bastard 'ere so that makes us even, so forget about it."

A faint sound from up ahead brought instant silence and reaction. Both he and the sailor had swung round, Stens at the ready. Bert held a warning hand out telling the 'red' to keep silent.

Seconds later Sergeant Riley crept into view. The moment he saw the cluster of bodies he dived to one side aiming his gun at them. He obviously felt it to be a trap.

"It's okay Sarge," Bert called softly. "It's only us."

The sergeant hurried to them and they lost no time in telling him what had happened and when they had finished he gave a low whistle of astonishment. He had wasted no time as they related their story. He quickly searched the two 'reds' and checked that the one Benny hit was indeed dead.

"My God old son!" the sergeant said after examining the broken skull. "You must have given him one hell of a clout."

"I didn't like the look of him," smiled Benny with a flippancy he did not feel.

"Well all I can say to that is, I hope you like the look of me," and the sergeant beamed at him in admiration. "Right, let's have a look at you."

"It's only a scratch Sarge," but there was no fooling this man.

"I'll decide if it is a scratch or not my lad," the sergeant chided. Benny did not see the look of concern he exchanged with Bert.

"Hmmm!" the sergeant smiled and playing it down told him. "You were very lucky old son, the fact that it went through the webbing and the possibility that Bert here knocked him out as he stabbed you probably saved your life. You almost certainly saved his."

"Don't you start Sarge," blushed Benny. "'E kept on about it long enough."

"We'll get you back to the chap with the first aid and patch it up as soon as we can," the sergeant told him. "Phillips, you shoot off and bring four men back here with you, quick as you can, explain to the lieutenant what has happened and tell him we'll be along as soon as we can make it, got that?"

The sergeant had placed the prisoner in such a way he could not escape easily and he watched him closely as he explained to Benny how things had developed so far. He believed these two had been planted to employ delaying tactics to allow the others to get clear away. That is if there were any more which was open to conjecture. He was not sure one way or the other.

Whichever way it was they had to press on regardless and the prisoner and the body would prove an hindrance. He lit a cigarette and offered Benny one. Benny declined.

"I'd forgotten, you don't smoke do you?" he puffed thoughtfully and was about to say something else when the group arrived. The sergeant wasted no time in detailing them off. The prisoner's hands were tied behind his back and a makeshift stretcher was made to carry the body.

Their comrades were eagerly awaiting them, keen to see and hear for themselves what had happened. They huddled around the dead man on the stretcher making diverse comments. They studied the prisoner who cringed in fear of his life. But mostly they made a fuss of Benny. Benny? Benny loved every minute of it.

"Well done you two!" beamed Lieutenant Fenton-Dowell. "Very well done indeed." He turned to Benny. "And how do you feel now Stretton?"

Benny felt quite important and lied. He was not going to let them see he wanted to collapse in a heap and sleep. "I'm feeling fine thank you sir!"

"I think we shall make a Grenadier of him yet Sergeant Riley," the officer said as the N.C.O. hurried forward with a guardsman carrying a small first-aid box.

They bathed the two inch wide wound with water from a bottle and wad of cotton wool then smeared antiseptic ointment in and around the wound, making Benny wince a little. Finally they covered it with a wad of lint which was fixed in place by sticky plaster. It still bled slightly but there was nothing more they could do at this stage.

"I think he'll live now," smiled the sergeant winking at Benny.

"Yes indeed," and the officer, keen to press on. "Right Sergeant! We'll move on while luck is with us."

"Sir!" he hissed out orders to his men. "On your feet everybody! Let's go!"

Benny's wound was giving him some stick now but he reckoned he could suffer it after the praise heaped on him. After all, was it not for good old king and country?

For two hours they pressed on but the terrain and undergrowth hindered progress as did the fact that they now had the additional burden of prisoner and stretcher-borne corpse.

As he plodded on Benny contemplated the incident that had resulted in this man's swift demise. In spite of accepting it could have been he who had died he still strangely regretted the outcome. He gazed at the butt of his Sten and marvelled that it had inflicted fatal injury.

He wondered what would happen to the corpse now. They could not carry it around for long surely, it would soon begin to decay in this climate. They could not delay long enough to bury it and to just dump it would hardly seem right and proper.

His heart skipped a beat as he saw excitement up ahead and the guardsmen dropping down, warning those behind. The corporal immediately gagged their prisoner and made warning signs that if he did anything stupid he would end up like his fellow terrorist.

Sergeant Riley had heard or seen something and now everyone crouched in readiness as he crept back to the officer who had been checking on the party with the stretcher. After hasty consultation the sergeant and officer moved up front and beckoned Gregory to join them.

They whispered and pointed and Gregory went off cautiously to investigate the cause of their concern. Several minutes went by. At last a voice was heard to cry out in the near distance. More agonising minutes dragged by. Benny's feelings were reflected on the grim faces of his fellows.

Sergeant Riley had returned to the prisoner and he watched him now without ever taking his eyes from his face. He meant to take no chances of him tipping off the enemy or of him taking to his heels.

Suddenly the beaming face of Sid Gregory told them all was well. He hurried towards his superiors to inform them. The officer and sergeant met him together at the front of the line.

"It's okay sir!" he said cheerfully. "It's 'D' platoon sir! They're camped out just up ahead sir!"

"Who was that calling out?" asked the sergeant.

"It was me Sergeant!" apologised Gregory going on to explain why. "I'm sorry but I had to. They'd left Simpson on guard and the trigger-happy pig was just going to blow my head off!"

"Hmmm!" mused the officer cutting in. "Have they made contact with the enemy at all?"

"Oh yes sir!" Gregory grinned happily with the news he bore. "Seems they had quite a skirmish with one lot. Killed two and wounded one and they've got him prisoner sir! Oh, and they wounded Lance Corporal Bird sir!"

"Badly?"

"Shot in the arm sir! The elbow I think sir!"

"Well Sergeant, seems we are getting some good results at long last!" he said. He turned to Gregory again. "Any news of the other patrols?"

"Yes sir! They are both on their way back to base sir! 'A' platoon had some bad luck. They lost Guardsman Collins during a skirmish and found him later sir!"

"Dead?" knowing the answer before asking the question.

"Yes sir! The usual petrol bomb between his legs while he was tied to a tree sir!"

"The lou..." The sergeant remembered and controlled himself. The officer and he exchanged determined glances.

"Did they take prisoners?" the officer wanted to know.

"No sir! But they're pretty certain they wounded at least three of the enemy sir!"

One hour later, having eaten with their colleagues in 'D' platoon, those that were not on look-out duties were stretched out on the grass resting and swapping tales of events.

Benny lay back awkwardly, trying to avoid more hurt to the painful, throbbing wound. Soon be dark, he reflected, and what a day it had been. It did not seem possible for so very much to happen all in the course of one solitary day. It seemed like a million years had passed since he left Consort.

Lieutenant Fenton-Dowell had expressed the wish for Benny to return to H.Q. with 'D' platoon but Benny persuaded him this would hardly be fair. He dearly wanted to see it through to the end, whatever that may be. Although the officer stressed they were likely to be out for several more days it did nothing to daunt Benny's spirit and determination.

"Very well then Stretton," conceded the officer finally. "I must admit you have come through with flying colours so far." He paused as he looked down at this young man. "But I must confess, I had serious misgivings at the outset."

"Thank you sir!" Benny preened himself, trusting it was all complimentary but began to wonder as he chewed it over.

They discovered there was a native village only half an hour's journey away, easily accessible by means of a wide track which ran down the side of the hill just a few hundred yards away from where they were camped. This wide path ran almost into the village itself.

Benny learnt that three men of 'D' platoon had been despatched earlier to this village to arrange transport and an ambulance in readiness for when the platoon reached the village later for the wounded Lance-Corporal Bird and the bodies.

The three men had recently returned and 'D' platoon were busy preparing to move out. They had been on ferret force for five days and were keen to get back to comparative civilisation.

They made their departure in two columns taking 'C' platoon's prisoner and corpse with them and Benny knew they were all glad to see the back of it.

The clearing in which they were camped was quite large. Only the odd tree or bush grew on it and the lush grass was quite dry since it was baked by strong sunshine. It was on a large flat shelf on the slopes of this sweeping hill curving gradually backwards up and away and around to both sides of them.

About twenty yards above them on a smaller shelf in the terrain was a huge metal black-painted tank and was almost full with water. From what the officer had been informed by his opposite number in 'D' platoon, it was a form of reservoir used by some obscure government department.

The top of the hill lay some fifty yards above them, flattish and covered with tall trees. The dense undergrowth through which 'C' platoon had made their approach lay a hundred yards to the left. Gazing downhill to the right, one could see clearly for two hundred yards before the jungle spread itself to control the ground it covered like some suffocating blanket. Directly below them was a mere twenty feet of grassland before the jungle which reached on until it bounded the Malayan village immediately below them at the foot of the hillside.

The site was ideally suited for a night's camping and after studying the position very carefully with his sergeant and corporal, the officer decided there were only two likely danger spots from which an enemy could spring an attack.

To forestall this eventuality they arranged for a sentry to be posted at each of these suspect areas. Benny offered his services but the officer flatly refused to allow this. "Get a good night's sleep Stretton, if we are still out here tomorrow and your wound is not troubling you we shall reconsider," he said.

With the coming of darkness Benny copied the others and made himself a frail covering by spreading his cape over a structure of sticks and small branches. With his groundsheet beneath him and pouches for a pillow he settled down to get a good night's sleep as suggested by the officer.

Benny hardly slept a good wink, firstly because he found it difficult to lie in a position that did not aggravate his wound and secondly because of the menacing sounds from the surrounding jungle. And then, worse of all, there were the mosquitoes hell bent on sampling his blood. Their high pitched whine all but drove him frantic. He had rubbed his bare flesh with his issue of insect repellant cream. But instead of repelling it seemed to have the opposite effect and they delighted on digging in their harmful proboscis where the cream was thickest.

Poor Benny. They nibbled at him unceasing but as fast as he flattened one another whined up to take its place. He could hear the Grenadiers talking softly as they huddled round the smouldering embers of the fire. He saw the glow from cigarettes as they were inhaled from. No one seemed able to sleep, or perhaps they were used to all this anyway. A good night's sleep? Benny grunted. What price now his hammock?

CHAPTER NINE

It was approaching dawn but still dark when Benny saw the officer rise in the glow cast by the fire. The glow created weird reflections everywhere, lighting up one side of the officer and men now being roused by the sergeant.

As Sergeant Riley stirred them the men quickly sorted themselves out ready to move. Benny was struggling to don his webbing when the sergeant reached him to ask, "How's your back this morning old son?"

"Not too bad Sarge, just a bit stiff that's all," he told him lying a little as before. "Good! That's the ticket!" and with a smile and friendly pat he was away.

Bert had come towards them as they spoke. "I reckon ol' Sarge 'as taken a shine to you mate," he grinned.

"Yeah!" agreed Benny. He sensed a genuine affection and bond and it was reciprocal too. "Yes indeed, 'e's a great guy," he said proudly. "You've said so yourself."

The platoon was ready to move off as the dawn light rapidly grew to almost daylight. The last look-outs had been called in to share cups of tea and guardsmen were busy digging holes in which they buried the fire's embers.

The ship's cook was curious as to why the officer had seen fit to place one guard to watch the path to the right and one to watch the left and yet had ignored the wide track leading off down to the village.

"Ah well!" he conceded. "I suppose the lieutenant knows what he's doing." He also had to admit to himself that the officer and his

141

sergeant displayed a most uncanny sense of timing for here they were ready to move off immediately there was sufficient light to do so. From being aroused until now, everything had gone with clockwork precision, not a moment wasted. He had been warned earlier that they would travel at night if circumstances warranted. As he scratched at his irritating mosquito bites he reckoned they might just as well journey at night for all the sleep he got!

The jungle was not nearly so dense now and they covered the ground at a fairly easy and quicker pace. As before they travelled in silence ready for any emergency. Benny was pleasantly surprised that in spite of his fitful night he felt quite bright and chirpy.

At last they came out of the jungle to find themselves on the edge of a large plain, stretching almost as far as the eye could see. They were grouped together studying their surroundings and Benny saw over on the left what he took to be some form of quarry workings.

Still further to the left were large buildings of corrugated iron sheets with wooden frames and supports and even though it was quite early in the day he saw people scurrying to and fro all wearing Chinese coolie garb and wide brimmed pointed straw hats.

Bert stood behind him as he gazed at these workings, full of curiosity. "It's a tin mine," he explained.

"Oh!" the ship's cook understood now. "Of course! I should 'ave guessed. Do you think we'll go near it?" he asked hopefully.

His question was answered, surpringingly, by Sergeant Riley, who called them together. "Right!" he barked having no fear of hidden enemies now. "We're going to give that little lot a good going over," he nodded towards the mine. "Remember! Do nothing to antagonise the workers but at the same time don't let them put you off making a thorough search, and I do mean thorough! You are searching the men and women for hidden arms not hidden charms or to see who has the best whatever!"

As they neared the building Benny saw that nearly all the workers were Chinese. This being so, any could be terrorist or terrorist sympathisers. How to tell was the big problem. He noticed their black pyjama-like cotton jacket and trousers, short in leg and sleeve and baggy. They hurried back and forth, on foot or cycle, along the many pathways.

The ferret force made directly for the main building and the officer demanded to see the person in charge. It proved to be the mine-manager who came finally when they managed to understand. He was English and at first wanted no part of the search but the officer tactfully pointed out that he really had no choice.

Benny understood the reluctance when he saw the workforce being rounded up and told to go to their living quarters in the largest building. It meant bringing all work to a standstill, naturally the manager was concerned.

When they had returned to their living accommodation the guardsmen entered the long dormitory styled building, two of them were strategically positioned to keep an eye on things outside.

"Jesus!" Gregory gasped and from the expressions of his fellows he voiced their feelings too. "It's stinking like a rotten opium den in here!"

"It is indeed Gregory," agreed Lieutenant Fenton-Dowell putting it rather politely. He coughed at the stench. "Though I feel the aroma is hardly to do with opium."

The air positively reeked with body sweat and a heavy pungent tobacco smoke. This, added to the sight of two tiered bunk-beds draped in mosquito nets, certainly created the impression that they had walked into an opium den.

The large building was in two sections, one housing the men and the other the women. The men were asked to form a queue near to the exit and two guardsmen searched them while another kept his eyes open to ensure nothing was passed from one to another. As the men were searched they were allowed outside to wait in a group just away from the buildings and in full view of the guardsmen out there.

Benny joined Bert and Moggy and the remainder of the guards as they made a search of the beds, cupboards, floors, ceilings, rafters, walls, toilets and corridors, leaving the anxious Chinese watchers in no doubt at all as to their intentions.

It was a nauseating task. So many perspiring bodies had slept in these dormitories during hot clammy nights with little or no ventilation that the stench, coupled with the evil smelling tobacco smoke and the oppressive heat, made it almost more than nostrils or stomachs could bear.

When all the men had been searched it was the turn of the women. It was obvious the guardsmen were uneasy having to conduct so personal a search but there was little else they could do. As the officer had pointed out, they might be cunning enough to realise the soldiers may well skimp the issue and therefore use the women to hide guns.

The operation unearthed no arms or ammunition, but as the lieutenant explained, the exercise would serve to keep these people on their toes and almost assuredly the terrorists would get to know and it could act as a deterrent.

They thanked the anxious manager who instantly ordered his workforce back to their duties before offering the troops refreshing drinks of lime-juice. They gratefully accepted and the manager rattled out orders in Chinese to a young coolie at his elbow. He returned with two others who carried trays holding tumblers of the iced drinks. Suddenly the smells of the immediate past were forgotten as they downed the most welcome drink.

Later, Benny overheard the officer expressing concern at the living conditions of those working at the tin mine.

"It really is distressing Sergeant," he was saying as they strode on side by side. "It's frightening the way some poor people are forced to live."

"Yes sir! And they probably work for next to nothing sir!" the N.C.O. said showing some compassion.

The officer sighed. "Ah well Sergeant! We are not here to act in the capacity of a visiting welfare committee," he said, refraining from using the word 'unfortunately'.

The terrain became hilly again but the jungle lay far off in the distance. They were crossing deserted farmland dotted with equally deserted huts and clusters of small buildings.

On one of these farms Benny spotted something growing that brought a whoop of excited pleasure and he ran forward to stoop and snatch at a pineapple. "Oh!" he cried holding his prize aloft for all to see. "Look what the navy's found!"

The others dived in to slice the pineapples through at their base with the machetes, there were seven or eight all together, ample enough for everyone.

"They're soddin' delicious," slobbered Bert through a mouthful of the juicy fruit. He had wasted no time hacking off enough husk to get at the edible.

Benny borrowed his machete and peeled his with slightly more propriety. He cut off a thick slice and offered it to the sergeant who took it with a wink and suggested that perhaps the lieutenant may appreciate a slice.

"Would you like some sir?" Benny asked. "I would indeed Stretton!" smiled the officer holding out his hand to accept the pineapple on offer.

It proved to be an entertaining interlude as they sat around enjoying the respite from the hunt. The fruit not eaten was stowed away for later and they were soon plodding onward once more.

They investigated every building and the surrounds but, although one hut had half a dozen chickens running around in it, there was no sign of human life.

Moggy suggested to the lieutenant that they should adopt the poor creatures and the officer queried this and asked, "Just what do you mean by adopt them?"

"Adopt 'em till we can bung 'em in the oven sir!" Bert chimed in, his eyes watching the birds running about on their long slender legs. As the laughter at this remark died away he added. "The poor things will only die if we leave 'em 'ere sir!" He could almost taste the chicken already but pretended he felt for them in their predicament.

After some debate over whether the chickens would be better taken by the soldiers or left to take their chances with the wild animals of the jungle Lieutenant Fenton-Dowell said. "Suppose we take the approach of Solomon? He would have taken the sensible solution. He would have said take half for yourself and leave half for the wild animals."

"Oh yes sir!" Bert was all smiles now he might be getting chicken to eat after all.

The sergeant turned to Benny. "Right Stretton grab the three fattest and do your stuff!"

"Yes sir!" cried the eager ship's cook and he set out to catch three of the unfortunate chickens aided by the eager guardsmen. With an expert snap of the neck Benny had killed them quickly and tying their legs together with thick grass he swung them proudly over his shoulder.

"Arrgh!" he cried letting them fall to the ground. In the excitement he had completely forgotten his wound and had clouted it with the chickens. The sudden pain took his breath.

The sergeant spotted his plight and he tossed the chickens to Bert saying, "There you are Smith! You wanted them, okay, you carry them!"

They travelled on. Since they had been crossing this plain they moved in a line abreast unlike in the jungle where it had been impossible to do other than progress in single file one behind the other.

The chickens had been tossed from one guardsman's shoulders to another as they took turns. They weighed little enough at first but after some time they created the impression they had suddenly been filled with lead pellets.

They climbed a hillock now, still spread out and as they neared the top the lieutenant signalled for them to take cover. A banging sound met their ears and they studied the landscape trying to see where it came from.

The sergeant pointed to a spot on the left of and slightly above their position. They crept stealthily towards the sounds until finally they could see exactly where they came from.

There on a level stretch of ground they saw more derelict dwellings. There was a large building and two or three smaller ones. As they listened it became clear the banging was taking place in the small hovel to the right of the site. It seemed that someone in there was throwing all manner of objects from wall to wall. The noise constantly changed in volume and pitch suggesting that whatever came to hand was immediately heaved at the walls. Whoever it was certainly did not care who came across them.

The sergeant crept around to one side picking out three guardsmen to go with him and they stole silently round to the right making their way behind the structure, always keeping at a sensible distance.

The officer signalled for the others to circle their way around from the front. When the officer considered they were close enough he signalled for them to lie low and they waited several minutes listening to the commotion.

The officer finally signalled to Sergeant Riley who could just be seen on the slopes behind the buildings. Instantly the N.C.O. and the guards with him ran full speed towards the building zig-zagging as they ran. The officer and men at the front aimed their guns to cover them should the need arise.

Within a few yards of their objective the sergeant and guardsmen dived down to hug the ground closely, lying as flat as they possibly could. They lay there waiting. Nothing happened and so up they shot and tore into the building with guns at the hip. Their comrades waited with bated breath.

Seconds later the sergeant reappeared to beckon them forward he wore a huge grin which suggested all was well. Still cautious and fearing a trap the platoon commander detailed two men to stand outside keeping their eyes peeled.

When the remainder crowded at the door of the hut they fell about laughing. There, plain for all to see, was a grunting, very hungry pig. It was painfully thin, its ribs sticking out visibly. The poor beast had been flinging itself at the sides of its prison in its determined bid for freedom and food. They let it out to grub greedily at roots and such as took its fancy.

"No one about then Sergeant?" -the officer asked more as a statement than a question.

"Doesn't seem to be sir!" the sergeant told him. "We've had a brief scout round but it might be as well if we gave the area a good going over sir!" he suggested. "You never know with these cunning hounds!"

"Hmmm! It does seem rather odd," said the lieutenant deep in thought. He sought the sergeant's opinion.

"It's the same old story sir!" explained the more experienced N.C.O. "The poor farmers are terrorised by these guerrillas and are forced to flee. The commies take over and live on the produce and any stock just as long as it lasts and they know they are safe."

"What a dirty way to wage war," said the pensive officer. "And of course that is why you believe we should burn these places down, to prevent the perishers establishing some sort of base and hiding place?"

"That's right sir! If we keep them on the move and keep hounding them it lowers their morale sir!"

"Do you really think there have been 'reds' here then Sergeant?"

"I'd stake my life on it sir!" and the sergeant said this with the air of a man who knows. "That pig for instance is a dead give away sir! If the people living here had moved in the normal course of events they would have taken the pig with them sir, it would be worth far too much to them sir!"

"Then why did we not destroy those few dwelling places where we found those chickens for instance?"

"No point sir!" the officer looked puzzled so the sergeant explained. "They would never use those places sir, too vulnerable out there in the open, we could surround them and starve them out, they would have nowhere to hide sir, in any case, they would never risk crossing the open plains and being seen."

The officer removed his bush hat to wipe the sweat from his brow as he chewed over the facts. "Well Sergeant, what do you suggest now, burn these places down?"

"I think we should give them a good going over first sir!"

"Very well Sergeant, call the men together and we'll get on with it without delay!"

When they were all present the officer told what was wanted and left it to the sergeant to detail the men off as to who was to search where. The lieutenant, Benny and a guard called Chambers were left outside keeping a sharp lookout.

The sergeant proved to be correct in his belief that terrorists had been here. They unearthed arms in more than one spot. Up among the rafters they found three boxes of ammunition. Under a pile of rubble and rubbish behind one outhouse they dug out a rifle wrapped in old sacking and well oiled, evidence of its being hidden and not simply discarded. Under floorboards in one of the small huts they found two Bren guns and a box of magazines. This find met with cries of delight, naturally.

They were most significant and important finds and it was proof beyond doubt that the 'reds' were using these buildings and possibly intended to return when it suited them. Well now the guardsmen could burn everything and upset their little plans.

The officer asked Sergeat Riley just why he had suspected this particular spot. "Well sir, this is the only place we have come across that we found stools, tables, food bowls, chopsticks and cooking pots," explained the N.C.O. "There were none of these things in any of the other places sir!"

"The next thing is to destroy these hovels," said the officer gazing over the area. "Let's not waste any more time. Burn the lot down Sergeant Riley!"

"Excuse me sir!" Lieutenant Fenton-Dowell turned to see Tim

Graham at his elbow. He had helped Benny and Bert and half a dozen others to get a short length of rope around the ribs and neck of the poor pig thereby affording them some control over the creature.

"We were just wonderin' what you're goin' a do about this 'ere pig sir?" the lad from Leeds told him.

Benny dived straight in with what he thought they should do with the pig. "We could eat it sir!" he beamed hopefully. The officer gave him an odd look but Benny pressed on regardless. "It would make an absolutely smashin' meal sir."

Benny explained they could cook the pig on a spit. "Same way they cook sucklin' pigs," he said. "Same way they used to roast the old ox in the day's of Robin 'Ood sir!" he explained thoroughly warmed up to the idea.

"I hardly see us as Robin Hood and his merry band Stretton," the officer told him, still to be talked into it. "And this creature is rather larger than a suckling pig is it not?"

The corporal strode up to instruct Benny, Bert and Tim to forget the pig and to give some help with the fire-raising. The officer intercepted him by telling him of their wishes regarding the pig. "Stretton believes he can make a meal of this creature Corporal!"

"I can sir!" insisted Benny determined to hang on to the chance. "I'll do it all myself sir! Kill it, scour it, gut it, cook it an' carve it an' all sir! And the meat would be delicious sir! Honest!"

The others warmed to Benny's idea, especially Lieutenant Fenton-Dowell. This served to encourage the ship's cook. "It's only the same as the chickens sir! We don't 'ave much choice. If we leave the pig it could end up feeding the 'reds'," he said.

The officer tugged at his ear lobe again. "Alright Corporal take those two but leave Stretton with me," he ordered and the corporal moved followed by Bert and Tim.

For a second or so the officer watched as flames began to sprout rapidly from buildings ignited by the sergeant and his men. He continued watching as he spoke. "Tell me Stretton? How do you propose we transport the beast if we do take it with us?"

Benny had thought of this too. "Easy sir! Just tie its legs to a long pole like they did in the day's of ..."

"Robin Hood. Yes, I know Stretton!" the officer had surmised what Benny was about to say and beat him to it. He had the look of a satisfied man now as he watched all the buildings burning fiercely.

Benny stood there holding the pig, unsure of what he should now say or do but he got a pleasant shock when the officer instructed the sergeant to detail two men off to go and find a long stout pole. It meant he would be cooking the pig after all.

"Right, the next question is, when and how do we kill the brute?" The officer looked to his sergeant for the answer.

"Beg pardon sir!" Benny had something to say on the matter. "It all depends on when you want it cooking. If you're goin' to cook it fairly soon then it won't hurt to kill it now, but if you don't want it cookin' for some time then it's best to keep it alive sir!"

"Oh?" said the officer adding, "Why's that?"

"Pork is a very funny meat you see sir! Kill it now and then carry it about for long in this 'eat an' it'll soon go off an' won't be fit for anybody to eat, sir!" explained Benny.

"Well Stretton," said the officer deciding to leave it all to Benny to advise them. "We shall be making our way back around this hill to the place where we were camped last night. We shall then have completed a circular search and with any luck we should make it back well before dark. The animal can be cooked then I suppose. How does that suit you?"

Benny preened himself at his sudden importance. "In that case you can kill it when you want to sir, it should keep alright for that short time." Benny explained that once the animal had been killed he needed to slit its throat to drain away the blood, leaving fine white meat.

"Fine! I am pleased it meets with your approval Stretton," the officer's tone sharply reminded Benny of his station in life. "Right Sergeant Riley, shoot it then!"

"Sir!" The sergeant took the revolver offered by his officer and he in turn held out a sheath knife taken from its place on the sergeant's belt. "Thank's Sarge!" said Benny taking it and running his finger gingerly along the blade he soon discovered it was indeed sharp.

With the men watching fascinated the sergeant wrapped a groundsheet around his arm and hand leaving a hole just large enough for the end of the revolver's barrel to poke through. They knew without asking that this was to deaden the noise of the report as much as possible.

Volunteers sprang forward to grab the pig and hold it steady. The sergeant raised the revolver and pressed the barrel up close, right between the eyes. A second of hesitation, perhaps for prayer, and the gun spat out instant death with a strangely muffled sound.

The instant the animal died Benny darted forward. He thrust the knife deep and cut a gap through the throat. Blood spewed out in all directions and they all dived away in their haste to avoid it. Once the main spurt eased off the ship's cook grabbed the pig's hind legs and raised them as high as he could to assist the drainage of blood.

Smith and Graham returned with two poles explaining that if one broke they would have another ready. Moggy stood gazing down at the dead pig as did the other guardsmen.

He shook his head and pulled a face. "I thought I might enjoy a bit of pork but I don't think I'll bother," he said turning his nose up.

"I know I shan't touch the bastard!" remarked Bert. "All the more for them as do want it," Benny told them not caring one way or the other. His arms were beginning to ache and the sergeant saw this.

"Take hold of it Phillips," he ordered Bert. Bert reached over to take the legs from Benny but he did not relish the task. "Take hold man, it won't bite you for goodness sake," barked the sergeant disgusted that a big chap like Bert should be afraid to hold a dead pig.

"That should do it Sergeant," said Benny as the blood slowed down to a drip or two.

Lieutenant Fenton-Dowell checked his watch, stared at the sky and surveyed the terrain. He studied his compass and map and called the sergeant and corporal to him. Now he spoke to them pointing first to the map and then to the probable direction they would be taking. Then they were off.

The line was headed by Lieutenant Fenton-Dowell who glanced constantly at his compass for guidance. He was followed by Sid Gregory, Bert Phillips and Moggy Reeves. The sergeant was next, then Benny, then Curly Compton and Willie Adams supporting the suspended pig between them, after the pig party came the three chickens slung about the neck of Ricky Mackenzie, Joe Currie, Pete Groves, Alan Smith, Tim Graham and finally bringing up the rear, Alf Brown and Corporal Sam Caddy.

They shared the task of carrying the pig, chickens and captured Bren gun. They never for one moment, however, forgot to keep alert.

They had travelled in a large circular fashion and Benny saw over to their left in the far distance what appeared to be another tin mine. For reasons best known to himself, the lieutenant chose to ignore it.

After around an hour they saw a small farm. It closely resembled the one in which they had found the arms and ammunition. This too lay to their left and this too was ignored. It was not possible at the distance to discern whether or not it was inhabited.

The going was relatively easy until they reached the bottom of a hill. The officer informed them when they were gathered about him, that over the hill was the spot they had camped at last night - if he had read his maps and compass correctly.

It was a difficult trek to the top of the hill and the journey took much longer than had been allowed for. Nevertheless, they finally stood surveying their objective below them. Glistening in the light of the evening sun they could see the big water tank.

They made their way down, still cautious, but in no time at all a new fire had been kindled on the site of the one they had extinguished only that morning.

While guardsmen busied themselves gathering firewood, fetching water and making camp generally, Benny was hard at work preparing the pig. The sergeant and Gregory busied themselves fixing a spit over the fire and as soon as the pig was prepared they forced a pole through the length of it and stuck it over the fire. They stood proudly watching, the dripping water left on it by Benny's cleaning caused the fire to splutter and spark at first but slowly the heat and flames took control and it was fat that dripped into the flames. Slowly at first but as Benny turned the spit the drips became constant and persistent.

Soon Bert took over turning the spit while Benny concentrated on the chickens which had been plucked, rather badly, by some of the guardsmen. The chickens, too, were prepared for roasting over the fire and Benny stood back quite pleased with his handiwork.

All the water had been carried from the crystal clear stream over the ridge of the hill, its source an underground spring. Benny stood drinking from a mug as he gazed up at the big water tank. He mused over it. This government reservoir could almost be a swimming pool. Why not? Benny made up his mind. He wanted a swim in this tank.

"'Ey Sarge," he cried, his eyes fixed on the tank. "Do you think anybody would mind if I went for a swim?"

The sergeant, who was sitting on his groundsheet arms wrapped around his knees as he watched the pig cooking, decided to pass the buck. "I should ask the lieutenant if I were you old son," he suggested with a smile that said. "This should be good."

Undaunted, Benny asked the officer. "Excuse me sir," he said walking over to the tent and asking politely. "Is it alright if I go for a swim sir?"

"But Stretton, we're in the middle of the Malayan jungle for goodness sake," he felt sure the heat had got to Benny. "Where the deuce can you possibly go for a swim?"

"In that big tank up there sir," Benny told him calmly.

"My God Stretton!" grinned the officer. "You are full of surprises man."

He turned to the sergeant. "I see no reason to object if the fellow wants to go for a swim, do you Sergeant?"

"I think it's a damned good idea sir, I might even join him myself," and the sergeant winked at Benny as he chuckled at the cheek of it all.

"Go and enjoy your swim then Stretton," the officer told him with pleasure and without further ado the ship's cook shot off up the hill.

He stripped naked, climbed up the side of the tank by means of the struts securing it to the ground and jumped into the cool water. He had completely forgotten the dressing on his wound but somehow it did not matter. It would soon dry off again.

The watching guardsmen cat-called and whistled as they observed him undress and climb in but he completely ignored them. He was thoroughly enjoying himself.

There were steel struts strengthening the tank from the inside but despite these he found himself able to swim a couple of strokes up and down. Had it not been for one extra stout bar spanning the tank across its centre he would have been able to really enjoy a swim. He was happy enough as things were. He found the water surprisingly clean and he realised it was quite warm from the heat of the sun. It had felt cool only on his introduction to it.

He should have known it could not last. No sooner did he lie back to float and relax than with a splash a guardsman had joined him. Then another, and another. Before many more moments had passed all the guardsmen bar two on sentry duty, were splashing about and having a ball in the tank, most grateful to Benny for the idea. He was something of a hero. Benny? It had suddenly become too crowded and he climbed out.

The dressing on his back was hanging on by one strip of plaster and as he bent to pick up his clothes and gear the sergeant strolled up.

"Better let me have a look at that old son," he said. Benny leaned his shoulder over so that the wound could be examined.

"It's okay Sarge, just a bit sore still," he played it down. The water had made it sting.

"Get your trousers and stuff on but leave your back till I've put a fresh dressing on it," the sergeant said. "Get yourself down by that fire my lad, you'll get a damned chill from the cool night air if you don't watch it."

"Good idea Sarge," agreed Benny. The last person he wished to go against was this big N.C.O. He struggled into his trousers and the sergeant went off to sort out the first-aid haversack. The mosquito bites were irritating and Benny scratched at them. The more he scratched the more they itched and in places he fetched the top of the bites off with his nails. It did not stop them itching though.

Once he had his trousers on he gathered the rest of his things and hobbled down to the fire. He rubbed the upper part of his body dry by using his cotton vest which he then hung beside the fire to dry. The sergeant was waiting to dress his wound.

"My God sailor!" he cried seeing the bites weeping. "You've made a right old mess of yourself I must say."

"I can't stop the bloody things from itching Serge," complained Benny twitching at the thought.

"You should have rubbed insect repellent on," said the sergeant dabbing at the wound to make sure it was clean.

"I did Sarge, that was one of the first things I did," he told him. "The soddin' mosquitoes seemed to thrive on the stuff." He flinched as he felt a stab of pain.

"Sorry old son," the sergeant apologised. "I can't understand that. I've never been bitten like this I must say."

"Do you use repellent?"

"Funny you should ask that," the sergeant smiled. "I don't as it happens."

"Well, there you are then," cried Benny.

Moggy had been loafing beside the fire trying to dry himself off.

He had views on the subject. "You don't smoke though do you sailor?" he said.

"I never 'ave," Benny informed him as the sergeant patted him on the back indicating he had finished with the wound, he now turned his attention to turning the pig and chickens.

"Well then, there's your answer, mosquitoes and gnats and that never bite them that smoke," explained Moggy. "Don't ask me why it is, I only know they can smell or sense the smell of smoke in the skin, honest."

"What a load of old cobblers," scoffed Bert having joined the growing band around the fire. "It could be somethin' special in Benny's blood that they fancy."

Benny sighed and still wanted to scratch and all their debate did nothing to ease his problem.

It was fast approaching darkness when Benny decided the chickens and pig were ready for eating. They tucked in eagerly and where their knives and forks failed them, they attacked the meat with their machetes. The meat was succulent and even Bert and Moggy, who had earlier declared they would not be dining off it, now tucked in as greedily as the rest.

Benny basked in the praise heaped upon him. He was on top of the world. Yes, on top of the world until brought crashing down to earth with a mighty bump by the sergeant.

"Right old son," he said completely out of the blue. "It's time for your spell of sentry go."

"Eh?" Benny choked on a mouthful of pork. "Sentry go? Me?"

"You said you wanted to have a go at it," smiled the sergeant and Benny hoped he was teasing. He wasn't. "It's a one hour spell. You relieve Mackenzie up there on the left, okay?"

"Okay Sarge," said Benny picking up his Sten and tried not to drop his lump of meat.

"We'll send your relief up when it's time old son," the sergeant grinned now. "And get rid of that," meaning the meat. "You can't do your sentry go with your hands full like that."

He checked his equipment by the light of the fire, aware that everyone, including the lieutenant, found the situation interesting and amusing. Finally he was ready and off he went in search of Ricky Mackenzie. He only knew he was somewhere out there in the darkness.

It was quite dark, for the clouds shut out all moonlight. He strained his eyes struggling to discern shadows and his bearings. He decided to risk calling softly. Besides, he did not wish to have himself shot by his own side.

"Ricky, where are you?" his voice sounded strangely remote.

"Over 'ere!" came the whispered response.

The lad from Consort crept forward cautiously, aiming for the voice. Then suddenly, he almost fell over the guardsman's feet. Ricky was lying face down looking away from the fire.

"Oh, it's you sailor, so they've roped you in as well have they?"

"Ah well mate, we've all got our cross to bear," said Benny as Ricky got to his feet. They whispered when they spoke and the atmosphere made Benny's skin creep.

"Don't look back towards the fire if you can help it sailor," advised Ricky helpfully. "Otherwise it takes a minute or two to get your eyes used to the dark again."

"Yeah, I know what you mean," said Benny. He settled down into much the same position Ricky had been in and the man he had relieved wished him luck as he turned and made his way down to the fire and company.

Benny was alone now and the reality of it all hit him. He made a mental note of all the things he had been told to do and not to do. One thing he knew for sure. He would not be sticking his head up above the skyline for any terrorist to make a target of.

His bites itched. His wound throbbed. His eyes and ears began to suggest a mixture of scary untruths. He told himself to count, breathe slowly and deeply. He did but he was still decidedly ill at ease and unsure. The sergeant had warned him about letting his imagination run away with him.

He felt the dampness coming up from the grass and hoped he would not get pneumonia from all this. The clouds began to thin out and he could see more in the silvery light. He twisted his head to gaze for a second at the scene below. Silhouetted figures squatted around the dying embers. The fire still retained a rosy glow and he saw the pig's remains hanging from the spit reflected strangely. No one bothered to turn it now. Of the chickens nothing was left.

Benny shivered and scratched, wishing he was back aboard

Consort snug in his 'Mick'. Or better still, in some cosy bed with a soft and warm companion nestling up to him.

The mosquitoes were hungry for more of his blood and they whined about him, tormenting the life out of him. He dare not risk slapping them hard, fearing the sound would give his position away. He wondered how the other chap on sentry go was feeling. He felt some of the bites. They were becoming quite swollen.

He ran his tongue over parched lips. God he could drink a pint right now. Groping for his water bottle he settled for a swallow of its lukewarm contents. All the time he struggled to keep a sense of proportion and tried not to make the slightest sound. He admitted to himself that he was a little scared.

His gaze was idly drifting over the terrain just ahead of him when he saw it. At first it was merely a white blur, disappearing as quickly as he saw it. There it was again. Then gone. His heart began thumping as he fought to get a grip on himself. Whatever this was he knew it was alien to his surroundings.

The sergeant's warning words echoed through his brain. "Don't let your imagination run away with you."

The blur popped up and down again. Benny tried to assess the exact distance in order to guess at the size of whatever it was bobbing up and down. It was hopeless. He took aim with his Sten, waiting for it to show itself. Could it be some kind of animal?

There it was again. Now it wasn't. What the hell could it be? It remained, each time now, only long enough for him to get it in his sights but the instant he had it lined up it disappeared. One thing he realised. It seemed to be staying in the one place.

In spite of the fact that this ghostly blur almost mesmerised him, Benny retained the good sense to keep a wary eye on other things. They were not going to sneak up behind him.

The moon peeped feebly from behind its flimsy covering of cloud and he saw it again. He took aim, got it in his sights. It was gone! Perhaps it was some sort of Malayan white rabbit or hare ... or an albino tiger! Get a grip on yourself for heaven's sake.

There it was again. This time he played it clever. He lay perfectly still instead of aiming at it. He guessed it was about twenty yards away from where he lay. He tried to keep calm. He wished more than ever that he had stayed on board the ship.

He knew delay could prove disastrous. It must be reported. Yes but how? Shouting was right out of the question. There was only one thing he could do. He must creep down the hill and tell Sergeant Riley. But that would mean moving and he felt much safer staying where he was. It was no good. He knew he should not desert his post but at least the sergeant would know the ship's cook had been keeping his eyes.

He wriggled snake-like down the slope to the others by the fire. "Sergeant Riley!" Benny called, his voice a dry hoarse whisper. "Sergeant Riley, are you awake?"

"What is it old son?" came the sergeant's voice from within.

"Sorry to trouble you Sarge but there's somethin' goin' on out there that's gettin' on my nerves."

The sergeant's head appeared. "How do you mean?"

"It's a bit 'ard to explain Sarge," Benny suddenly felt extremely foolish. "There's somethin' sort of white or whitish. When I get it lined up in my sights it disappears." Benny hoped a hole in the ground would swallow him. "I was just wondering what I should do Sarge for the best."

"There is only one thing you can do sailor," Benny knew when this term was used that he was in trouble. "Get back to your post and investigate!"

He was almost back at his post when the truth of what he had to do next hit him. He had to investigate! Benny lay down facing the spot he had last seen this blur. It was still playing games.

He fought to pluck up courage. Indian style, he crawled forward. Only about a foot but that was enough for now thank you. Nothing happened as he waited, nerves tingling, heart pumping and pulse racing. Taking encouragement from this he edged forward another foot or so. Still nothing happened. He watched, waiting for the blur to show itself.

There it was again but even now he could not distinguish what it was. It bobbed down out of sight and he crawled another yard nearer. He saw now that the ground rose slowly about two feet, running up the hill. He knew that he was only a few feet from it, or him, or them, now. His heart was up in his throat choking him.

Patiently he waited and just when he thought it would never pop up again, it did. Poor Benny. When he saw what it was our gallant naval hero wanted to curl up and die. "Oh no!" he cursed through clenched teeth. He felt so downright ashamed of himself he could have cried.

There right in front of him on the ground lay nothing more than a sheet of newspaper. As he stared at it in utter dismay the breeze wafted the newspaper up at one corner where it remained dancing for a few seconds before the same breeze let it down again.

Lying there, he cursed the idiot who was the cause of the newspaper's being there, he cursed the elements for having the gall to provide just sufficient a zephyr to waft the paper up and down as it did. And when he had done, it registered with him that all the fun and games was not yet over.

"'Ow the piggin 'ell do I explain to Sergeant Riley?" The sergeant was bound to ask him what it was had caused him to seek his advice. How could he possibly admit it was nothing more than a piece of newspaper. Yet if he did not tell the sergeant the truth it meant he must tell him a lie and he knew he could not lie to him. Even if he did what could he tell him it was?

Still cursing his luck he crawled back to his original spot. If the truth did come out he would be a laughing stock. A slight sound behind him had him spinning round aiming his Sten. "Who's there?" he hissed venomously.

"Relax old son, it's only me," said the sergeant himself. "Everything under control I see."

"Yes ta," said Benny wondering if the sergeant would mention 'it'.

The sergeant did. "Did you go and investigate?"

Benny took a deep breath. This was it, better get it over with, no good beating about the bush. "Sarge, promise me you won't laugh ..."

"Now why should I laugh?" even in the poor light Benny sensed the sergeant was smiling. "You seem to forget old son, I've been on quite a few guard duties in my time."

His words gave Benny a lift. He still expected the worst but he reckoned without the warm understanding of this man. He explained exactly what had happened, how he had been afraid, worried he would let the side down, ashamed to have left his post, he left nothing out and when he had finished he waited for the ridicule.

Instead the sergeant said softly and kindly, "It's funny how the old mind works at times like this old son, plays some rare tricks on you doesn't it?"

"Uh! You can say that again," readily agreed Benny.

"Honest." He stood up to go. "Don't worry about it old son, there's only you and me know." He studied the illuminous dial of his watch. "You've only got another ten minutes or so to go, see you then."

If he had expected to be relieved he was to be disappointed. No one took his place for they were packing up in readiness to move on. It was Sergeant Riley who came up to tell him his turn of sentry go was over and they were leaving.

"Movin' off?" gasped Benny flabbergasted. How could they do this to him? "But Sarge, it's the middle of the night."

The sergeant shrugged his broad shoulders. "That's the way it goes old son. You can't stop fighting a war just because it get's dark. It's all to do with the element of surprise."

They were with the rest of the guardsmen now and Benny, sadly, began to fold his gear up.

"Did you see that farm and tin mine we passed in the distance on the way back here?" asked the sergeant standing by Benny as he sorted out his few odds and ends.

"Yeah, I wondered why we never bothered with them."

"Yes, well there may or may not have been 'reds' there," explained the sergeant helping Benny sort his webbing out. "We think there are and we hope they watched us go by, if they did they will be feeling pretty safe at this moment and we can catch them with their trousers down can't we?"

Benny chuckled at the thought but he still did not fancy struggling through this damned jungle in the dark. It was bad enough in daylight.

The remains of the meal Benny had cooked were thrown into the bush and quickly they were ready for moving and the officer called everyone to him. "Keep reasonably close, we don't want to lose anyone in the darkness," he said. "Get lost in the dark and you could well stay lost." He gazed about to see that they were listening and understood. "You have all been briefed as to why we are moving at night and where we are going, any questions?" No one had a question. "Right Sergeant, let's move out."

It was only natural that progress was slow. Traversing this jungle in daylight was problem enough but in the moonlight extra care had to be taken.

Lieutenant Fenton-Dowell did not intend to approach the farm or mine by the direct route. He reasoned that if 'reds' were there and had seen the guards passing by then they might be expecting just such a move as he now made. Instead of the shortest method he led his men in a wide sweep intending to come at them from the rear.

They had worked their way around and were now some distance from the mine, studying what they could see of it in the dark. The lieutenant gave the order for everyone to lie low and keep their eyes peeled for any movement when he fired his Very pistol.

Benny was astonished at this. He simply failed to understand how anyone could plan to take the enemy by surprise and yet advertise their presence well in advance by illuminating the heavens.

They were spread out as the officer hissed, "Here we go then!" and fired the pistol, holding it high above his head in the general direction of the mine. The flare exploded to light up the sky. For the few seconds it took to float down to earth the mine buildings and all the surrounding area were exposed fairly clearly. The guardsmen scanned intently and eagerly every inch they could for the least sign of life or movement. With a splutter the flare hit the ground and after a few moments of struggle gave out. With that the darkness returned only now it seemed total. Once their eyes grew accustomed to the light again they moved forward.

When they arrived at the mine workings, they were surprised to see no one apparently sleeping. They conducted a thorough search as at the other mine and again were glad to get it over with. There was the same awful, nauseating smell.

At this mine however there was one big difference. Here the workers bent over backwards to offer them gifts. Even though against the rules some of the gifts were accepted. They included watches, wines, cheap brandy, cigarettes and even, for a ridiculously low fee, women.

Lieutenant Fenton-Dowell was as polite as ever and apologised for the disturbance, reminding them that it was, after all, in their own interests for all the obvious reasons.

Benny mentioned the fact that they seemed to be expecting them and so many of them were wide awake. It was explained to him that these people had two or three hours off during the heat of the day and slept then most likely and of course the flare from the Very pistol would have warned them of their coming.

Benny smiled at this. Had the officer fired the pistol deliberately? He asked Bert's opinion. "I shouldn't think so," grinned Bert. "After all, ain' that what we're tryin' to do, catch 'em with their trousers down?"

Having satisfied himself that his men had once again conducted a thorough search, the lieutenant led them off to continue elsewhere. In what little moonlight there was they could make out the shimmering waters of paddy fields. Bullfrogs croaked their odd chorus, the sound floating out over the water. The clouds had returned and at intervals, the light from what moon there was, dimmed to varying degrees of darkness, sometimes so dark as to blot out even the very narrow paths between the fields.

These slender pathways, at times barely wide enough to keep a foothold, separated the fields in a criss-cross pattern and Benny, keeping the required distance from the man in front, almost lost his balance on more than one occasion.

Carefully picking his way along the narrow tufted path, Benny heard a muffled oath and gazing ahead saw that the tall guardsman in front of him, Willie Adams, had stumbled upon shallow water and was now wading through it to regain the path some three yards beyond.

The guardsman hissed a warning. "Watch it mate, there's a break in the path just here."

Poor Benny! He had seen Willie stumble slightly and heard his whispered warning but he forgot to take into account the great difference in their height and disaster resulted.

He gingerly put one foot in front of the other when without any warning, the ground beneath his leading foot gave way to water. "Wha..." the rest of what he was about to say would have been uttered under water for that is where poor Benny was.

He struggled to regain an upright position but only succeeded in making matters worse. Each time he put weight on a foot it slid out from under him and under he went again.

Willie and Bert rescued him from his predicament. They took a shoulder each and hoisted him up, coughing and spluttering on a mixed mouthful of water and greenery.

The water was only two foot deep but poor Benny had simply lost his balance and gone right under. His pouches were full of water and he looked sadly at his Sten once they had planted him on the firm path on the opposite side of the breakage.

The guardsmen were almost hysterical with laughter as they struggled to keep quiet. When Benny held out his dripping Sten gun and asked if they thought it would still fire they laughed even more. Perhaps the doleful expression on his face had something to do with it.

"Talk about a bleedin' clown," laughed Bert shaking his head in time with his laugh. "What the bloody 'ell 'appened to you?"

Benny stared back at him, poker faced and said sarcastically, "I got fuckin' wet!"

This served to create more merriment. The ones at the rear of the line had caught up and were also enjoying the laugh at Benny's expense.

"What made me laugh," said Willie, "was seeing this arm coming up out of the water holding a Sten gun. It was just like a modern day version of Excalibur," and he laughed louder.

"What in God's name is going on here?" snarled the sergeant having doubled back to find out what had gone wrong.

Instantly all frivolity ceased. "Benny very nearly drowned 'imself Sarge," Bert hastened to explain.

"I didn't," retorted the ship's cook annoyed at such a thought. "I saw Willie go in an' I thought I'd be okay but silly bloody me forgot about 'is soddin' great long legs didn' I? I just lost my balance completely and in I went."

Even the sergeant smiled now and shook his head in disbelief. "Well, just as long as it's only your pride that's hurt old son," he reached out and lifted muddy grass off Benny's head. "I think there's enough room in these paddy fields for this without trying to grow it on your head, don't you?"

This remark melted some of the icy look in Benny's eyes and then at last he gave in to a grin and the party moved off once more.

As he trekked along he tried getting rid of the mud and water. He tipped his pouches upside down and watched as the water poured out. A lot of water was retained in his jungle boots and made a loud squelching sound as he walked.

The others were waiting about thirty yards from the huts. Lamps burned low just inside the main building. Outside, in front of a large sieve, sat a youth, his back leaning against the building. He seemed oblivious of their presence as he busied himself with a huge mound of objects resembling a form of bean.

Even when the guardsmen fanned out about him to make their search he gave no sign that he knew of their existence. It puzzled Benny, this strange total indifference to the middle of the night invasion of his privacy. Could he be trying to hide something? Was it simply great fear? He shrugged his shoulders as the young man carried on with whatever it was he worked at and went off into the larger hut after Bert and Moggy and the sergeant. The rest of the guardsmen were busy checking the grounds and other buildings.

It amazed him to discover that here too everyone was awake and dressed. Benny took a swipe at the mosquitoes buzzing around in the lamplight's immediate glow. "Bastard things!" he cursed softly and with good cause.

His comrades were searching everywhere, as before, and he gazed all around taking stock of the hut, its shape, size and occupants. He saw a very old man with long grey beard, talking to an equally old lady almost bald. She appeared to do all the talking and at great speed. He saw two or three very demure, quite attractive, young girls, two young mothers with babies at their breast, a small boy, three middle-aged women and one other young boy.

"God's truth!" gasped Benny. "'Ow the 'ell do they all manage in 'ere?" No one listened to him. He stooped down and undid the laces of his boots. Realising water would spill onto the floor of this home he went outside to remove the boots and tip the water out.

As he held up the boots to drain the officer strode past to join his sergeant. "I'm damned if I know what to make of this place sir!" the sergeant said softly lest the occupants spoke any English. "It doesn't add up sir, firstly there's that youth outside, then there's only a boy and an old man in here," he made a sweeping movement with his arm, taking in the women, "yet there's all these womenfolk sir, it just doesn't make sense."

At this the old man stepped forward having heard and understanding every word. "I essplain to 'onlable officer plis, men all wor' 'ard a' tin mine, you un' erstan' sir?"

"I understand, yes," the officer told him glancing at his sergeant

164

with a question in his eyes. The sergeant read the question and shrugged his shoulders. "It might be the truth sir, how can we prove it, that's the thing?" he said.

"It tlue 'onlable sir," insisted the old fellow bowing low. The two knew they had to take his word for it, unless they unearthed weapons.

For the first time Lieutenant Fenton-Dowell saw the sorry state Benny was in. "Good God man!" he gasped eyeing the ship's cook up and down. "What has happened to you?"

"I lost my balance and fell in the paddy-field sir," explained an embarrassed matelot. He was trying to wring water from his trousers. It would have been easier if he had removed them first.

The old Chinese gentleman pottered forward with a cup of hot tea and Benny took it. The cup was quite small and there was no milk but all Benny cared about was the fact that it was wet and hot. "Thank you very much," he said and returned the bow the old man gave him as he took it.

The Grenadiers went over the place from top to bottom but found nothing. Finally the lieutenant called off the search, obviously disappointed at finding nothing and they moved on towards a small hill just visible against the skyline.

CHAPTER TEN

Benny did not feel well. He ached all over and his senses seemed oddly numb. Even Bert noticed and asked what was wrong. "I reckon it could be these wet clothes Bert, I'm shiverin' wi' the cold."

"It's a pity you couldn't take 'em off an' dry 'em ain' it?" said Bert.

"Aw, not to worry, they're dryin' out on me but it's a long bloody process ain' it?" He had said not to worry but that was precisely what he was doing. He did not like the way he felt at all.

"'Ere, 'ave a drop of this," said Bert producing a bottle of inferior brandy which had already been well and truly sampled.

Benny tipped the bottle and filled his mouth. It was raw and stung but he swilled it round, allowing just a few drops to run down his throat at a time. He passed the bottle back and Bert told him he had 'picked it up' at the last tin mine. He winked as he said this and left Benny wondering.

"I told you, do you the world of good," smiled Bert deciding to have a mouthful himself before passing it back to Benny. "'Ere, pass it on to Moggy an' tell 'im to 'ave a sip."

Benny caught Moggy up and handed him the bottle. Moggy pulled a face as he sniffed at it and replaced the cork without touching a drop. "No thanks sailor, rot your guts that stuff."

"Tell 'im to pass it on," hissed Bert from their rear.

"Bert say's pass it on," said Benny relaying the message and Moggy duly sought out the man ahead of him. The bottle passed back and forth in this way but no one really fancied the brandy once they saw the label and smelt it and it was soon back with Bert and he and Benny indulged themselves. Each time they had a drink they screwed up their noses and suffered. It didn't stop them emptying the bottle however.

"I suppose you acquire a taste for it," said Bert having another drop. He was the last man in line and the two were not bringing up the rear quite as well as they should have been at the moment. Each time they drank they stopped to do so and since they stopped regularly and often they rather fell behind.

The platoon was now crossing almost barren wasteland. Even the ground beneath was a fine deep sand which tended to give way under foot. Here and there could be seen clumps of tall grass and a few sparse bushes were dotted about like lonely sentinels silhouetted in the moonlight.

They plodded on for half an hour before coming to an embankment alongside a river which was over twenty feet wide at some parts.

Lieutenant Fenton-Dowell called a halt and the men flopped down onto the sandy bank with relief, leaving their superiors studying maps, checking compass and getting their bearings.

It was getting light quickly now as the two brandy drinking stragglers finally caught up with the party. Benny held the bottle tightly but he had no need. It had long since been emptied. Bert had been content to let his navy pal drink the best part of it since he felt his need to be greater.

Benny's clothes were still damp and he found himself shivering in fits and starts in the early morning air. He felt worse as each hour went by and the brandy had done nothing to help. And there was to be no rest for them. As soon as they were on the point of settling down on the sandy bank the officer and sergeant called to the men and moved on. Bert cursed his luck and Benny had a few choice words of his own but it made no difference. They were off along the river bank which veered round to the left.

Moggy hesitated when he saw the state of Benny. He rounded on Bert. "You stupid twat!" he snarled. "Fancy getting him pissed like this."

"'E ain't pissed," Bert told him. "I think 'e's got a fever or somethin'."

"Moggy," sighed Benny striving hard to stay with it. "I ain't pissed, I ain't honest mate."

Bert, realising there was nothing else for it, got one side of the ship's cook while Moggy got the other and between them they helped him along. Being so much taller, when they put their helping arms around him they all but lifted him completely off the ground as they hurried after their comrades.

Benny wanted no more of this. "Wait!" he shouted at them. "I'm okay now, I'm okay, just put me down please."

They stopped and gently let go. His head thumped and his eyes refused to focus for more than a split second at a time. "You've got to believe me," he begged them. "I'm not pissed."

The guardsmen looked at each other at a loss. "Look, just let me walk an' I'll prove it." Benny was determined not to let the navy down. He fought so desperately hard to fight off whatever ailed him. He would prove to them he was ill, not intoxicated by a mere drop of brandy. He went to move forward. Mercifully, he passed out.

Moggy and Bert grabbed him before he fell into the water for a second time. "Quick! Shoot off and tell the sergeant or somebody," Moggy cried. Bert was already in full flight.

The lieutenant ordered the platoon to halt. He left the corporal in charge, then hurried back with the sergeant and Bert to where Moggy kept a worried eye on Benny.

When Lieutenant Fenton-Dowell saw the bottle still clutched in the matelot's fist he went white and raised his voice. Never before had he been known to do this by the battalion. He sniffed at the neck and snapped at Bert and Moggy, "Did either of you know he had this?"

Bert knew he had to come clean. "I knew 'e 'ad it sir," he said quietly.

"Do you know where he got it from?"

"I gave it to him sir," admitted dispirited Bert.

"You damned idiot!" the officer was white with rage. "How much did he drink?"

"Only about a cupful sir," said Bert. Moggy was looking the other way pretending he heard none of this. The sergeant was on one knee attending Benny.

The lieutenant's voice was low and menacing as he thrust the bottle right under Bert's nose. "Are you really expecting me to believe he got like this on just one cupful of this rubbish?"

"Yes sir," said Bert adding quickly, "it's the Gospel truth sir," when he saw the angry glare return. "We passed the bottle round for everyone to have a drink sir," he reconsidered the implications involved in this remark. "Well, that is, a couple of us sir."

"Just a couple of you?" The officer looked from Bert to the inert figure of Benny, now propped up in a sitting position by the sergeant. "Was this bottle full to begin with?"

"Yes sir!"

"Oh?" the lieutenant was obviously making a point. "Then if Stretton drank only a cupful and only a couple of you have had a drink, what's happened to the remainder?"

Bert felt trapped. If he implied the platoon had shared it, they could all be in trouble. If he admitted he and Benny had shared most of it he would be in trouble for lying from the start. He could think of nothing to say and so he said nothing.

"Just how much did you drink Phillips?"

Benny groaned, stirred, shivered violently but remained dead to the world. Bert stared down at his sailor chum wishing he had never tried to warm him with the brandy. "I 'ad about the same as 'im sir," he said.

"Then can you explain how he lies unconcious while you're still on your feet!"

"I can't explain it sir," Bert's anguish was plain to see. "'E was saying 'e didn't feel very well sir, that's why I thought a drop of brandy might do him good sir."

"Why didn't you say he complained of feeling unwell in the first place man?" He joined the sergeant now by dropping on one knee beside Benny.

"He did say he wasn't well sir," Moggy said coming to the aid of Bert.

"He certainly looks a peculiar colour," mused the officer "What do you think Sergeant?"

"He could be under the influence sir but I don't like this shivering one bit." Sergeant Riley had been busy tending Benny from the moment they came to him. He had not really listened to the reprimanding tones of the lieutenant. "It's probably due to the soaking he got in the paddy-field sir," he said as he leaned Benny's head right forward. "His clothes are still fairly damp sir."

The officer displayed understanding by telling Bert, "I realise your intentions Phillips but in future let me decide whether or not brandy

169

is the solution, alright?"

"Yes sir, I'm sorry sir," said Bert not feeling so bad about it all now.

The officer turned his attentions back to his sergeant and Benny. "You know Sergeant, we are forgetting that young Stretton isn't used to all this, it is possible he's burnt himself out, all this trekking, guard duty, getting soaked."

"It certainly won't have helped matters sir," agreed Sergeant Riley. "He's bound to be very tired I should think and the brandy might just have been enough to knock him over sir."

They spent a few minutes talking, shaking, massaging, even tried throwing a drop of water on his face but all they got were grunts and groans. His eyes did open once but they were sightless and promptly blinked shut again.

"Well," decided the officer. "We have delayed far too long." He took out his maps and glanced at his compass. From the light of his pocket torch he studied it for some moments before calling the sergeant.

"Over in that direction, about half a mile away, is a village, we'll take Stretton there and see if we can get any advice or help. If they have salt we might be able to induce him to vomit and bring back the blessed brandy." He sought the opinion of his sergeant. "What do you think Sergeant?"

"There isn't much else we can do sir, if we can get some of that muck up off his stomach he might be alright."

"Good, that's the way I see it," said the officer. He turned to Bert and Moggy. "Right you two, we'll need to carry him so pick him up and let's get off."

They swung their Stens over their shoulders and round their backs out of the way and picked Benny up. The sergeant carried Benny's Sten and the party strode off after their comrades. When they joined the rest of the platoon there was no shortage of volunteers willing to take a turn at carrying Benny. They all had the chance for half a mile under these circumstances is a long way. Daylight was well upon them now. The village comprised of no more than eight or nine straw huts and the occupants had turned out to greet them at the edge of their village, led by the headman.

Lieutenant Fenton-Dowell introduced himself and his platoon, explained why they were at the village and asked for salt or salt water or anything else that would induce Benny to vomit.

The headman spoke English and when the introductions and requests were finished he clapped his hands and yelled out orders in Malay. At once people hurried off to do his bidding, eager to be part of it all. They returned with enough salt and salt water to serve the desired purpose a hundred fold.

The officer took one tumbler and vainly tried to get Benny to drink. He was in a sitting position, propped up by the strong legs of Sergeant Riley. There was absolutely no response from him at all.

Seeing what they were about the headman clapped his hands and in seconds a chair had been provided for Benny to sit on. Once the headman had Benny sitting on the chair he offered advice on what he would do about the situation.

Lieutenant Fenton-Dowell graciously accepted, failing to see what else he could do. He had the sergeant tilt Benny's head right back and pinch his nose between finger and thumb. Forcing Benny's mouth open the officer slowly poured the salt water down his throat.

Surprisingly Benny gulped down the saline fluid greedily. After a moment as they stared at him, his eyes opened and he gazed with a strange distant look at the officer and startled him with a request for more.

They responded by giving him fresh water. Benny's demand for water proved astonishing for he downed three cups before a worried officer called a halt. "My God! We daren't give him any more Sergeant, we could be doing more harm than good."

The sergeant agreed. The villagers milling about them grinned broadly as they watched this figure in jungle-green gulping down all this water.

The officer put a stop to their grinning by telling the headman he intended to make a thorough search of all the dwellings in the village. The headman mildly protested but knew he had no choice.

Leaving the corporal looking after Benny who seemed to have improved some, the Grenadiers carried out their search. However, as they searched, the corporal watched as Benny slipped in and out of consciousness.

The search completed, the sergeant and officer came to ask if there was any progress. The corporal shook his head sadly.

"Hmmm!" said the officer tugging at his earlobe as a means of helping him think. "It begins to look as if it may be other than the brandy Sergeant Riley," he said. What could they do?

As it became obvious that the matelot had not made, and did not look like making, any improvement, the sergeant proposed that they should look for help quickly. The officer agreed and so a stretcher was made from poles and spare tunic shirts slung between them. They used lengths of rope supplied by the headman to strengthen the stretcher. The headman also handed over a bundle of straw, to be used, as he explained, as a pillow and bedding. Everyone seemed keen to make Benny's journey as comfortable as they could.

The distinct possibility that Benny was not intoxicated but really ill was now accepted. They lifted him gently onto the stretcher when the time came to go. Despite the search, the villagers had provided refreshments for the troops and they waved as the platoon bade them farewell and set off for their temporary camp which they knew to be not far off.

Benny knew little of the journey. In his wakeful moments he gazed up past the faces of his bearers to the moving maze of leaves and branches and the clear blue sky beyond. He struggled to talk and turn his head but failed on both counts. The only thing he wanted to do was close his eyes and sleep.

It was past mid-day when the guardsmen arrived back at their temporary camp. With the aid of groundsheets and long branches they set up a canopy to protect Benny from the sun. They also lit the fire to dry his clothes and to provide hot drinks as he alternately shivered with the ague and burned with fever.

The sergeant and lieutenant sat beside Benny hoping the warmth and drink would bring him to something like his senses. After perhaps two hours of patient watching he looked up at them. He even managed a smile.

In a flash the sergeant was with him. "Hello old son," he said cheerfully. "How do you feel now?"

"Please Sarge," he croaked through parched lips, "I'm dying for a drink."

The officer leaned over him smiling confidently and told him they were making a cup of tea. Benny, however, pleaded for water and the sergeant went to get some for him.

The officer asked, "Do you think you can tell me what happened to you Stretton?"

"I 'aven't a clue sir," Benny said trying to sort his jumbled mind. "I can remember thinkin' I was sickenin' for somethin' because I didn't feel at all well sir."

"Was that before Phillips gave you the brandy?"

"Oh yes sir, ages before then. Bert only gave me a drop of brandy because I felt cold sir," explained Benny remembering that much.

"Ah, good," said the relieved officer.

The sergeant returned and held out the water. Benny drank as if his life depended on it. He flopped back then as if even the effort of this had exhausted him. "I don't know what 'appened sir, I seem to remember walking on a sandy slope somewhere and my feet kept slidin' away from me an' then, I don't know sir, I'm sorry," he said weakly.

"It's alright Stretton," the officer assured him.

"You know what," sighed Benny talking to no one really. "I ain't got an ounce of strength in me." Even as he spoke his eyes rolled and he began to shiver again, uncontrollable, his teeth rattling like someone playing the bones. Every part of him shook with a frightening intensity. "Quickly sir! Let's move him nearer the fire." He did not stand on ceremony but his officer ignored the fact that his N.C.O. was giving instructions. They lifted the navy lad and placed him nearer the fire. Guardsmen sitting around watching shot forward to help with the groundsheets and such.

"Cold old son?" the sergeant asked. He spread his tunic shirt over him and smiled trying to cheer him up. "The tea will be along any minute now."

Benny shivered far too much to be able to speak properly so he settled for a nod and hoped it would not be mistaken for the shakes.

Then, as quickly as it began, the shivering ceased and in a few seconds Benny was asleep or unconscious.

By now the officer was certain Benny was seriously ill and was becoming concerned. "Let's have another look at this blessed map," he said taking it from his pouch. Moggy came up with mugs of tea. The officer took one and placed it on the floor beside him. As he studied the map he asked the sergeant a pointed question. "Do you suppose he could have pneumonia Sergeant?"

"I've wondered that too sir. I should hate to think it's that."

"So should I Sergeant, so should I. Aha! It seems there is an Englishman living not too far from here, a government official, a botanical expert if my memory serves me correct. I have heard he is a most remarkable chap, lives in a rambling great mansion. Come to think about it I do believe that water tank up there is all part of what he does. Why the devil did I not think of it before?" He drank his tea and stood up.

"Sergeant, what do you say we take young Stretton up there? After all he may know something about his condition or have medicine?"

"In any event he might be in a position to fix the lad up with a dry bed and a roof over his head sir," said the sergeant secretly hoping this may be possible.

"Then let's get off now Sergeant," said the officer, obviously not a man to waste time once he decided on something. "If the track is reasonable we could make it in thirty minutes."

The sergeant called the guardsmen to him, explained the situation and asked for six volunteers to act as stretcher-bearers. He got ten, including the corporal and the only two not volunteers were those on look-out and they knew nothing about it. They decided to draw straws for the job of carrying Benny and without any further delay the mercy mission set off.

Fortune was with them for this track was a good, easily manageable one. They started off down the hill at first, as if they were going towards the village they could see in the distance. It was the same path that 'D' platoon had taken two days ago.

They reached the residence in very good time. What a fine place it turned out to be. There were beautiful gardens leading all the way up the long drive to the house. It was built Georgian style, the sun enhancing the white walls. The lieutenant and his men saw a much wider path joined the one they were on at the approaches to the massive gates leading to the last hundred yards of driveway and the house itself. This clearly went down to the village and was of sufficient size to take a motor vehicle and evidently did so.

Formidable iron railings stretched away from either side of the gates. Along the top of the gates and railings ran a double string of barbed wire. Set in the right-hand, brick built post, was a large brass plaque boldly sporting the name, Dr Lionel A. Hubertson. D.Sc. F.R.M.S.

"Looks quite impressive sir," observed Sergeant Riley.

"Hmmm!" the lieutenant studied the large white button with the word 'Press' imprinted across in gold letters set into the gate. He pressed it and even as he did so they saw a European striding towards them and doddering along behind him came a small Malayan gentleman.

The European raised his arms waving them about, calling to them as he did so. "It's alright, I'm coming. My man told me you were here, shan't keep you a moment gentlemen," he carried a large key which he inserted into the big lock which held the gates firmly shut.

Swinging the gates open wide he stood back to allow them entry. "Come in gentlemen, quickly," and once they were all inside he locked the gates behind them.

"Let us go in gentlemen," he said leading the way hurriedly to the house. "I am Doctor Hubertson."

The lieutenant began to introduce himself but was promptly cut off by this man of letters. "Later young man, later ... Let's hurry inside if you please."

It was a novel experience for the guardsmen to see one of their officers treated in this fashion and they were quite enjoying it. Lieutenant Fenton-Dowell did them proud and took it all in his stride.

Dr Hubertson was a short stocky man, middle aged with a hint of grey in his otherwise longish black curly hair. His smart, check shirt was open at the neck and the sleeves were neatly rolled up. He wore a pair of very baggy, knee length khaki shorts, almost hiding his brown knees and almost reaching his long socks. He wore a big, bright kerchief around his neck and to complete the picture smoked a large meerschaum. With his thick soled shoes he might easily have been mistaken for a Bavarian. The little Malayan was never far from the doctor's elbow.

He ushered them through the ornate front door, which was wide enough to allow the stretcher and bearers through quite easily. The doctor's man closed it behind them.

"In here," cried the doctor pointing to a reception room and they filed through to place Benny and the makeshift stretcher gingerly down on the highly polished floor of marquetry blocks.

"My good lady wife is preparing tea gentlemen, it will be but a moment," he said leaving them briefly.

Everywhere was spotlessly clean and highly polished. Suspended from the ceiling above Benny was an enormous, three-bladed electric fan. It rotated slowly, without a sound. It was effective though for after the heat of the journey the big room was pleasantly cool and fresh.

The doctor returned. "That's that gentlemen," he said and turned and gave instructions to his man in fluent Malay and with a low bow the man hurried off.

Only now did the doctor condescend to know who these guardsmen were and why they had called on him. They shook hands with each other with polite formality.

For the first time the man of letters showed interest in the man on the stretcher. He was just about to lean over Benny and ask about him when the tea trolley arrived, wheeled in by the doctor's man. Moving to the trolley, he said, "Help yourselves to milk and sugar, there are biscuits in the barrel."

As they drank Lieutenant Fenton-Dowell was becoming anxious and he glanced at Sergeant Riley over the top of his cup, swivelling his eyes stretcherwards. The sergeant got the message and shrugged his shoulders. What could they do? Had Benny been badly wounded and losing a lot of blood things would have been totally different but he appeared to be fairly comfortable as he lay there sleeping.

The doctor read their thoughts. He stood gazing down at Benny who was in a semi-conscious state and had started to shiver slightly now. "Hmmm!" he mumbled and crouched down to put a hand on the matelot's brow and to feel his pulse. "Hmm!" he repeated standing up but still gazing at Benny lying there. "Hmm! Malaria," he said with casual calmness. "He is having a malarial spasm."

The lieutenant was stunned. "Malaria sir?" he gasped.

The doctor mistook this for contradiction. "That's what I said young man," he retorted. "Seen far too much of the cursed thing in my time not to know what it is. You must take my word for it gentlemen, this poor fellow has malaria." He was adamant.

"Get me a cup of tea for him, not too hot mind," he ordered, leaving it for anyone to obey. He crouched down beside the stretcher and gently lifted back Benny's eyelids. It was obvious he knew what he was doing.

He saw the painful looking bites on Benny's arms. "The blighters have certainly made a meal of him," he said shaking his head with slow deliberation. The sergeant handed him the tea. "Here you are my boy," he said to Benny raising him up gently for him to drink.

Benny was utterly confused. He squinted through pain-racked eyes trying to see who this stranger was. "Who are you?" he croaked feebly.

"It's alright Stretton, he's a doctor," said the lieutenant telling a white lie.

"Yes yes, I'm a doctor," said the man. "I'm a doctor and I'm telling you to stop this blessed fussing and drink this tea."

Something in his manner did the trick and Benny drank the tea. "That's just fine," said the doctor patting him on the head. He went to stand up but before he could move away Benny feebly caught his arm.

"Please doc, what's wrong wi' me?" he said pleading to know.

It was Sergeant Riley who answered. "There's nothing wrong with you old son," he said smiling trying to instill some spirit into the matelot but not really succeeding. "You just relax and try to get some sleep."

The doctor had been out of the room and he returned carrying a small, cream coloured tin. He removed the lid and held out the tin to Benny. "Take one of these and suck it," he told him. "They work wonders for a dry mouth."

Benny treated this offer with suspicion, trying to see what it said on the tin. "Tell you what my boy, take it with you, you will enjoy them I'm sure," said the doctor. The matelot grasped the tin and squinted at the lettering on it. Finally he made out the words 'Old English Humbugs' and smiled. "Thank you doc', thank you very much," he said letting the tin fall from his grasp. "It's very kind of you."

"Rubbish boy! We have oodles of the things," said the doctor. He took out a sweet and unwrapping it popped it into Benny's mouth. The matelot smiled faintly. He was aware of the taste but it was all too much trouble, he only wanted to sink into nothingness again.

The doctor stood up and beckoned the lieutenant to one side. "That boy must get medical attention quickly. Have you any objection to my calling up security headquarters for advice young man?" adding before the officer could reply. This was not a question. "I'll give them a buzz on the radio transmitter at once," he turned to gaze down at

Benny lying there.

"That's why we came here, to ask your advice," the lieutenant told him. "We had no wish to go to the village for reasons of security."

"Wise man, no need to let the devils know any more than we have to," he said as he left.

"He's a character sir," the sergeant said as the lieutenant helped himself to another tea. "Yes Sergeant," agreed the officer stirring his tea. "What a blessing he has a radio transmitter here."

"A Godsend sir!" The sergeant thought about it. "Strange he should have one sir?"

"Hmmm!" the officer too thought about it. "It is rather strange yes." he agreed.

When the doctor returned the lieutenant stood up and went towards him, hopefully. He was not disappointed. "Well gentlemen, there is an ambulance on its way from the military hospital at Kuala. Now, if all goes well, it should arrive at the rendezvous point in one and a half hours. The journey from here should take only thirty minutes and so we have an hour to wait gentlemen." He spread his hands apologetically. "I'm sorry but that is the best I can do I'm afraid."

"But that is marvellous Doctor," and the beaming lieutenant reached out to take the doctor's hand and shake it. "It is most kind and considerate of you."

The doctor was embarrassed by all this. "Dear me, I do wish everyone would stop making such a fuss."

The officer remembered the two-way radio. "Excuse me sir, I never realised there were any two-way radio sets for miles."

His words briefly caught the doctor off guard. "You are not to realise anything young man," he said. "Furthermore," continued the doctor, "I absolutely insist that the matter is forgotten." With that he turned his attention to the guardsmen. "Get yourselves a book or magazine from the bookcase there, it will help you pass the time gentlemen, if any of you wish to go to the toilet, my man will show you where it is." He then surprised the officer by coming to him to whisper as the men went to the bookcase to help themselves to reading matter.

"All top secret you understand," he told the bemused officer. He watched to see none of the others heard. "That's why all the aerials are hidden away from sight."

He beckoned the sergeant and they left the room. They were taken to a small study and out came the brandy decanter. Lieutenant Fenton-Dowell smiled and looked at his sergeant. They shared the joke and explained about the brandy incident to the doctor. He chuckled and assured them his brandy was rather different to the muck sold locally.

"Tell me doctor, have the 'reds' ever attacked this house?" asked the lieutenant.

"Good gracious me yes!" he sat back staring at the ceiling as he recollected. "They got rather a nasty shock I'm pleased to say. I have a most efficient staff here. There were about twenty or so of the blighters, tried to climb the railings silly beggars, just like sitting ducks they were," he chuckled loudly, enjoying the memory. "They've not been back since but we take no chances. We fetch all our requirements in the car and we have a reliable system keeping us in the picture I assure you." He raised the decanter. "More brandy anyone?"

"Isn't it risky taking your car along these lanes sir?" asked the officer holding out his glass for a refill.

"Not really young man," said the doctor watching the brandy as he poured. He said it as if it were quite normal when he told them. "Bullet-proofed and armour-plated of course." He had a twinkle in his eye now.

"Do you have many servants sir?" asked the officer watching the doctor refill the sergeant's glass.

"Young man, you are far too inquisitive," the doctor told him.

"You too sir, if I may say so, also seem to know a lot more than is normal for a man in your position."

"Perhaps, Lieutenant," the doctor had lost the light hearted manner of a moment ago. "Perhaps my position as you put it is not all it appears to be eh,?" His words were full of hidden meaning.

Before the officer could make further comment there was a tap at the door and a very attractive woman entered the room. She was perhaps thirty or thirty-five and had the bearing of refinement.

"May I join you dear?" she asked politely.

"Yes my dear, do come in and meet our guests," she glided forward and he made the introductions.

"How nice of you to call on us," she said sweetly. "Would you care for tea or anything?" she asked.

The three men looked at each other. The doctor raised his hand with the brandy glass in it and she got the message. "Oh, I see you already have a drink. I'm sure you would prefer that to tea," she smiled.

"Darling," the doctor said. "Ask Moon to make sure those chappies in the reception have tea and biscuits would you?"

"Of course dear," she said going to the door.

"Oh yes dear," he added and she turned waiting. "Do have a look at the boy who is ill for me will you?"

"Yes of course dear," she said and went.

"Moon," explained the doctor, "is my man, my dear wife says his round face is a moon face and so she calls him Mister Moon, rather quaint."

In the other room his wife squatted beside Benny. She caressed his brow and spoke to him softly and caring. "My goodness me, what have you been doing to yourself young man?" she asked.

"I don't feel so bad thanks," said Benny. She was hardly able to hear his murmur. His mouth was so dry his tongue felt twice its normal size. He lied too. He felt dreadful.

She reached for the tin and took out a humbug which she held by his mouth. "Everything will soon be fine," she told him in an effort at consoling him. "Once you get to hospital they will soon have you back on your feet."

"'Ospital?" Benny vainly struggled to sit up. "Who said I'm goin' to 'ospital? I'm stickin' it out to the end wi' Bert an' Moggy an' ..." he gave in, spent.

The doctor had decided to have another look at Benny for himself and came into the room in time to hear his last words. He was followed by the officer and the sergeant.

"What is wrong dear?" the doctor asked.

"I'm afraid I've put my foot in it and mentioned hospital," she explained. "The poor darling doesn't seem to like the idea."

The doctor kissed her fondly on the cheek. "You are always putting your pretty little foot in it my darling, never mind, I still love you," and as he kissed her again he patted her on her rump. He then turned his attention to Benny.

"Now then my boy, what is all this nonsense?" he asked stooping

180

down.

"Doctor, please ..." Benny's eyes searched the doctor's face. "You can fix me up wi' a couple of tablets or somethin', I'm not goin' to no 'ospital."

"You just listen to me my boy," the doctor wagged a finger under Benny's nose. "You are ill, got that? And the place for people who are ill is the hospital and to the hospital you are jolly well going."

The sick matelot was visibly upset by all this. "But you don't understand doc, I mustn't let the side down?"

"You are not letting the side down Stretton, I promise you," said the lieutenant coming to lean over from the other side. "In fact we are all proud of you, aren't we men?"

He got a chorus of full agreement from the concerned guardsmen. He thought of Benny's wound. "By the way, how's your back now Stretton?"

Benny stared back at him. He was at a loss.

"His back Lieutenant?" the doctor was interested. "What's wrong with the boy's back?"

"He has a knife wound doctor, but luckily not too deep, his webbing strap took most of the blow," the officer informed him.

"Good God man! Let's have a look at it," insisted the doctor. He sought their help in turning Benny over.

They removed his clothing sufficient enough to see the wound. It was quite clearly inflamed but Benny seemed not to notice. "Please my darling," the doctor stood up to instruct his wife. "Hot water, antiseptic soap, lint and bandaging if you would dear."

Having bathed, cleaned and dressed the wound, they carefully lay him back on the stretcher and covered him as well they could. It would soon be time to leave. The Grenadiers settled down to their reading. The doctor, his wife, lieutenant and sergeant, retired to the study where the brandy was. Over drinks the doctor explained to them the route they needed to take and where the ambulance would be expected to arrive if all went well.

It was to come through the village and along the lane leading up to the house. For reasons of security it was to come only halfway. This would shorten the time otherwise required so that any 'red' observers would not have time to establish an ambush. By the time they realised it, the ambulance would be well on its way back to the hospital. There was also an ideal turning point and if they timed it correctly they would meet up there without either one having to wait for the other

The time to leave came and all the handshakes and farewells were made in the house at the doctor's insistence. They hurried to the gate which he had gone in front to open. Once they were through he locked it, then quickly moved back into the house again while the guardsmen kept looking back until he had disappeared from sight indoors.

"He doesn't believe in hanging about does he sir?" observed the sergeant.

"Sensible fellow Sergeant, he know's how easily he could be picked off by a sniper's bullet," a thought occurred to the officer. "Do you realise Sergeant, I do not recall seeing any arms in the place."

"Funny sir, now you mention it, he didn't even carry a revolver did he sir?"

The khaki-painted ambulance with its big red crosses displayed for all the world to see was just turning round when they arrived. There was an armed escort sitting beside the driver and two more sitting inside the ambulance.

As the driver jumped out, the escort did so and he faced away from the vehicle, gun at the ready. They certainly took no chances. A stretcher was pulled off its runners and placed on the ground beside Benny. Quickly but carefully they lifted him on it, covered him with blankets and tucked him in. A pillow was placed under his head and with swift deft movements the stretcher was lifted up and pushed back along its runners into the ambulance.

"Quick as you can please sir," begged the driver as the Grenadiers gathered round to say their farewells.

Benny was barely able to understand what was happening to him but he did manage to smile for them.

"Well, goodbye Stretton, take good care of yourself," said Lieutenant Fenton-Dowell patting him on the head.

There appeared to be a tremor in Sergeant Riley's voice as he said his goodbyes. He gripped Benny's hand firmly in his own. "Cheerio old son, mind 'ow you go," he said forcing a smile and winking. Bert and Moggy could think of nothing more to say than, "So long sailor!" and "Be seein' you mate!" but their expressions told their own story.

182

As he drove off down the hill the waves and shouts followed him, even though Benny never heard them and would never know. He had wanted to tell his chums how sorry he was to let them down like this but the words stuck in his throat.

He was so proud to have known these men of His Majesty's Grenadiers. He was not to know they stood silently watching the ambulance bump and jolt its way out of sight. Even when they could no longer see it they hesitated. It was the sergeant who made the first move. "Right you lot, let's be having you, we have a lot of ground to cover," he barked. Bert and Moggy and the others swopped knowing looks and with one last glance, they turned and followed their sergeant.

CHAPTER ELEVEN

As the ambulance rumbled along on its journey to Kuala Lumpur Military Hospital, Benny slept on. He knew nothing of the journey or his companions. The driver had commented on how poorly his passenger looked and wasted no time at all in getting him to the hospital.

He drove directly through the main gate and up to the reception block. Staff awaited their arrival and in no time at all Benny was lying in a bed in the medical ward. The duty medical officer had examined him, his wound had been dressed and he had been given a hot blanket-bath. Now, in clean pyjamas, the lad from the Royal Navy slept.

He slept, almost without interruption, for three whole days. The only time he woke at all was when the duty nurse tried to get him to eat or drink. They wasted their time. Benny, lying flat on his back, would gaze up at what he considered to be the vision of an angel in her white uniform.

This angel would plead with him to eat or to drink the milk she brought, or the lime juice, or the tea. Everything was unreal and no more than a dream to Benny. They would tend his wound but he was unaware of it.

On the fourth day he began to wake up. For a few minutes at a time his eyes would open and things would add up, just a little but it was a start.

In the evening, a male orderly who was passing Benny's bed, got a surprise. The bed was placed length-ways down the ward, between the beds running down the ward in normal hospital fashion, it was right in the centre of the ward near the end where the offices were situated. As this orderly passed the bed, Benny spoke.

"Excuse me," Benny had said.

"Oh!" gasped the young Royal Army Medical Corps man. "You gave me quite a start," he said regaining his composure. "How do you feel?"

"A bit weak ta. Where the 'ell am I?"

"Don't you know?" and when Benny shook his head he told him. "You're in the military hospital at Kuala."

Benny rubbed his face with his hands and suddenly remembered his glasses. "Oh God," he gasped. "I've lost my glasses." He was not to know that throughout they had been carefully looked after from the moment Bert had picked them up when he had first passed out.

"I think the sister has got them for you," the orderly him. "I'll bring them for you when I go down to the office. That is if they let you have them."

The orderly walked off leaving the matelot listening to the whispers of his ward-mates. He struggled to lift himself up on to one elbow but it was as much as he could manage to raise his head so he stopped as he was.

Sometime later the sister came to see how he was and, like the majority of qualified nursing staff, she was most prim and proper. She had that familiar air of authority and efficiency and stood five feet two. Cosily plump, her hair tucked up neatly beneath her cap, she spoke to Benny in a friendly manner but one that implied she stood for no nonsense.

"Hello, young man," she said tidying his bed.

"'Ello," said Benny forcing a smile he did not feel. "The orderly said you might have got my glasses."

"Yes, they're safe," she stood arms folded staring down at him. "Why?"

"Could I have them please?"

"No!" she said, wasting no time letting the matelot know she was in command. "When I can be sure you are in a fit state and not likely to break them you may have them back, okay?"

"Yeah, okay," sighed Benny.

"Now, how would you like a nice drink of Horlicks?"

"That would be nice thanks," he said feeling very thirsty.

"Aha!" she cried having struck gold. "At last you must be getting better. That is the first time since you came in here you have accepted a drink without us having to force it on you." She was obviously pleased about it and smiled happily. "Good, I'll go and get it before you have time to change your mind."

"What the 'ell's wrong wi' me sister?"

"Nothing that a few day's rest can't cure," she said. He gazed at her with a look that said he did not believe her. "You're simply completely worn out," she insisted. "I promise, in two or three days, you will be as good as new and ready to return to that ship of yours, okay?"

"But what about goin' back to the platoon?" he asked.

She shook her head and in her eyes was a warning. "Platoon?" she snapped. "I should think you have had enough to last you a lifetime," she said as she recalled the state he was in when admitted. "It nearly cost your life in fact."

The orderly arrived with his drink and shook him gently back to awareness. "Uh!" he gasped. Seeing what it was he attempted to sit up but it proved beyond him.

A fellow patient from across the ward got out of bed and came across to help the orderly raise Benny to a sitting position. They held him while he held the drink. "Thanks," he said, forced to sip because the drink was hot.

This simple effort had taken more out of Benny than he liked. His head had started thumping, his heart was racing and he fell back eyes closed.

"That 'Orlicks'll do you the world o'good me ol' cock, git a good night's kip an' y'll be right' 's ninepunce in the mornin', be'cha," this ripe Cockney voice belonged to the patient who had helped him sit up. He shifted Benny's pillows, making sure he was comfortable before going back to his own bed. Benny failed to see how a good night's sleep would see him as right as ninepence when, after all the sleep he had had, he still felt awful.

The sister's voice called out from the office end of the ward. "Goodnight everyone, see you tomorrow." Those patients awake and so disposed bade her goodnight in return. She switched off the main lights, leaving only the emergency light for safety, and left the ward.

Benny slept like a log. Why not? He had practised enough these last few days and nights he should be expert at it.

This military hospital turned out to be no different at all to any

186

other hospital. As is the universal practice, everyone was awoken at a most unearthly hour. They were compelled to wake whether they wished to or not, the only exceptions being those critically ill or severely wounded.

Two male orderlies hurried took pulses and temperatures, a night sister doled out pills and medicine from her trolley, checking her board as she did so. Those patients referred to as 'walking' wandered back and forth to the toilets at their leisure, unless some administered concoction persuaded them to speed things up a bit.

"What the bloody 'ell's goin' on," groaned Benny pulling the bed-clothes over his head. "It's worse than Picadilly soddin' Circus!"

"That is quite enough of that," snapped a voice whose owner whipped the clothes right off him.

Benny saw the middle-aged sister standing there holding out a dose of Milk of Magnesia. She almost dropped it when he winked and said, "Come an' give 's a kiss an' I'll say I'm sorry."

She snorted, "It's plain to see you're getting better my lad," she thrust the glass at him. "Here you are, get that down."

He took it but she had to lean over to help him up in order to drink it. She held the glass and he gulped it down. "Urgh! he pulled a face. Before she was aware of what he was about, he had an arm round her pulling her to him and had kissed her on the cheek. She freed herself, dislodging her cap in the process.

"You devil you!" she stormed blushing. She turned away so that he should not see the smile playing at the corners of her mouth. Straightening her cap she reached into her apron pocket and brought out his glasses. Turning back to him she handed them over. "These are yours I believe," she said tartly.

"Oh thank you darlin'," he said putting them on and making a show of admiring her. "My God! You are even prettier now I've got these on," he said.

"Which is more than can be said for you," she retorted moving to the next patient, careful not to let him see her smile.

As the sister left from one side of his bed, one of the orderlies stole up on him from the other. "Here you are then," the orderly cried tapping him on the shoulder. He held a thermometer. "Just stick this under your tongue," he said.

The slim medical orderly took his pulse as he waited for the temperature to register. Benny was dying to ask a question and the instant the tiny glass tube was taken from his mouth he asked point blank, "'Ey mate, what does it say is wrong w' me on that board?"

The orderly was already writing on the board in question. "It doesn't say," he said with complete indifference.

"Aw bloody'ell mate, come off it," sneered Benny. "Don't be a clown all your bloody life."

The orderly coloured up and stared at Benny in annoyance. Then suddenly, after a quick glance up and down the ward, he whispered, "Psycho-neurosis."

"Psycho what?" scoffed Benny leaving the orderly waving his hands downwards in a frantic bid to tell him to keep it quiet. "Quiet please, you'll get me shot," he cried. He was glad the sister was up the other end of the ward.

"Some bugger ought to shoot you," said Benny. "I'm no more bats than you are chum, you must be lookin' at the wrong board. My name's Stretton," he pointed out thinking it would help. It didn't.

"I know what your name is and that's what it says," the orderly said. "If I'd known you were going to kick up a fuss I wouldn't have told you."

"Load of bollocks!" snapped a disgusted Benny. What next?

The unhappy orderly decided it was time he got off out of it and he did by seeking the next patient whose temperature he must take.

"What's wrong you ol' china?" asked the Cockney character from across the ward as he came to have a look at Benny.

"That dozey idiot reckons it say's I'm a bloody nut-case on my board," a disgruntled Benny told him.

"Yeah? Well, it ain' is fault nar is it? 'E carn 'elp it, if I wuz you I'd ask the doc' when 'e comes rahnd 'is morning'," suggested the Cockney. "'Sides, 'e's the geezer what wrote it down on yer board in'a firs' place so 'e ough'a know."

"I will see 'im, don't worry," said Benny hoping he would be awake when the doctor made his rounds. "What time does 'e come round?" he asked.

"Abaht ten."

"Cheers!" Benny said. It struck him then that he could drop the orderly in a bit of trouble.

"Ere, I can't ask 'im can I? 'E'll want to know who told me it's got psycho-neurosis on my board won' 'e?"

"'At's no bovver, tell 'im I told yer," grinned the Cockney.

"But that's goin' to drop you in the shit," said Benny.

"Nar, I shall jus' plead innocence won' I?" his broad grin suggested he would enjoy the challenge. "In fact tosh, I'll tell 'em I told yer 'ow's 'at?"

"I can see I'm goin' to get on wi' you mate," and Benny grinned now too.

Benny surprised everyone, including himself, by devouring his food when it arrived. The day-sister pointed out to him that he must be on the mend when she made her rounds and wishing them good morning. She watched Benny stuff the last bite in his mouth. "Did you enjoy that?" she asked knowing by the way it disappeared from sight that he did.

"Yes ta!" he told her smacking his lips noisily.

She pulled a face, tutted and shook her head. He was curious about the letters shining on the epaulettes of her starched, spotless white coat.

"What do the letters stand for on your shoulder sister?" he asked pointing.

"They stand, my boy," she said, implying he would be no wiser when she had told him, "for the Queen Alexandria's Royal Army Nursing Corps, satisfied?"

"Yes ta!" he told her beaming.

Benny was able to sit up now but never once had the awful throbbing pain in his head eased off. His eyes pained him too, especially when any bright light met them. They had hurt when he tried focusing on the medal sister wore, it was a replica of the one the night-sister sported but whereas he asked about the letters on the epaulette it did not seem right or proper to ask about such things as medals.

He was growing impatient waiting for the doctor and as the sister made her way back down the ward he called to her. "Sister."

"Now what is it?"

"Would you say I was a nut case?"

She smiled. "I must admit I have to wonder about it," she said amused.

"I'm not laughin' Sister, I'm serious," and the expression on his face told her so. "I want to know why they've put it on my chart?"

189

She was no longer amused. "Put what on your chart young man?"

"About me bein' a psycho."

The sister glared at him, arms akimbo. "Stretton! You have absolutely no business at all knowing what is or is not on that chart," she wagged a finger towards the end of the bed. "That chart is there solely for the benefit of the hospital staff, not the patients!"

He was not to be intimidated. "But if I'm supposed to be mental I want to know who say's so," he said, "and why an' all."

She turned to move away, changed her mind and had softened. "Don't fret yourself Stretton, I can assure you, nobody is of the opinion that you are mental and what is written on that board certainly does not imply you are a ... psycho, as you put it."

Some time later he saw the doctor and matron commence their rounds. He had suspected they might be on their way when the same orderlies had flitted in and out checking everything was as it should be.

He saw that the doctor was a captain in the Royal Army Medical Corps and the matron was also in the Q.A.R.A.N.C. The party seemed to spend precious little time with any of the patients. Just a cursory, "Good morning," and "How are you?" before moving on, not really stopping at all.

Benny played it cool and feigned sleep. He did not wish the Cockney to accuse him of getting cold feet and the sister had as good as warned him off any further questions. At least for the time being.

He regretted not asking once the doctor had left the ward however. It would have been far better had he asked and put his mind at rest. The day passed. He ate, drank and cursed his aching head for not letting up. It was not like a normal type headache. A dull, painful, heavy, eye-squinting headache it was. "Per'aps that's what they mean by psycho-neurosis, I'm off my 'ead but don't know it," he told himself and fell asleep worrying about it.

The night came and went and Benny knew nothing about its passing. The orderly that took his pulse next morning, informed him that he may be able to get up for a spell during the day, from what he had heard the sister saying.

"She's got to be jokin'," scoffed Benny opening his mouth for the thermometer. "I'm knackered sittin' up to eat an' drink."

"Well, don't say I said anything for goodness sake or you'll get me shot," the orderly said. He had a quick look to make sure no one was about. "But I heard the M.O. and sister talking and apparently they want you back on board that ship of yours in two days," he paused to check the thermometer, entering the reading on the board, "and so they want you on your feet as quick as they can."

"What are they tryin' to do! Kill me?" Benny moaned not understanding. "Besides," he told the orderly thinking he had a valid point. "If I'm mad they won't 'ave me back on board." He gazed across the ward seeking help and advice from the Cockney chap. He was not there, having been discharged whilst Benny slept.

The orderly's words proved prophetic for sure enough when the M.O. and matron made their rounds they informed Benny it was time he tried getting up and about. Benny did get up and promptly folded at the knees. Patients, orderlies and sister rushed to his aid.

"Bloody 'ell," he gasped. He remembered there was a lady present and modified his language. "My flamin' legs just melted away from under me."

"You should not have got straight up like that for goodness sake," the sister snapped. "You have been in bed for several days my lad." She helped the others sit him on the edge of his bed. "You must take your time and do it in stages."

He sat in the chair dangling his legs, his head thumping. He did not wish to appear ungrateful but he preferred to lie down and go to sleep. While he was sitting there they moved the locker containing his bits and pieces and took it over to a bed beside the wall. They were moving him now that he was getting better.

"They tell me you're in the navy," said a voice at his elbow.

Benny turned to see a little chap had pulled up beside him in a wheelchair. "Yeah," he said, "I am." Benny didn't like chatting.

"What's a sailor doing out here?" asked the little chap having no imagination.

Benny looked at him and sniffed. He let out a great sigh and said, "You tell me mate." It was totally out of character for the matelot to behave like this but he did not feel up to a friendly inquisition.

"Where do you come from sailor?" the little chap tried again.

"My name's Benny," he informed him not liking the way this chap called him sailor, "an' I come from a place called Nuneaton."

"Well I'm blowed," gasped the wheelchair occupant. "I come from

Rugby so I guess that makes us near neighbours."

The little chap rattled on and on as Benny knew he would. He didn't have the heart to tell him to go away and leave him in peace.

"'Ello there, I see they've got you out of bed then," said the stocky, balding patient who had walked the length of the ward to timely interrupt the chatterbox. He had a real handlebar moustache and just had to be an R.A.F wallah.

"'E comes from Nuneaton, Ces," the little chap piped up.

"Oh? I used to work in Cov' during the back end of the war," the newcomer said perching on the corner of the table beside Benny's chair.

"Do you come from Cov' then?" he asked admiring the great moustache.

"No. Leamington Spa. That's another reason I packed up working in the factory and joined the R.A.F," explained the airman. "All that rail travel to and from work got me down in the end."

"I've asked him how a sailor comes to be in this place," said the little chap determined not to be left out, "but he can't tell me, funny because I'm sure there are no ships this far inland."

Benny ignored him and addressed himself to the R.A.F. type. "I was attached to the Grenadiers, everything went wrong I guess," he shrugged his shoulders. "Ah well, teach me not to volunteer in future."

This small talk continued until lunchtime and Benny found himself sitting at the table. He struggled through the meal, his head was giving him hell and finally he was forced to stagger back to bed and in a few minutes was sound asleep.

He was only asleep for a few minutes for as soon as the sister spotted him shook him awake. "Now now! Come along Stretton, this will not do at all you know."

"What the 'ell's goin' on for Christ's sake?" groaned Benny squinting against the light and the pain of his eyes and head.

"That's enough of that blaspheming and you've had enough sleeping too," she snapped at him. "Come along, out you get. You really must walk about and get some life into your limbs. Buck yourself up my lad, we hope to return you to that ship of your's tomorrow. Come on, out you get!"

"Aw God Sister!" he moaned. "I've got no life to put into my limbs,

I'm bloody ill let me tell you."

"Yes and I'm telling you to stop that swearing," she glared at him defying another word of it. "You never will get well if you don't pull yourself together my lad. Come along, let me see how far you can walk. Better still, get your towel and toiletries and get yourself a good hot soak in the bath." She called an orderly over and instructed him to assist Benny in and out of the bath.

Each time Benny put his foot to the floor a sharp pain ran through his head and eyes. But he was not going to let it beat him. In spite of almost passing out half way to the bathroom he pressed on. No slip of a silly sister was going to say he was not trying.

She was right about the bath, he felt much better for it. It certainly eased his aching limbs even if it did fail to restore his lost energy.

The R.A.F. type was near his bed when he got back. "My God," he told him. "I feel as if I've been belted with a soddin' sledge 'ammer."

Bristle-face grinned. "Tell you what sailor, the length of time you were asleep we were all thinking you'd been hit by something."

Benny called to the orderly passing by. "Do me a favour will you chum," the orderly raised his eyes asking who it was. "Bung me a plaster on my back will you please?" The old plaster had come off in the bath.

"Can you hang on a minute, I've got to do everybody in a tick so I'll do you then," said the orderly.

Benny was about to sit down but that pest of a sister was behind him again. If she kept it up he was going to have her for victimisation.

"I thought I asked you to walk about young man?" she said.

"I 'ave been walkin' about darlin'."

"Oh have you darling?" she sneered "Well sitting down on that chair is a funny way of walking my lad."

"I wasn't sitting on the ..." he almost swore but stopped in time, "chair."

"Tell you what Stretton, if you want to sit down why don't you walk up to the end of the ward and through the doors onto the grass outside. You can sit in the sun, it'll do you far more good than sitting in here." She took his elbow to lead him on his way.

Benny was glad to go to get out of her way. He felt awful still but refused to give in. He felt he had given in to this thing too much already. Yet again, there had been nothing he could do about it. Once out there he collapsed onto a deckchair.

As he lay there dozing in the sun's warmth a sombre thought struck him. He was willing to bet that this weird sensation of his head drifting away from him would be exactly like one's soul drifting up and away when one died. He shuddered.

He gazed about at the grounds of the hospital. It had beautiful flower-filled gardens. The French windows through which he had come, opened out onto a wide verandah and as he gazed now he thought what a truly peaceful scene this was. What was more natural than that he should fall asleep?

He was aware of a shadow across his face. He had no idea of time or of how long he had slept but he knew instinctively the shadow belonged to sister. He opened his eyes. He was right.

"'Ello my darlin' come to share a bit of sun w' me then?" he said smiling.

"Now you just look here my lad, I will ..." as she wagged her finger beneath his nose his so very comical expression compelled her to stop and she gave a faint laugh. "Really Stretton! You are incorrigible, you really are," but he knew by her little laugh that he had won her over.

She changed the subject. "I just can't see you being fit enough to leave tomorrow if you're going to do nothing to help yourself," she said.

Benny lay back in the deckchair and closed his eyes. In spite of putting on this show of carefree good humour he knew all was not as it should be. He knew in his bones something had gone wrong. He knew too that there was no possibility of his making the journey back to his beloved Consort unless there was a drastic improvement in his condition. He fell asleep leaving them to worry about it.

A patient came out to wake him and inform him that sister had sent him to tell him it was teatime.

"Cheers mate!" Benny said making a feeble attempt at stretching. Funny sister had not come herself. An idea came to him and he smiled. Off he went to struggle round the flower beds collecting half a dozen of the best blooms as he went.

Holding them behind his back he entered the ward and pottered down towards the sister. Reaching her he swung the flowers out graciously and held them beneath her nose. "All for you my darlin', a token of my undyin' love an' devotion."

The patients watching this whistled and cheered and clapped. Sister soon put a stop to that, "Stop that nonsense at once! All of you!" She turned to glare fiercely at Benny. "And what about the gardener?"

"Just tell 'im you don't love 'im any more darlin'," smiled Benny.

"Now look here Stretton!" This time Benny's expression did not throw her off balance. "I must warn you that if I have any more of this frivolity I shall have no alternative but to report you to the matron. I will not be made a fool of. Is that quite clear?"

It was Benny's turn to be serious now. He tried to explain his reasons for doing what he had. "I 'ave no intention of making a fool of anybody, least of all you. I know what a difficult job you 'ave at the best of times an' I was only tryin' to brighten things up a bit, that's all. I'm truly sorry if I 'ave offended you, I didn't mean to, honest."

She said nothing but stared hard at him for long seconds. Then quite surprisingly she reached out and took the flowers from him. "These might just as well go in water now I suppose," she said. She turned and waltzed off towards her office, smelling the flowers as she went. They were not to see it but she had a proud look on her face.

After tea, Benny attempted to read from a novel but it became too much for his eyes after only a few words. His eyes simply refused to focus. He tossed the book from him. The chap from the R.A.F. asked him if he fancied a game of draughts. He did not really but had to do something so found himself facing the massive moustache across the table.

"I think it's only fair to warn you sailor," said the R.A.F. wallah, preening himself smugly. "I'm pretty hot at this game," He rubbed his hands together cockily. "I've never been beaten since I've been in here."

Benny thought this feat should not be hard, seeing how many in the ward appeared capable of tiddlywinks, let alone draughts. "Don't worry whiskers ol' cock," he said. "I shall probably fall asleep while I'm playin'."

Whether he minded being called 'whiskers' or 'old cock' or not, the man from the R.A.F. did not say. He was too pre-occupied preparing to take another scalp.

He did not take Benny's scalp however. The rest of the patients cheered when a very surprised matelot beat the moustache easily. Had the R.A.F. wallah been over-confident? He was so embarrassed at losing, he declined Benny's offer of a chance to get even. He made some excuse he had other things to do and left.

The next morning, when the M.O. and matron made their rounds, they stopped at Benny's bed for a change. He secretly hoped it had nothing to do with the flower episode of yesterday. They stood at the foot of his bed talking in subdued tones. They studied his chart as they talked.

Finally the M.O. came up to him. "Hello," he said simply. "G'mornin' sir!" said Benny politely, wondering what was coming.

"We think you should be alright to rejoin your ship today," the M.O. said. "How do you feel about it?"

Benny wanted to remind him that he was the flaming doctor but felt it best not to. "If you say so sir," he said. He reasoned it out that if this M.O. said you were fit, then fit was what you were.

"Yes Stretton, but how do you feel now?" the doctor asked.

"Not too bad sir," Benny was surprised the fool had bothered to ask. He hadn't bothered before so why now?

Benny decided it was high time he took the bull by the horns. "What exactly was wrong wi' me sir?" he asked remembering he was a captain.

"Hmmm, yes," murmured the captain biting his bottom lip in thought as he looked at the board. "Yes, I see. Well Stretton, it seems you were admitted suffering from complete nervous, mental, and physical exhaustion, that's all."

The M.O. handed back the board and sidled towards the next bed. "Now you've had a jolly good rest everything should be fine. You should take things easy of course, get back into the swing of things in slow stages."

"'Ow about the wound in my back sir?" he asked, hardly daring to.

"Oh that?" the M.O. said it as if it was not worth a mention. "Nothing wrong with it is there?"

"Well no, not really, but ..." damn it! Benny was not going to leave it at that. "Excuse me sir but I'm worried there's more to it than you say."

The M.O. stopped and turned to stare at this man who dared to challenge his knowledge and authority. The matron stared with him, equally aghast. What more natural than that the sister should copy them? Benny? Strangely, he did not care a hoot.

The M.O. now had a disgruntled frown. "What do you mean Stretton?" he asked coldly.

"Well sir, I feel so tired and the pains I get in my 'ead and across my eyes is murder, it never seems to let up sir."

"Good grief man! What do you expect?" snapped the M.O. The matron smirked. The sister glanced away. "You are bound to feel tired until you get back to your old self. As for the headaches, that's all part of it. It will probably last a few more days but don't worry about it. You'll soon be fine," and with that declaration which did nothing for Benny, the M.O. continued his rounds. Matron tossed Benny a haughty look and followed him. Sister just smiled.

When rounds had been completed, one of the orderlies asked if he would like his wound dressing again before he got dressed. Benny told him no, it had been done that morning and he preferred to get out of the place without further delay. Deep down he felt aggrieved. He simply did not believe all the aches and pains and problems of these last few days were due solely to the fact that it was nothing more than fatigue.

The orderly pulled the screens around the bed for him to get changed into the jungle-green gear provided by the Grenadiers. It had been washed and pressed and even the boots had been cleaned. He asked what had happened to all the webbing and pouches and the Sten gun. No one could tell him. As far as they were aware, the gear he had now was all he had had when admitted.

Shortly before lunch, the driver detailed to collect him called in at the sister's office to tell her the ambulance was ready. Benny sat chatting to some of the other patients when she came into the ward to beckon him.

"Well, so long you lot!" he called out waving to them all as he walked steadily off out of the ward.

"Come along Stretton," smiled the sister warmly. She had obviously forgiven him the flower incident. "Your carriage awaits." They walked out together to the waiting ambulance. Just as he was about to climb the steps the driver unfolded for him, he took the sister completely by surprise by planting a kiss on her cheek.

Unable to prevent the kiss, she nevertheless managed a hefty smack across his backside as he mounted the steps. "You are a cheeky beggar, Stretton," she smiled as she said it.

The doors were shut now and he sat there thoughtful. The armed escort sitting opposite offered him a cigarette which he declined. "No ta, I don't smoke."

"What's been wrong with you then?" the escort asked being friendly.

"Accordin' to the quack I've burnt myself out but it makes me wonder if 'e's in the right bloody job."

The escort chuckled. "What makes you say that then?"

"I don't know really, I just feel so soddin' yuk all the while," Benny told him. With nothing else to do as they journeyed on he gave the escort as much of the story as he could recall. The longer they travelled, the worse Benny felt. When the driver pulled up at a village between the hospital and the Grenadiers' camp he asked what they had stopped for.

"We only come so far," explained the escort. As he spoke the driver opened the door and lowered the steps. The escort who had been in the driver's cab came to join them.

"What the 'ell's goin' on?" the matelot asked

"It's alright mate," the driver told him quite unconcerned. "The truck'll be along any second."

"What bloody truck?" gasped Benny still reluctant to get down from the ambulance.

"The truck from the Grenadiers' camp. It's coming to pick you up. In fact, I'm surprised it isn't here yet."

Benny shook his head and let out a disgusted sigh as he climbed out. "Balls to this for a game of bloody soldiers," he said. "Why the 'ell didn't the truck come and pick me up at the 'ospital? Talk about a bloody pantomime!"

The ambulance driver explained that it was a procedure adopted to keep the terrorists in the dark.

"It's certainly keeping me in the bleedin' dark," snapped Benny. He felt groggy and none of this was helping. The shocks, however, had not finished.

"I'm like you mate," the driver said closing the doors. "I think it's all a complete waste of time, but like you, I have to do as I'm told."

The escort from the cab had returned to his seat and the driver started to walk back to the front of the ambulance.

"'Ere 'old on a minute," cried Benny not believing what was happening. "You're never leavin' me 'ere on my soddin' own?" They did.

"Don't worry mate," the driver called as he climbed into his cab. "You're as safe as houses while you're in the village." He slammed his door shut as Benny tried hurrying towards him. "So long then!" he waved and drove away.

There was nowhere to sit. The wide, dirt road, was lined by small, dwellings and shops, without windows or proper fronts. There was no pavement since there was no real road. People and children drifted about aimlessly along with the odd animal. He saw they were a truly cosmopolitan people in this village. Indians with their barber shops and spices, their wooden carvings and sari shops. Malaya and Chinese with their bright carpets and tapestries hanging from every available spot. Hard as he strained his eyes, he did not see the truck he waited for.

The overpowering smell of the orient, poor sanitation and pungent spices and curries and burning incense and camphor wood, was getting to Benny.

He tried walking away from the smell of cooking and spices but there was no escape. He kept telling himself to snap out of it. He was in the Royal Navy was he not? Mustn't let the navy down in front of these people.

When the truck finally came it tore towards him at a frightening speed, scattering the villagers in all directions. A soldier jumped out and helped Benny clamber in. He tossed a Sten gun to him as soon as he climbed back with him and the truck swung round, to speed back the way it had come.

They covered the trip at this same breakneck speed. Benny and his escort were bounced and jarred unmercifully. It did not bother the Grenadier but poor Benny did not know where hurt the most or how he survived. Benny could not for the life of him understand why they had to travel so damned fast. Were they dodging terrorists? As far as he was concerned they need not bother. A terrorist bullet would put an instant end to all this suffering. He was feeling sorry for himself.

The truck jerked savagely to a halt at the gate. It was given clearance and off it shot, twisting along the camp's narrow roads until finally braking hard to stop outside the transport shed.

The guardsman acting as escort climbed out. "Here we are then, Butlin's holiday camp, all change." His humour was wasted on Benny, the one who normally made his own similar brand of life's amusing observations.

"If I were you I'd go straight to the orderly room first," the driver said to him.

Benny tried to remember just where the orderly room was but gave up. "Where is it?" he asked.

"It's back there near the gate," said the driver tightening up straps on his truck.

Benny was far from amused. "Why the 'ell didn't you drop me off there?" he asked letting the driver see he had a bee in his bonnet.

"Sorry, I never gave it a thought," said the driver. He immediately offered to make amends. "Tell you what, jump back in and I'll drive you down there."

"No thanks," said Benny. He had had more than enough of his driving. The relatively short walk to the orderly office was still a long way when your legs were made of lead and your head was threatening to explode. He thought he would never reach it but he did.

The guard standing outside remembered Benny but Benny did not recall him. "Hello there," he said greeting the matelot with a cheery smile. "I was wondering where you had got to."

"Hi!" said Benny dying to lie down somewhere. "Is the orderly officer in?"

"Yeah!" the guardsman told him. "Go on in, you'll see him in there."

"Cheers!" said Benny making his way through the door. As he entered a young second lieutenant looked up from his paperwork, his expression said, "Well?"

"I've just come from the hospital at ..." he got no further for the officer jumped up.

"Ah! Yes of course," he beckoned to a chair. "Sit down. Tell me, how are you feeling now?" he asked kindly.

"To be perfectly honest sir, I don't feel well at all."

"Hmmm! I must say you don't look very well," he was gazing at Benny most sympathetic. "I'm sorry your stay with us ended so disastrously," he said. "All of your shipmates left us two days ago. They were wondering what had happened to you."

"The platoon you were with went back out again this morning," the sergeant sitting at a desk in the corner told him. His words perked Benny up a little. "They were hoping to visit you in the hospital but of course when they had to go off on patrol again that put paid to that."

"But they must 'ave just come back from patrol?" gasped Benny feeling for them. "Poor devils, fancy 'avin' to go straight back again."

"Ah yes," said the lieutenant. "That's how it goes unfortunately. Sometimes we may spend days doing nothing but routine stuff and then suddenly everything happens at once. Still, that is what we are here for after all."

"So you're not too happy the way things turned out then?" the sergeant said getting up and coming to where Benny sat.

"Uh!" grunted Benny. "The bit I remember was great, I really enjoyed it." He sighed. "I only wish I knew why it all went wrong."

"I shouldn't worry old chap," the officer smiled. "You'll soon be back on board your ship."

"Yes, I suppose so," agreed Benny but right now he wanted nothing more than to curl up and go to sleep.

"Take him along to pick up his belongings will you Sergeant?" the officer instructed. "I shall probably see you again before you go, if not I'd like to wish you all the very best," the officer said warmly.

Benny walked so slowly the sergeant was forced to keep holding back. He stared at him, concerned. "Are you alright?" he asked.

"I'll survive I suppose," Benny told him but not really believing it.

Once inside the tent he had shared with Bert and Moggy, the matelot sorted out his own naval clothes and changed into them. The sergeant sat on a bed smoking while he waited. His naval uniform looked anything but smart. It was as he had left it. There was nothing he could do about it. It was all he had so what it looked like did not come into it.

His head was spinning madly and again he was reminded of feeling just like this when he had been accused of being drunk on the brandy. Only this time he was determined to hang on.

He must have presented a sorry sight for the sergeant stood up to peer into his face. "Are you sure you are alright son?" he asked, he was obviously concerned.

"To tell you the truth Sarge," he said quietly. "I just don't know 'ow the 'ell I'm managing to stay on my feet."

"Well I must admit you've got me worried, come on son, let me take you to see the M.O."

"I'm okay Sarge, really I am, it's just at the moment I feel knackered, that's all."

But that was not all. As Benny left the tent with the sergeant he blacked out.

CHAPTER TWELVE

Benny did not regain consciousness until much later that evening and when he did he was lying in a bed in precisely the same ward he had been discharged from that very morning.

As his eyes began to focus he realised he was in the cot-bed in the centre of the ward exactly as before. He was naturally confused. He wondered if he had dreamed all that about going back to the Grenadiers' camp. He did not really care, he only wished to sleep and get rid of the pains in his head.

He lay there, eyes screwed up against the light, when the night-sister commenced her rounds. She saw that he was awake and came to lean over. "Hello there," she smiled shaking her head. "I don't know what we are going to do with you, I really don't."

He reached up feebly and caught her hand. She went to pull it away. "It's alright darlin', I just wanted to see if you were real," he said, no life in his voice.

"Oh I'm real right enough," she smiled. "Now, you just try and relax while I finish my rounds. Then I'll come and have a look at you, okay?"

Half an hour later she returned with a drink of Horlicks and watched as he drank greedily. "My goodness, that didn't take you long," she said reaching for his pulse. She spent a second checking it then placed his hand down gently. "Now, is there anything you want before you settle down for the night? By the way, I've got your glasses."

"No ta Sister, all I want to do is sleep." He certainly didn't want his specs.

She pulled the bedclothes up over his chest and tucked them in. "There we are then, I don't want to hear another sound from you all night, okay?" She stood there smiling down at him. Benny? Benny was sound asleep.

He was still asleep when the orderlies started their daily routine next morning. They had obviously been told to leave him alone and this they did. They didn't bother with his pulse or temperature and he slept on. Even the matron and M.O. passed his bed without a second glance.

It was lunchtime nearly before he stirred. He tried to sit up but a sweet young nurse hurried from the office and restrained him.

"Now now Mister Stretton," she said mildly rebuking him. "You just lie still, there's a good man."

"Well I'll go to the foot of our flippin' stairs," sighed Benny staring at her in disbelief.

"Whatever made you say that?"

He heaved a sigh and she looked back at him puzzled. "Only a little while ago my darlin', you people were insistin' I get up off my backside an' get fit to go back to my ship. Now you come along an' tell me to flippin' well lie still."

"Well I'm sorry but I'm only following the doctor's orders Mister Stretton and he said you are to have absolute rest and quiet."

"It was the flippin' doctor who ordered me up an' about in the first place. When I told 'im 'ow I felt 'e just said somethin' about it bein' natural because I was flippin' exhausted," he told her, browned off with the whole business. "All 'e was interested in was gettin' me back to my ship."

"Now look here," the young nurse said firmly. "You must stop getting upset. I'm sure everyone is doing their best for you and it's no good if you're not going to help by being sensible."

He apologised. "I'm sorry darlin', it's just that I feel so kna..." he remembered, "worn out an' my 'ead's killin' me."

They were bringing lunch round and a patient helping the orderlies brought Benny's over. He managed to eat some of it before giving in and settling down once more.

He was awoken by the moving of his cot. It was a young, very attractive nurse and an orderly who were wheeling the cot across to the side of the ward. They stopped by an empty bed, removed a side rail and invited Benny to transfer himself to the bed. As he struggled from the cot to the bed, he kept glancing at the nurse. Now here was a woman he could go silly over. He opened up the chat by asking where the sister was that had been there yesterday. She told him it was her day off.

"Aw, don't tell me we've only got you for one day," he said trying to sound broken hearted.

"No," she informed him bluntly. "This is my ward."

"Funny, I don't remember seein' you before."

"That's not surprising," she told him. "I was only transferred here today."

"I'm glad you've come to let us look after you."

She appeared not to have heard this remark. "It's all part of the training we have to do you see. I'm hoping to sit my exams soon and we have to spend so much time in each ward."

"Oh bother! And 'ere I was thinkin' you would be spendin' the rest of your life with me," Benny said, still trying to catch her eye as she busied herself.

"We have to go into the laboratory as well, and the theatre."

"The theatre?" Benny knew what she meant but he made it sound as if he thought she meant the theatre of the entertainment world.

She giggled and stared at him. "The operating theatre silly."

"Oh! I thought you meant the other kind of theatre, you know, the one where they have all those lovely dancing girls," he teased her.

"No!" she laughed a tinkling laugh. She looked at her watch. "Goodness, it's nearly teatime," and with that she waltzed away in the direction of the ward offices to the envious looks of most of the men in the ward.

"Jeezus!" sighed Benny. Dying or not, he fancied her.

The fellow with the moustache came over to have a chat with him. He told Benny he was due out the next day and the matelot hoped he had better luck at getting out than he had had. They chatted away until the tea came round, Benny had been content to just lie there while they talked.

Shortly before it was time for the nurse to go off duty, a sister from another ward came in. Together, she and the nurse went all round the ward remaking beds and checking the patients were comfortable.

Later, the night-sister came over to have a look at the matelot lying there feeling sorry for himself still. "Aha!" she said with a cheeky look on her face. "I see you're still alive then my lad?"

"Oh 'ello darlin'," he said ignoring the flippancy.

"Is there anything you want dear?" she asked most kindly.

"Not really thank you Sister, not unless you've got a cure for me?" He was quite pleased when he heard her call him 'dear'. So nice and friendly with it too.

"Oh we'll cure you alright," she told him tidying his bed to give her hands something to do. She made to leave to have a look at her other patients. "Don't worry yourself about that dear, we shall cure you, I promise."

The days came. The days went. Each was much the same as the day before and the day before that. New patients were admitted. Cured patients were discharged. Dead ones were wheeled out.

Whenever Benny slept, which seemed to be constantly, they left him to it. They never took his pulse or his temperature as far as he knew. The matron and M.O. would pass his bed with a nod and "Good morning, how are you?" moving on, not caring to wait for his answer, if he was awake. If he was asleep they simply exchanged knowing looks as they passed his bed.

He was allowed to get out of bed but only to go to the toilet or for a wash or bath. Not that he cared. He really thought he may be dying for instead of improving he got steadily worse. The short, mild spasms of ague had increased both in duration and intensity. No longer did he flirt with the sisters or the nurse. He only wanted to lie there.

He once asked the doctor for a tonic. He knew that what the doctor gave him contained iron but it served no purpose as far as helping him get well. He thought of the sister's words. She had said they would cure him but where was this cure? He had even heard the whisper about having him having sleeping sickness and he believed it. What else could be wrong?

Benny was very sick. One moment he would be so cold and would shiver violently. There were other times when he would perspire freely, his head throbbing violently and his eyes feeling as though someone had them in the palm of their hands squeezing the life out of them. His entire body would burn with a fierce heat, the aching pain of the fever sending him almost delirious.

Finally he could take no more. In one of his calmer spells he knew he must take the initiative. Seventeen days had passed since he first collapsed on that river bank. He had begged the orderly to take his temperature but he was too scared lest the sister caught him taking it. He explained that he was only permitted to take the routine ones. However, this young orderly did promise to mention it to the sister, when she returned from her tea, that Mister Stretton was not feeling too grand.

"Not feelin' too grand!" gasped an exasperated Benny. "I'm bloody well dying for God's sake!"

Benny listened for sounds coming from the sister's office. There were none. This was what he had been waiting for. He struggled out of bed determined to succeed with his plan.

It was agonising. A million and one gremlins were banging away inside his head for all they were worth. That sadistic monster was crushing his eyeballs again, the light penetrating his eyes sending red-hot needles through to his brain and right down his neck causing him to squint in an effort to blot it out.

Every step was torture but he would die rather than give up now. The other patients were watching, spellbound. One of them, realising the matelot was making for the office, called out to him softly. "Don't do it sailor! You'll get shot if you get caught in there."

His warning went unheeded, Benny was already fumbling with the door knob. Another patient scurried over to him trying to deter him. "Come on my old fruit, it's not worth the risk. If you get caught you'll be in real trouble."

Benny stared at the speaker. "Do you think I give a monkey's toss what these bastards do to me now?" he croaked. "Don't you think the bastards 'ave done enough all ready?"

"What is it you want in the office anyway?"

"I intend to prove that I'm ill," Benny told him still struggling to open the door. "That's all I want to do, show 'em I'm ill."

"Yes, I know," the patient was keeping one eye on the door leading outside. "But what do you hope to do by going in the office?"

"It's too much bloody trouble for this shower to take my temperature so I'm goin' to take my bleedin' own." Benny told him. "An' nobody's goin' to stop me so there."

Seeing the grim determination on the matelot's face the patient realised it would be wiser to humour him. He reached out to open the door for him and helped him inside. The thermometers were in a glass jar on top of a filing cabinet. Making a poor grab at them, Benny almost knocked the lot over. Only the quickness of the patient now helping him, saved them.

The matelot collapsed into the sister's chair behind her desk and allowed the patient to pop a thermometer into his mouth. Benny had no intention of allowing his new won ally foiling him and he snatched the thermometer out before the patient had a chance.

He fought to read the markings, twisting it one way and the other until at last he saw the mercury proclaiming what he had known all along. That he had a high temperature. He could not believe the reading and sat down with a thud.

"Oh God no!" he moaned. He crossed his forearms on the desk and lay his head on them.

As he sat there the man gently took the thermometer from his fingers and read it for himself. "God almighty!" he gasped and replacing the fragile glass tube in the jar he hurried to persuade Benny to leave the office. "Come on my old sport, let's have you back in bed quick. I'll see the sister for you when she gets back, and that's a promise."

"I was right wasn' I?" said Benny knowing he had satisfied his own mind.

"Yes you were sailor, dead right," agreed the patient helping him through the office door.

He got him back in bed just in time for as he pulled the clothes over Benny the orderly entered the ward. "Hey up Chris!" the patient called out to him.

The orderly sauntered over, mildly curious since he was always being called over by patients and nearly always for the most trivial things. "What is it now?" he asked.

"Just have a look at this bloke here Chris," he stood aside. "He's in a bad way mate."

The orderly looked down at the delirious figure of Benny and turned his nose up. "Hmmm! He does look middling."

The patient who had stuck his neck out to help Benny nearly exploded. "Middling! Fuck me Chris!" he fumed. "A pissing blind man could see how bad the chap is, open your bloody eyes for Christ's sake!" Without stopping to think what he was saying he blurted out, "He's got a temperature of a hundred and bloody four point eight!"

This shocked the orderly out of his affected, unruffled manner. "How do you know what his temperature is?" he asked loftily.

"Because I took the bastard!" snapped the patient angrily. All this was slowly bringing him to boiling point.

"You'll be in trouble if you have," the orderly told him, loftier now.

"Yeah!" the patient stuck his face up close to Chris's, ice-cold eyes glaring into his blinking ones. "But believe you me mate! It will be nothing to the trouble I shall kick up if anything happens to that chap!" he added, pointing to Benny.

The orderly was not to be denied. "Look Reg, you must have read it wrong. It can't be that high."

Reg had had enough. "Now you listen to me chum," he spoke with a menacing slowness. "You had better get his temperature taken yourself and then you will know for sure, right! And let me warn you, if anything happens to him," he pointed again with his thumb, "I personally, will kick up a bigger bloody stink than a cartload of bleeding skunks and you will be top of the list! So, if you value your miserable life, move your arse!"

How the orderly moved! Chris sensed Reg meant every word he had said. He was back with a thermometer in a flash. He held it up to the light, checking the reading before placing it under Benny's armpit. There was no way he was going to risk putting it in the matelot's mouth.

"He feels very hot," he said, waiting the required time. Reg said nothing. He watched as the orderly retrieved the slender pencil of glass to hold it up and read it. Seeing was believing, his face fell and he turned white.

"Well?" snapped Reg.

"My God!" gasped Chris. "It's nearly a hundred and five. I'll get hold of the sister right away," said Chris suddenly keen to get things moving. "She should be back by now anyway." He hurried back to the office intending to phone the sister, when she walked in.

After a brief conversation she came out to hasten to Benny's bed. Chris followed behind. Sister placed her palm on the matelot's forehead and felt his pulse. She was calm and professional. "What did his blood tests show?" she asked Chris.

"I have no idea sister," he said. "I'm sorry."

She ignored his apology. "Who took his temperature, Simpkins?"

"I did sister," he told her, automatically assuming full responsibility. "I saw how feverish he was and thought I ought to make sure before I troubled anyone," he glanced at Reg hovering in the background.

"Good for you Simpkins, now stay with him please. I'll get over to the lab and check right away." She turned to Reg still hovering anxiously.

Reg walked up to Chris and placed a fatherly arm round his shoulders. He gave them a friendly squeeze. "Thanks a lot Chris, you ain't such a bad bugger underneath are you?"

When sister returned from the laboratory she was clearly fuming. In her hand she held a thin, narrow tin and a small wad of cotton wool which she placed on Benny's locker. She opened the tin and withdrew a needle and a small glass slide and took a sample of blood from Bennyís middle finger smearing it onto the slide. She then placed the slide inside a special container and passed it over to the orderly.

"Right Simpkins," she said grimly as she dabbed cotton wool to the tiny pin-prick. "Do you know why you could not tell me the result of his blood test?" She continued without waiting for an answer, "It appears our Mister Stretton has never had a blood test. Some incompetent idiot neglected to do their duty correctly." It was clear she was fuming beneath the calm exterior but realised the implication of what she was saying and used her eyes to warn the orderly not to speak. She walked off towards the office, orderly on her heels.

"Close the door please," she said once inside the official retreat. "As I was saying Simpkins, because of someone's incompetence that poor man out there may die, that is a distinct possibility. Even I must accept some of the responsibility." She stood looking up the ward to where Benny lay. Chris was worried but he failed to see how anyone could blame him.

"I should have checked it all out," she paced up and down, as angry with herself as with anyone. She realised Chris had the slide. "Get that over to the lab quickly, tell them I want instant action on it, that I said so and tell them that I am on the warpath."

The sister came out to take Benny's temperature again. She held his wrist taking his pulse, her eyes studying his face. This done she hurried back to the office and picked up the phone.

The patients watching from the ward saw her angry gesticulations through the windows and knew the phone was red-hot. Slamming down the receiver she stormed out of the office to come and have another look at Benny. She sat down to watch Benny, willing him to hold on.

He raved about nothing in particular and everything in general. He was still at it when an army doctor came in and walked up to the bed. "How is he now Sister?" he asked reaching for the stethoscope in his smock pocket.

"He is still delirious Doctor. I'm still waiting for the results of the blood test."

The doctor examined Benny thoroughly and replaced the stethoscope in his pocket. He had a grave look on his face and was about to say something to the sister when matron walked up to them.

Reg, sitting beside a fellow patient's bed, remarked quietly, "You see, they're all shitting themselves now." The other patient agreed they all were.

"Good evening Doctor, good evening Sister, how is our young sailor? asked the matron leaning over the bed to see.

"He seems to be holding steady Matron," the doctor told her.

"Good," she said holding her hands clasped in front of her. She motioned to the doctor that she wished to speak to him on one side.

"You do realise of course that I shall be obliged to make a full investigation into this whole affair. A full report will have to be made. It is regrettable of course but I have no other choice. I must consider my nursing staff."

They had reached the sister's office and went in. No one was going to admit being responsible. They both knew that. Just as they both knew a blood test should have been carried out in the very first instance. And they both were concerned that any patient could be in the hospital as long as Benny had been without having either a blood test or thorough examination. Both knew something had gone disastrously wrong with the system.

The blood test proved positive. Doctor Lionel A. Hubertson diagnosed malaria many days ago and now he was proved right.

It was all systems go now. The hospital staff pulled out all the stops in their determination to atone in every way. No effort was spared. They did a remarkable job.

The first major problem created a dilemma They had to give him mist-quinine. Trouble was, what dosage did they give? Benny's was no normal case. He was so full of malaria, if the dosage given was insufficient the bug may overcome it. If they gave him too great a dosage this could kill him. They had to get it right.

The doctor explained the two types of malaria and told them which one it was Benny had. He deliberated over books and past histories and finally came to Benny's bed carrying a glassful of mist-quinine for him. As usual with this type of fever, it has its 'valleys' and 'peaks'. After the burning delirium, Benny was now aware and shivering.

"Here we are," smiled the doctor putting a hand behind Benny's head to raise it so that he may drink.

The sister came to help. Benny's eyes rolled from her to the doctor. He could not be bothered to utter a word. He just opened his mouth and as they tilted the glass to it, he drank. It was vile stuff but down it went. It clung to his teeth and tongue and whole mouth, so bitter. They lay his head down on the pillow with tender care and left him. He closed his eyes, the light was too much.

Moments later the nurse and sister arrived with hot water bottles and an extra blanket. They were about to begin what was to be a long cycle of opposites which were vital if Benny was to survive. Now he was cold they would struggle to maintain his body temperature by means of these. His temperature would be constantly checked and rechecked and the instant it showed signs of rising the bottles and blankets would be removed. As his fever mounted they would bathe him with ice-cold water to strive to keep his temperature down. Then, once it began to descend they would repeat the process in reverse then back again and so on and so on until hopefully, their efforts, coupled with the quinine, would see Benny well on the road to recovery.

During the 'valley' spells he would perspire so freely the sheets on the bed became saturated and they would change them time and time again since this was the time they needed to keep him warm and dry. Yet when he was at fever pitch he would burn and as they bathed him liberally with the ice cubes the bed clothes were unavoidably saturated by they themselves. Not once did anyone grumble about all this extra workload. They were only too pleased to help.

Slowly but surely they began to win the battle. The extremes of heat and cold were drawing in by degrees. His temperature had not risen above a hundred and one for several hours and they prayed it would continue to improve. It did.

That first night, the sister explained to the pretty young nurse the task lying ahead. "We have a very long way to go, Nurse Bourne," she said. "He will need most careful nursing during the night, the highly critical times will be when his temperature is at its lowest."

The sister turned down her offer to stay with Benny. There would be plenty for her to do the following day.

As she left, the night-sister arrived. Without bothering to go into the office she walked directly to Benny's bed. "What's wrong with our sailor boy then?" she asked having seen the screens which had been placed around his bed.

"Good evening Sister, he's very poorly with malaria."

"Oh no!" gasped the night-sister. "I wonder how long he has had that?"

"Heaven knows," sighed the sister soon to be going off. "He is absolutely riddled with it poor man. He must have been suffering some time. Why he did not complain is a mystery."

"Oh, I think he complained alright," said the night-sister. "He was often saying what terrible headaches he had," she shrugged and spread her hands. "If only I had realised," she said feeling a little guilty for not doing so.

"Shhh! That will do," her opposite number chided her mildly. "It has all been gone into a hundred times and the least said at the moment the better." She sat by the bedside and rose now.

After going through the ward paperwork, the day-sister helped change Benny's wet bedding and a few minutes later as they stood gazing down at the sleeping sailor, they knew from experience the battle his body and system faced before this was all over.

That night, Benny's temperature dropped very low and the perspiration positively oozed out of him. He shivered violently with the ague again, his teeth rattling uncontrollably, almost shaking themselves out of his throbbing skull. The night-orderly never stopped sponging him down but could not prevent the sheets becoming sodden.

When sister saw this she explained how vital it was they keep him warm and dry. She was happier now she had completed her rounds and could keep her eye on the matelot.

In a little while Benny woke and gazed around, he seemed to be trying to add it all up. His sheets were wet again and he began to cry.

"Hey!" cried the sister jumping up to console him. "What's all this about then?" She pushed his hair from his forehead and stroked it back, tender, caressing strokes. She smiled down at him, a friendly, comforting smile. There was no violent sobbing or whining. He just lay there looking at the sister with a pained expression, an unmistakeable plea, begging forgiveness, written in tear-filled eyes. "Whatever's wrong dear?" she asked seeking to put things to rights.

"I'm sorry I wet the bed," he said ashamed that he should do such a thing.

The sister sat back laughing softly and shaking her head. "Well I never," she said turning to share relieved feelings with the orderly. The orderly bent over Benny hoping to stem the flood of tears. They had feared much worse.

"You haven't wet the bed silly," he turned to the sister.

"No of course not, silly man."

"I 'ave sister, I can feel the bed, it's wet through, I'm sorry, I didn't know I'd done it," the tears flowed afresh.

"But you haven't you silly man," laughed the sister quietly. "The sheets are wet because you are perspiring like billyo."

Relief ran through Benny and his tenseness left him. Relaxed now, he went back to sleep. He was not to know but this show of depression was all part of the fever. The night passed. The sheets were changed, and the constant vigil maintained. Those little men with big hammers persisted in trying to break out of Benny's skull and the monster with his eyeballs was determined as ever to crush them to pulp. When he slept, terrible nightmares engulfed him, causing him to toss and turn and cry out loud. The sister and her orderly would do their best to comfort him, careful to see he did not fall from the bed.

Both Sister Plant and Nurse Bourne arrived for duty next morning much earlier than the required time and went directly to Benny's bed to ask after progress. Once they had set their minds at rest they went about their normal ward duties.

Before the matron and M.O. made their rounds, the sister and nurse found themselves busily bathing the sick matelot with cubes of ice once again. His temperature was high and delirium had taken over as before, the rich naval vernacular not for delicate ears. The young nurse, not as worldly wise or experienced as sister; blushed deeply and tried to hide her embarrassment.

"If you think the sailor's language is bad just you wait until you hear people coming round from the anaesthetic, that will open your eyes my girl, and your ears," the sister told her.

"Really?" the nurse was drying Benny's feet, rubbing in between the toes. She thought how even the sailor's feet were quite hot. "Do all men swear when they're coming round then sister?"

"Oh! Don't run away with the idea it is just the men who swear young lady," they were pulling the thin cotton sheet over Benny now for decency's sake. This was all that was required while the fever raged. "You would never believe how even the sweet and innocent-looking can let go when they are coming round."

The doctor who had given Benny the quinine was far from happy. Normally that one good dose should have had some affect on the fever, however slight, even allowing for a brief upsurge at the outset as the medicine challenged the malaria.

The matelot was still so poorly the doctor called in colleagues for consultation. They got their heads together over volumes of medicines and tropical diseases combining ideas, notes and experience. Sadly, experience was rare for most of these young army doctors when it came to malaria. It was something extremely rare to hospitals back home. They nodded their heads. They finally agreed.

The doctor informed sister he was giving a stronger dose of quinine to Benny and it would be repeated if considered necessary until signs of some improvement.

This time it was sister who administered the dose. As before it clung relentlessly to his teeth, tongue and mouth. She saw the face Benny pulled and fixed him up with a drink of warm sweet tea. This however did not take away the taste of the bitter quinine.

For the next two days, Benny's temperature see-sawed up and down until at last they knew the battle had been won. Benny was going to be fine. The malaria would always be with him, when they had cured him of the fever this time the bug would lie dormant in his blood to possibly surface in the future.

He had survived this first terrible attack without apparent damage to his liver or kidney or other vital organs. In this at least he was lucky. On the first day after the passing of the crisis Reg Greenhough, the man who had helped Benny when he took his own temperature, came to have a look at him.

"'Ello my old cock, 'ow are you now?" Reg asked. He was as pleased as anyone that Benny was on the mend at last.

"A lot better thanks," and Benny even smiled to prove it.

"You never told me you come from Nuneaton," said Reg.

"Why, do you know it then?" asked the matelot surprised.

"I should 'ope so my old cock, I come from Bulkington."

"Honest? Bloody 'ell," said Benny even more surprised.

"Where did you do your drinkin' then?" asked the older man. Obviously a man who enjoyed his pint.

"Give me chance," smiled Benny. "I wasn't really old enough to go boozin' before I joined the navy, I joined up as a boy!"

"I used to prefer a bike ride out down the country lanes to the little country pubs myself," Reg told him, dreaming of it. "I used to spend some 'appy times in the Blue Pig at Wolvey, nice little place that." He dreamed some more. "Or was it the Blue Boar? I ain't been back there for bloody years." He reached out his hand for Benny to join with him in a handshake of greeting. "Anyway, now that we've met, my name's Reg Greenhough, 'ow do you do."

"Hi! My name's Benny Stretton. Pleased to meet you." He was tired but felt he owed it to Reg to be polite and made an effort at conversation. "What are you doin' in 'ere then?"

"You might well ask. I'm in the Coldstreamers an' I was teachin' these young conscripts 'ow to use a Sten correctly an' 'ow careful they'd got to be when like a daft arse'ole I went an' shot myself through my foot," Reg told him grinning all across his face as if it was all a huge joke.

"You didn't?" and even Benny managed a chuckle. "Come on, tell the truth. The terrorists did it didn't they?" guessed Benny, always the romantic.

"No, honest," Reg decided to come clean. "To tell you the truth old cock, we were on patrol and I was just givin' this 'alf soaked conscript a right cussin' about being careful wi' 'is Sten when I slipped on this grass slope. I'd got my Sten under my arm with the muzzle pointin' down, of course as soon as I jolted the bloody gun off it went. The bullet went clean through my foot." He laughed as he added, "Damned good job it was only a single shot else I'd have shot my bloody foot off altogether wouldn' I?"

This little tale was as good as all the tonics and Benny really appreciated it."I bet the bloke you'd been tellin' off 'ad a good laugh didn' 'e?"

"Not 'alf, that bugger 'urt more than the bullet did," laughed Reg.

The diversion had helped, at the same time the laughing, slight as it was, had tired him. He pressed on however. "'Ow long 'ave you been in 'ere Reg?"

"Four weeks tomorrow my old cock, I 'ope to be out soon else I'll be in 'ere for Christmas."

"Christmas?" Benny was surprised. "You won't be in all that long surely?"

"What do you mean? It only wants a couple of weeks, that's all."

"Good grief, don't the time fly," gasped Benny. He had lost all concept of time in here. "I ain't been in 'ere that long 'ave I?"

"Now, stop upsetting my patient please Sergeant Greenhough if you don't mind." Sister had come to disturb their chat. She beamed at Benny, happy he was better.

"I was just goin' Sister," the sergeant lied patting Benny lightly on the shoulder. With that he limped back to his own bed.

After tea Benny lay back feeling decidedly better. The fact that his dreadful headache had virtually disappeared played a big part in this. He was thinking about what Reg had said, wondering where he would be spending Christmas when suddenly a frightening thing happened. From the region of his heart came a strange fluttering. It took his breath away. Just when he thought he might have imagined it, it happened again. This time a more definite flutter and a little more pain.

Instantly he thought it was his heart. It happened again and this time he thought he was going to choke. "Oh God!" he thought. "I'm 'aving a heart attack. I'm going to die." His heart was thumping now but not from any attack other than fear. Benny truly felt his time had come and Benny did not want to go.

"Please don't take me yet Lord," he prayed fervently but silently. "I won't be able to say goodbye to my mother."

Just as soon as they came, the flutters and pains stopped. He began to relax and was able to reason things out. He now accepted that if he was dying there was absolutely nothing he could do about it. He became serenely calm as he accepted the inevitable, a remarkable peace filled him.

He made a mental note of what he had to do. The first thing was to offer a little prayer to God. When he had completed what he had to do he would offer up a big prayer, make his peace and await his destiny. And he had never been more serious in his whole life.

He whispered a small prayer and then called to the sergeant in the bed opposite. "Hey Sarge!" There was no answer. He tried again, louder this time.

He still got no response from the sergeant but he did get some from Nurse Bourne who came to see what it was all about. "Stop all that shouting Mister Stretton! What on earth are you after?"

"I'm sorry nurse, I only want a word with the sergeant, that's all."

"He is asleep, what did you want him for?"

"It doesn't matter nurse, I only wanted to ask him to do me a favour, that was all."

Nurse Bourne smiled her sweet smile. "Can I be of any help?" she asked.

Any other time the sailor would have smiled back just as sweetly and made the obvious answer but not now. He said simply, "Sorry nurse, it's sort of private and personal."

"I see," she took no offence. "Promise me you'll let me know if I can help at all."

She must have told the sergeant that he wanted him, he came over to ask what was wrong. He made Reg Greenhough promise not to laugh at what he had to say.

The look on Reg's face told the matelot he was in earnest and wishing to see him get well would do anything to help him.

"It's like this you see Reg, to you, or anybody else, it might seem like a big giggle but believe me," he paused, "it's very important to me."

"Well? Go on old cock."

"I want you to do me a big favour if you will," he had overcome the mental barrier and was now able to explain precisely what he wanted him to do.

"Of course, anything, just say an' if it's within my power I'll do it." Sergeant Greenhough was a man to be trusted.

"Cheers. Let me put you in the picture first Reg. After tea, I was just lyin' 'ere when all of a sudden I got this awful sensation an' pain right 'ere," he placed a hand over his heart. "I honestly thought my time had come. Honest, I've never been more frightened in all my life."

"I can just imagine old cock," said Reg soberly.

"I don't want you to think I'm barmy. I've never been saner or more serious than I am at this minute. What I'm askin' you to do is this, an' I mean it Reg, just in case anything should 'appen ..." Reg nodded "... I'd be ever so grateful if you'd drop my mam a little line tellin' 'er I was thinkin' about 'er when I went, that I love 'er an' miss 'er an' ... aw bloody 'ell Reg, you know the sort of thing I mean."

"Yeah! Of course I do, you just stop worryin' an' leave it to me." He leaned over and ruffled Benny's hair. "Is that all that's been worryin' you?" he asked with a grin.

"Ain't that enough?" gasped Benny.

"God's truth Benny lad, you needn't have worried about that. Tell you what, if anythin' does 'appen to you, I'll not only write to your mam, I'll call an' see 'er at the very first opportunity, an' that's a promise."

A lump had found its way into Benny's throat. "Aw! God bless you Reg. I'll let you 'ave 'er address. You don't know how much it means to me. Thanks mate." The matelot was doubly relieved. Firstly his mother would now know and understand. Secondly, and this was almost as important to Benny, Reg had listened to him and taken him seriously.

Reg had an idea. "'Ere, tell you what, why don't you 'ave a word wi' the doctor when 'e comes round, see what 'e says."

"No bloody fear," Benny considered this to be out of the question. "'E'll think I'm off my rocker for Christ's sake."

"You will be off your rocker if you don't tell 'im, that's what 'e's 'ere for. Besides, if you don't tell 'im, I will," threatened Reg. "It's better if it comes from you, besides, you reckon 'ow worried you are about your mam, what do you think she'd say if she knew you 'adn't played ball wi' the quack?"

"Alright, I'll tell 'im," he accepted it was in his own best interest to confer with the doctor. "But I bet 'e laughs 'is cock off."

The doctor did not laugh. In fact as he pulled his stethoscope from pocket he wore a solemn expression. He also spent a good five minutes examining the matelot. He then took the sister's arm and led her to the foot of the bed, out of ear shot, removed the board and wrote something on the chart, at the same time talking softly to the sister.

Benny could restrain himself no longer. "Is my ticker okay doc ... sir?" he had to ask.

"Your heart is fine Stretton," smiled the M.O. replacing the board. "I imagine you had a touch of indigestion."

Benny was astounded at such a suggestion. "Indigestion? Aw come on doc, who are you tryin' to kid?" The matelot did not call him 'sir' this time, how could he when he had the temerity to imply all his worrying was over nothing more than indigestion? "I've never 'ad indigestion before."

"Well, there has to be a first time for everything Stretton, now, I'm going to prescribe a few tablets for you to take, for the indigestion," he said quickly just in case Benny got the wrong idea. "For your own sake you must stop this worrying. It will do you no good at all, the sooner you cheer yourself up the sooner you will be fit again."

"Thank you sir," said Benny. What else could he say? The doctor sounded so positive even Benny found himself believing it. But Benny was not to see the hidden wink given to the sister as they walked away.

He had two repetitions of this fluttering and pain but told himself not to be silly and worry over it. He even smiled at himself for stupidly thinking his number was nearly up.

The tablets the orderly brought shortly after the doctor's visit were promptly swallowed, to be flushed on their way by the nightly beaker of Horlicks.

CHAPTER THIRTEEN

Benny never looked back from that moment on. Two days later he was sitting up taking stock of his fellow patients. There had been many changes of course but Reg was still with him.

Now that Benny no longer had the terrible head and eye pains he was his own nosy, chirpy self again, almost. He wanted to know how Reg, a surgical case, happened to be in a medical ward.

"Ah well, that's easy," Reg told him. "When I was admitted the surgical ward was full so they bunged me in 'ere an' I've stopped in 'ere since," he donned a suitably serious look as he went on to relate how there had been a spate of surgical cases, including a good number of wounded and several had been admitted to the medical ward.

"They ain't all wounded that's in the surgical ward then?" asked Benny.

"Christ no old cock," Reg cried. "If they relied just on the wounded they would 'ave to shut up shop at times! There's all bloody sorts in there"

At that moment a tall, exceedingly thin young man walked slowly by. So thin was he that when Benny saw him he felt compelled to ask Reg about him.

"Who?" asked Reg craning his neck to see. "Oh, you mean young Terry there. It's a cryin' shame for 'im, 'e's got that Addison's disease."

"Addison's disease, what the 'ell's that?"

"Somethin' I wouldn't wish on my worst enemy old cock, I ain't too sure but it's named after the doctor who discovered it nearly 'undred years ago. It's somethin' to do with the kidneys I think, an' anaemia ..." He shook his head. "There's no bloody cure for it, not yet anyway."

"No cure for it?" Benny turned to glance after the unfortunate Terry who had just reached his bed. "Does that mean ...?"

"Yeah, that's what it means alright. It's very rare they tell me and it's a bloody good job accordin' to what I've seen 'appenin' to that poor sod. You just keep wastin' away until there's no more left to waste away and, well, that's it, you're dead."

"'E's just like one of them poor bastards from Belsen ain' 'e?" said Benny. "'Ow did 'e get it?"

"Buggered if I know, I don't suppose they do really, it might not be somethin' you catch, it might be in your system. It's got somethin' to do with all the goodness in the food you eat goin' to the liver or the blood from the liver or kidney or ..." Reg gave up guessing. "God know's what it is but whatever it is that poor bastard's got it."

Benny's heart went out to this unfortunate soldier who was doomed to die and there was nothing anyone could do for him. "Is it catchin' Reg?" he asked.

"No, thank Christ," said Reg, "an' it's a fuckin' good job it ain't an' all if you ask me."

"Jesus, it must be bloody awful to know you've only got a little while to go," Benny shuddered and recalled his thoughts of two days or so ago. "I know Reg mate, I've 'ad a taste of it."

"Yeah, you did didn't you," agreed Reg getting up from the chair. "I'd better shift, nurse's comin' to gi' you your blanket-bath you lucky sod."

"My goodness me," the nurse beamed placing the bowl of hot water on his locker. "You're lookin' a whole lot better I must say sailor." They had all taken to calling him sailor now, even the matron and Benny was secretly proud of being the only member of the Royal Navy in the establishment.

"I feel a lot better my darlin'," he told her truthfully. "It makes all the difference not 'aving that flippin' 'eadache."

The next afternoon the serenity of the ward was rudely shattered by a bluff red faced fellow standing in the double doorway leading out onto the gardens. It needed only a casual glance to realise he was drunk.

He stood there swaying, singing at the top of his voice. Singing?

He no doubt thought so but it was a terrible din.

The patients loved it. But Sister Plant was most certainly not amused. In fact, she blew her top!

"Mister Jenkins! You idiotic nincompoop!" she yelled at him. "I have warned you for the last time, you silly, useless man. This time I intend to see you are severely punished for this disgraceful behaviour."

But the drunken Jenkins was past caring. He stared, grinning back at the sister and placing thumb and fingers in the general direction of his nose, and blew a loud 'raspberry'.

A most unladylike sound came rumbling up from within her throat, and she shouted for the orderly. "Simpkins!"

Hospital etiquette out of the window, Simpkins came running. He had no intention of falling foul of sister in this mood. He reached her side and she pointed dramatically to the wobbly Jenkins.

"Simpkins, get hold of Parker and run a cold bath and I do mean cold! You will then see that this drunken oaf is placed in the bath. Ask Nurse Bourne to make some strong black coffee too. We shall see how Mister Jenkins likes blowing 'raspberries' when I have finished with him."

Then she reached out and grabbed Jenkins firmly by the ear. He was too far gone to offer even token resistance. The patients did not help his case when they cheered.

"Now Jenkins, you and I are going for a little walk," her voice was full of menace. "You are going to show me just where you hide this drink you keep pouring down yourself, and you are going to tell me where you get it from"

Sister Plant led the hapless Jenkins out through the double doors in search for his hidden booze. Jenkins was past caring for what the sister said or did, he started singing merrily.

One or two of the patients had followed to the door to watch their progress with interest. It stopped after a few yards. Jenkins was making so much noise he had become an acute embarrassment to the sister and she was forced to concede defeat and make a strategic withdrawal. They were, after all, in the grounds of a hospital and she had no wish to be placed on matron's report. She pushed the drunk roughly but firmly before her and finally handed him over to the waiting orderlies. "Make sure he suffers or by all that is holy, you two will." She then set about a search of her own for the illicit drink.

Reg told Benny that Jenkins was a long-serving soldier who over the years had developed a great passion for drink. He was forever under its influence and as a result was constantly in trouble.

Tom Jenkins was serving in the Royal Electrical and Mechanical Engineers and only a few months left to serve to complete his twenty-two. The reason he happened to be in hospital was understandable. Ulcers. They did nothing to dampen his desire for alcohol and even under treatment in hospital he seemed quite able to equip himself with ample supplies. Marvel was he had not been thrown out long ago.

This time he had really excelled himself. None of the patients could recall seeing him quite like this before. The noise echoing out from the bathroom indicated that Jenkins had not taken kindly to his cold bath.

When it was over and the orderlies emerged with the cursing Jenkins held tightly between them, they looked a sorry sight. Their hair was dishevelled and their uniforms saturated. They held him down, or at least tried to, while Nurse Bourne poured the coffee into him. When the first cup was empty she promptly refilled it and had another go.

Satisfied they had done all they could, they now took a rather more drastic step. For both his own protection and to stop him disturbing his fellow patients, they strapped Jenkins in a straightjacket which had been provided by the sister at the outset. In the meantime, she had returned from the gardens and the expression on her face told the patients she had drawn yet another blank.

She stood now over a cursing Jenkins. Her face close to his she strived to get her message across as she threatened him with a stay of at least a week in the straightjacket if he did not desist instantly. Her warning must have registered because he became quiet if a little sullen.

Benny felt for the man. He had often been the worse for wear over drink. He remarked to Reg that Tom would have a rare old hangover when he sobered up.

"I shouldn't think 'e will," Reg said expressing doubt. "'E got used to the stuff years ago."

"What do you reckon will 'appen to 'im now then?" asked Benny.

"Lord above knows, they were talking about doin' some sort of operation on 'im if all the diets an' medicines didn' 'elp," Reg snorted. "Mind you, 'e don't give 'em much bloody chance to 'elp does 'e? 'E's a fool to 'is bloody self, ulcers are bad enough to get rid of at the best of times."

"Like you say Reg mate," agreed Benny feeling a little tired. "'E's a fool to 'imself." He settled down meaning to have a doze. "There's one thing about it, you do see life, even in a bloody 'ospital."

They were not to know it then but they were due to see even more 'life' very soon. It started the next day just as the doctor and matron began their morning rounds.

The phone in sister's office rang and she excused herself to answer it. Almost at once she hurried back to where the doctor and matron were and interrupted them. Whatever it was it caused them to speed up the remainder of their routine and directly they had completed the morning ritual all three hurried back to sister's office.

They held a brief consultation and then matron and doctor left, telling sister they would be back as soon as possible. The sister called her nurse and orderlies into the office and the patients knew instinctively that something was afoot.

Having put them in the picture, all four came hurrying out into the ward where they promptly set about making up four beds. The inquisitive onlookers now knew four new patients were soon to be admitted. Indeed, hardly had the beds been made up before the patients walked, unaided into the ward.

Later the ward gossip revealed that the four were all from the R.A.F. base and had been admitted as suspected dysentery cases. They each had severe diarrhoea and were causing the orderlies all kinds of extra work. They were confined to their beds and as a result there was a steady coming and going of bed-pans and orderlies. Screens were around the beds and sister had instructed they remain there to facilitate matters.

Samples went to the laboratory where tests proved positive in all cases. The unfortunate airmen did indeed have amoebic dysentery. Now would start the search for the cause. If luck was with them they would find it quickly before it spread out of control.

Luck proved to be with the authorities this time. The four airmen had all dined at a small cafe in Kuala Lumpur two days earlier. It transpired the locally made lemonade they drank contained contaminated water and was the carrier.

These unfortunate airmen would now undergo a long series of injections and enemas and tablet-taking and a whole lot more before overcoming their dysentery.

Tom Jenkins got a great laugh out of it all when he heard about it next day. "Serves the silly sods right for drinking the filthy muck, if they'd drunk a man's drink it wouldn't have happened to 'em," he proclaimed loudly.

"Huh!" snorted Reg. "You've got room to bloodywell talk, just take a good look at yourself before you start criticisin' others. You're on the carpet good an' proper you are mate."

"That pompous old cow don't frighten me none, she's only jealous 'cos she can't enjoy life herself, the frustrated old bitch her," scoffed Tom.

"She ain't all that bad Tom," smiled Reg. "Not once you get to know 'er."

"Balls!" snapped Tom. "She just want's to be top bloody dog that's all. I sussed her out right from the start mate. I've always enjoyed a pint, always, and it's never done me no harm before."

"I daresay old cock, but you've got ulcers now an' booze an' ulcers don't mix," Reg tried explaining.

"Bullshit!" snarled Tom. He had had enough and stormed off in the direction of the double-doors and the flower beds.

This was the moment Sister Plant had been waiting for. She had made up her mind she was going to find his hiding place. Since she had failed to find it by constant searching she now reasoned the obvious — let him lead her to it. She had long since faced the fact that he would continue to drink and thwart all attempts to heal his ulcers. So, cut off the drink and presto! They could concentrate on the cure and then she would be rid of him.

But Tom Jenkins was much too wise to be caught napping. He suspected the sister was up to something and to foil her he simply sat down in one of the chairs on the verandah. He lolled back, eyes closed but aware of her as she hid behind the curtains.

Sister Plant, too, knew a few tricks of her own. Making certain she stood where Jenkins could not see her, she beckoned to Nurse Bourne with one hand whilst bidding her be very quiet by placing a finger of the other hand across her lips.

Words were whispered and young nurse nodded and smiled. She retraced her steps with equal caution until she stood some way down the ward. Turning, she paused but only for a second. Then in a suitably loud voice she called out: "Sister! Sister Plant!"

The sister feigned annoyance knowing full well that Tom Jenkins heard it through the open doors. "Nurse Bourne," she snapped, at the same time exchanging impish looks of delight with her. "I shall not tell you again about rudely shouting down the ward. How many times must I remind you that this is a hospital? Do not let me have to warn you again."

"Sorry Sister," her voice expressed regret but her face told otherwise. "The lab is on the phone, they would like to see you as soon as possible about the dysentery cases."

"Drat!" cried the sister. "Just when I was rather busy with something."

Tom Jenkins chuckled to himself. "Rather busy, the lyin' old cow."

"Oh well, I had better get over there I suppose," sighed the sister loudly. With that, she and the nurse walked off down the ward together. Jenkins watched them through a chink in the curtains, careful not to let them see him. As soon as they were out of sight he got to his feet and made off along the concrete path lying between the flower beds, humming a little tune. Had he but known it he would have been cursing himself for letting the sister outfox him for outfox him she had.

At that very moment she watched him from behind the very curtain through which he had just peeped.

The moment he had disappeared behind a corner of a building beyond the flower beds the sister scurried off in hot pursuit. She halted cautiously at the corner where Tom had gone from view. Peering round it she was just in time to observe him entering the gardener's shed.

Satisfied she retraced her steps and returned to her office. Once there she lifted the receiver of the telephone and made a call.

Tom may well have been a little afraid of sister for he was back inside the ward much sooner than he normally would have been but it was evident he had been at the booze yet again. The nosy parkers of the ward were left to stew. They could only guess at what had tran-

227

spired.

Visitors were permitted on three afternoons a week and that afternoon several turned up at the ward. On each occasion visitors were
allowed, Tom never failed to have someone call upon him. Lucky
man. Sadly, today, luck was to desert him thanks to Sister Plant. She
had laid her plans with meticulous care. All she had to do now was
wait patiently for the dividend her craftiness deserved.

Benny could now get out of bed to the toilet or to sit out for a short
spell and had persuaded sister into letting him sit on the verandah.
Today he was helped by Nurse Bourne.

She helped him down into the chair and he could not resist a quick
peck on her cheek. She blushed and for one moment looked as if she
was about to slap his face, hard. Changing her mind she said instead,
"Just you wait until you are better, that's all."

"Oh, why, will you let me kiss you passionately then my darlin'?"
he said grinning up at her, teasing. He felt one hundred per cent better already. Yes indeed, Benny was on the mend.

He lay back in the wicker chair and relaxed. He was almost asleep
when the sound of someone running startled him. Benny rubbed his
eyes. He surely must be dreaming. He saw what he thought he could
not be seeing. The runners were three 'red-caps' and they shot past
him, along the path and out of sight around the corner. They were off
to the gardener's shed.

Benny's nose twitched annoyingly but he knew he dare not risk
moving away from the chair. There he sat, ears and eyes straining for
the slightest sight or sound. He wished some other patient would
come along so that he might coax them into having a stroll around
that corner.

The military policemen themselves walked back along the path
after a little time. This time, however, they escorted two R.E.M.E. pri-
vates and a diminutive Malayan.

The Malayan was protesting most strongly, arms going like an
orchestral conductor. All of this failed to impress the poker-faced M.P.
who now held him. He carted him along like some boy unwilling to
go to school. The party walked quickly past to circle the ward and out
of sight towards sister's office.

Shortly after this the sister and another 'red-cap' and an officer
from the military police came from her office, through the double

doors, and past the reclining figure of Benny. They too were lost beyond the corner as they went to the gardener's shed.

When they returned, the officer and 'red-cap' carried a large, heavy box between them. They took the route around the outside of the ward towards the front, sister herself wearing a very smug, self-satisfied look, went past the curious Benny to her office.

He dozed, waiting for something else to transpire. Nothing did. He closed his eyes and lulled by the sun's warmth he was soon asleep.

He was awakened by Nurse Bourne calling to him softly, her lips close to his ear.

With one swift movement his arms were around her waist and he had pulled her down onto him. He growled savagely and playfully bit her ear before letting her go. She had blushed alarmingly.

She struggled upright and tidied up her uniform angrily. "One of these fine days you will go too far," she snapped.

"Oh yes, let's," he teased.

"It's all very well, but whatever would the sister say?"

"Don't worry about her my little darlin' I've got enough love for the two of you so she needn't be jealous." He wore that cheeky, loveable grin again.

"Oh have you, in that case you should have ample enough energy to make it back to your bed without any help from me then," she snapped standing back out of harm's and arms way.

"Okay then, if that's 'ow the land lies," he said defiantly settling back in the chair. "I shall just 'ave to sit 'ere till I rot shan't I?"

"You will not! You will kindly come along in and get your tea, if you please." Neither of them had heard the sister approach.

"I was just comin' Sister, honest," Benny told her struggling up. Nurse Bourne could do no other but help. It did not stop her making a face at Benny but he simply grinned and winked back at her. Sister saw none of this, she was already halfway down the ward.

After tea, Reg popped over to have a chat to Benny who had been ordered back to bed. "Fancy 'em whippin' poor ol' Tom off like that," Reg said as soon as he sat down by Benny's bed.

"Whippin' Tom off?" Benny asked at the same time glancing towards Tom's bed. It was empty. "Where 'ave they whipped 'im off to then?"

"Blimey," Reg ignored Benny's question. "You missed all the fun an' games while you was outside, you should 'ave seen it."

"Well, don't keep me in bloody suspense."

"It seems Tom 'ad a visitor with 'im at the time see, anyway, 'e suddenly cried out in pain and must really 'ave been in agony. They sent for the doctor, 'e ordered 'im straight into the surgical ward, no messin'," Reg was enjoying telling the tale. "I reckon 'is ulcers 'ave burst or somethin'. I 'eard they've got to operate on 'im bloody quick else it's goin' to be too late."

"Poor ol' bugger," said Benny feeling genuinely sorry for the man.

"That ain' all," continued Reg eagerly. "While all this was goin' on, the 'red-caps' came in an arrested the bloke who had been visitin' 'im."

"'Ey!" Benny was getting excited now. "I saw some 'redñcaps' earlier on, they'd got two pongoes an' a Malayan bloke wi' 'em. The Malayan was playin' 'ell up wi' 'em. After that another 'red-cap' an' an officer went out back there somewhere, they came back carryin' a box between 'em."

"Bloody 'ell old cock, it does get excitin'," gasped Reg. "I wonder if it was the beer from the gardener's shed?"

They were just like two old women now, revelling in it. "Is that where 'e kept the booze then?" Benny asked.

"Yeah, from what I can make out Tom used to pay his mates to bring the beer wi' 'em when they came to visit 'im. One of 'em would sit an' talk to 'im while the other two smuggled it into the shed. The gardener dug a great big 'ole in the ground, in the shed. They dropped the box in it an' covered it wi' some boards. The gardener got paid to keep 'is eye on it an' 'is mouth shut."

"It's bloody marvellous 'ow they got away wi' it for so long ain' it?" said Benny.

"Oh don't worry, they'd got it all well planned old cock," Reg assured him "They had a false top on the box just in case. They'd got soil on it wi' bulbs an' plants an' that, then if anybody did 'appen to stop 'em an' ask what they'd got they just show 'em the little garden arrangement in the false top see."

"I'll be buggered," gasped Benny, impressed at such ingenuity.

"It was only because the sister followed old Tom and saw 'im go into the shed," explained Reg. "They would never 'ave found out otherwise old cock, sister phoned the matron an' told 'er all about it and she phoned the bloody authorities."

"What do you think they'll do to 'em?" asked the matelot, feeling sorry for them in a way.

"It all depends I suppose," mused Reg. "Especially if anythin' 'appens to poor old Tom." He shook his head. "I imagine the gardener will get the sack for a start." He thought about this. "Mind you, I don't really know what they can charge the poor bugger with."

"Bloody 'ell," cried Benny. "The old Sister really started somethin' didn't she?"

"Yes, but she did it for 'is own good," Reg reminded him. "She warned 'im time an' time again but 'e just laughed in 'er face an' now look where 'e 'is."

The next few days came and went, as did the patients come and go. Benny was making fine progress and was able to potter almost anywhere he chose now. He spent time in the patients' library, in the garden or walking about to have a chat with the other patients. His favourite pastime however was to wander out to where a large number of guinea-pigs were kept in a big, spotlessly clean pen with ample space to run free.

These guinea-pigs came in all shapes, sizes and colours. At first it had saddened him to think that such loveable little creatures may be made to suffer in the cause of humanity. But then he thought of the poor chap with Addison's disease and the many more like him who may be saved by these little creatures in a roundabout way. The scientists had to strive continually to find cures and surely it was better to try possible cures on animals until they were sure they would work and were safe. It still left him feeling sad however. He reckoned it had to be worse for the person responsible for looking after such animals, especially if they were together long enough to become somewhat attached.

Terry, the young guardsman with the Addison's disease, was very weak now. He never moved from his bed and the screens were around him constantly. The ward's gossips told of how samples had been taken from his breastbone to help find out exactly what shape he was in. Benny wondered if this were true and if so just how this would tell them. No one was certain of this and whenever the subject was approached it was always done so in subdued reverent tones. One thing was certain, Terry was sinking fast.

Benny was forever chasing young Nurse Bourne and flirting with the two sisters. He had also found a new love, the dear old lady who came round the wards with a trolley laden with hobbies and handicrafts and all suchlike and on occasions library books for those patients unable to get to the library proper.

She was a civilian welfare worker and the moment she discovered Benny to be a sailor she brought him a pile of needlework to go on with. One was a duchess-set with a pattern of pansies. Benny and her had many a happy natter and got along splendidly.

Three days before Christmas there was quite a stir. One of the night orderlies was caught with an R.A.F. patient in the middle of committing sodomy.

They were found by the night-sister who wanted the orderly for something but could not find him. She poked her head into one of the bathrooms and there could be no mistaking what they were up to.

Everyone knew the orderly's sexual preferences. He often flaunted the fact and many stories were told of him including how he would dress in women's clothes and would parade the streets of Kuala Lumpur touting for business. He loved his reputation and preferred to be called Veronica, even in the ward on duty. When hauled before his C.O. on one occasion, he told him it had not been his wish to serve in the army. He was a National Serviceman and resented as much being compelled to serve as he did being sent to Malaya. Furthermore, if the C.O. was not happy to have him would he please send him back home without delay. What the C.O. said is not recorded.

Be all that as it may, something had to be done now that sister had made her discovery. The patient was promptly transferred elsewhere and 'Veronica' was locked away. For how long and where, no one seemed to know.

The following day, Terry's suffering came to an end. He died peacefully in his sleep. The passing left the ward in a subdued state, no one wanted to make conversation and when they spoke it was in hushed tones, even though his body was no longer in the ward. Strange, many of them had lost their appetite too.

Someone immediately suggested a whip-round and enough Malayan dollars were soon collected to purchase a very fine wreath. Members of the staff also dug deep into their pockets for him.

After breakfast on Christmas Day, Sister Plant came into the ward carrying a box full of decorations, all those patients able to gave her a welcome hand to trim up the place. They had a ball as they busied about adorning the ward, instructed by the sister who, true to her sex, changed her mind countless times until at last a Christmassy atmosphere prevailed.

The sister jokingly held out a heap of balloons for Benny to take, saying, "You always seem to have plenty of wind sailor boy, let us see you blow this lot up."

"You should 'ave kept Veronica 'ere sister," he told her.

She was wary. What was he up to? "Oh," she said. "Why?"

"A great big 'puff' like 'im would 'ave 'ad 'em blown up in a jiffy," he said much to the delight of the patients.

"Now now," she chastised mocking him. "There's no need for petty jealousy to creep in sailor boy."

That did it. He snatched up a balloon and began to blow it up, accompanied by a chorus of cheers when he succeeded. He tried to give the impression it irked him but he really revelled in it. They could not see him suffer to blow the lot up and between then they soon had the balloons blown up and hanging decoratively about the ward.

The Christmas dinner which had been laid on was a veritable feast. It would have done credit to anyone and the hospital staff waited at table. Cigarettes and cigars were handed round, nuts were cracked, crackers pulled, drinks poured and wishbones tugged. Only the wine and other drink was carefully monitored, everything else everyone indulged in. They even sang a few carols and thoroughly enjoyed themselves. Yet, in spite of, or perhaps because of all this, thoughts were of home and the people they missed and loved.

Benny, naturally, was in the thick of things. Wearing a gaudy paper hat he mingled with all the ladies, and there were some smashers, kissing them beneath the mistletoe he held aloft. Matron loved it when he included her.

Into the midst of all this gaiety strode three very tall, very smart Grenadier Guardsmen. When Benny saw them he froze to the spot, unable to grasp what his eyes told him. A huge lump clogged up his throat threatening to choke him. Tears threatened to flood forth. After that first initial shock, he ran forward eagerly, trying to keep control of his emotions as they all but took over. His arms were reaching out a welcome before him as he ran.

"Lieutenant! Sergeant Riley! And Bert!" there was a tear or two now. "I don't believe it! Oh my God! What a great, fabulous Christmas present ... aw, I don't believe it." He was shaking hands and making a great fuss of them. He had not realised how close he felt to these wonderful characters. He had difficulty getting his words out, he was so choked.

They stood smiling down at him, pleased he was better and that their presence had made his Christmas even better. "I'm speechless," gasped Benny. "I never thought I'd see you big buggers again. Aw God! What a fantastic surprise." As the back slapping, shoulder thumping went on the lieutenant was apologizing to the matron and her staff for their intrusion. He introduced himself and his companions and went on to explain why they were here.

"You must admit Lieutenant, our sailor friend is certainly overjoyed at your coming," the matron said. "Would you care to join us in a little wine?"

"That is extremely kind of you, matron, thank you," he watched as she went to get the wine. The others joined him and together with Benny they raised their glasses to a merry Christmas and happy New Year.

The matron told them how Benny was forever going on about his 'ferret force' friends.

"Yes, but I must admit we did not feel very friendly towards him when we thought him intoxicated Matron," the lieutenant told her, smiling down at Benny who winked back at him.

"That was one time I was delighted to be proved wrong," Sergeant Riley said placing a fatherly arm around Benny's shoulders.

"I'm sorry about all that sir," Benny said. "I really am."

"You're sorry?" said the officer. "Good heavens Stretton, we're the ones who should be apologising, we were the ones who were proved wrong," he turned to his sergeant. "Isn't that right sergeant?"

"Dead right sir."

The officer explained they were limited for time but had been determined to see the matelot before he left for his ship. They considered today would be an ideal time to visit him and so, here they were.

"You see Stretton, we of the er, platoon, thought you might appreciate a little something as a token of our friendship and all that er, jazz," he was slightly embarrassed and turned to Bert for help.

"Phillips, you tell our friend Benny what we have done."

Hearing the officer use his Christian name led the matelot into thinking perhaps he had had too much wine. But no, the lieutenant was being humble for the moment, besides, he had a great liking for this young man from the navy and was it not Christmas after all?

"Sir!" said Bert. He now addressed Benny. "Well, Benny old mate, we all clubbed together and bought these few little odds and ends for you, we 'ope you like 'em," he held out the small parcel he had been carrying.

That lump was in his throat again and he felt unsure of what he ought to do. Sergeant Riley and the other two egged him on. "Come on then old son, take it."

"Yes," said the officer. "We should consider it an honour for you to take it, Benny."

Bert thrust the parcel at Benny. "Come on, it's gettin' 'eavy," he grinned. The patients had gathered about them, all keen to share Benny's surprise. He reached for the parcel, hesitant, glancing around at their faces, seeking some sign that they had contrived some joke at his expense. He scanned Bert's face but saw only warm sincerity.

The second he finally had the parcel in his hands, Reg sang out at the top of his voice, "For 'e's a jolly good fellow, 'e's a jolly good fellow" ... and not unnaturally, the others all joined in, giving it full volume.

Benny could do nothing but stand there, emotions tugging at his heart strings. This just had to be one of the most memorable Christmases he had ever had.

The singing came to an end and immediately someone shouted for three cheers for Benny. They gave out three rip-roaring cheers and Bert decided his matelot mate should make a speech. "Speech! Speech! Speech!" he chanted and this was taken up on every side.

Lieutenant Fenton-Dowell held up his hands and called for quiet. When he got order he turned to Benny. He said nothing, simply looked at him and waited for him to commence whatever speech he was going to make.

"Here you are," said a patient trying to be helpful. He pushed forward with a chair which he placed by Benny. "Climb up on here and do the job properly."

The matelot grinned and climbed onto the chair. "Alright. I can see I'll get no peace till I make a speech."

He stood there and suddenly could think of nothing to say. He wanted so much to thank them and tell them how much all of this meant to him. They stood smiling back at him as he sought words that would do justice to the occasion, this moment called for special words.

"Well, first of all I would like to thank each and everyone of you for all that you've done for me. I know it might sound corny but ... well, I mean it from the bottom of my heart, I must be the luckiest guy in the world to 'ave so many wonderful friends." He silently prayed the right words would come to him. Without understanding why, he felt very humble, thought of Christmas, and decided that since he was so thankful he must offer thanks through prayer.

"I wonder if I could ask you all a special favour? I feel the only way I can say thank you properly is to say a little prayer and I'd love you to pray with me ... please." Without waiting for them he clasped his hands in front of him and closed his eyes.

"Dear 'Eavenly Father," he began. At this moment he sensed a spiritual glow, it flowed through him, a wonderful feeling of inner peace. His words came from the heart and he meant every syllable he uttered. "I want to thank you for all the many wonderful blessings you 'ave given me and for letting me know so many marvellous friends."

He knew, even though his eyes were closed that they prayed with him and now he prayed for them. "Dear Father in 'Eaven, please watch over everyone 'ere and protect and comfort them and their loved ones, wherever they may be. Please look after all the 'ferret forces' especially those in 'C' platoon and comfort all those in 'ospital and all those who look after them with such tender care and devotion Lord. Please God, let there be an end to all wars, let the teachings of your Son, Jesus, show us the way ..." He could think of nothing else and so concluded with a simple "Amen."

For a few, very dramatic, moments a pin would have been heard dropping on a thickly carpeted floor. The silence was shattered by a resounding cheer as Benny stepped down from the chair. They crowded round to pat him on the back and make cheery comment.

"Come on ol 'cock," urged Reg. "Open your parcel."

Others echoed these sentiments and so Benny obliged. As he removed the wrappings he tried to guess the contents. When he discovered what they were he was overjoyed. A huge box of chocolates, six large bars of Brazil nut chocolate, a tin of Old English humbugs and on top, in neat Christmas wrapping, a shiny Grenadier Guard's badge. This last item said it all. Proudly he held it out to admire it, looking from one to the other of the three men who had brought it. His eyes and expression told them how he felt about it.

"We thought you might like the badge as a souvenir Benny old son," the sergeant told him. "Not quite the same thing as a blow-pipe but then, it doesn't take up as much room does it?"

"Oh my God yes, the blow-pipe," cried Benny remembering. He gazed at the badge again. "What can I say? It's fabulous. I really appreciate what you've done for me," once more his gaze wandered over the three of them. "I promise you all one thing, I shall treasure this as long as I live." Reg held out a hand hopefully. He wanted to admire the badge too. So did the other patients, in spite of the fact that it was just a normal army badge, it somehow had acquired a magical property. Benny? There was no other badge in the whole universe to compare with his.

"You know sir," Benny said to the officer. "There is nothing I can think of that I would rather have than this." He held up the badge which had now come back to him.

"The humbugs were Sergeant Riley's idea," explained the officer. "He felt you must have a real fancy for them after the way you polished off the ones given to you by Doctor Hubertson."

"Well, what can I say?" Benny knew no words could express his feelings.

"You don't have to say anything," the officer told him. "It is all our pleasure I can assure you, is that not so Sergeant Riley?"

"Quite right sir."

The lieutenant turned to Bert. "Pleased to do it, are we not Phillips?"

"We are indeed sir," agreed Bert winking at Benny. "Honest Benny, all the blokes wanted to chip in and get you somethin'."

"Yes and they all send their kind regards and hope you're better," added the sergeant.

"Well, I would really appreciate it if you would thank them all for me and wish 'em a merry Christmas an' all that, tell 'em I'm often thinkin' about you an' the fun an' games we 'ad." He glanced over to see matron circulating.

"Fine, fine," Lieutenant Fenton-Dowell patted him on the shoulder and turned to look for matron. She caught his eye and came towards them. "Well matron, I fear we have taken up enough of your time and we do have to push on so ..."

Matron raised her hand to stop him. "I simply refuse to let you go without your first having a mince-pie and a drop of the good stuff gentlemen," she said firmly.

"Since it is Christmas, and since you put it so sweetly, we shall be pleased to accept a pie and a drink for the road as they say," smiled the officer. He clicked his heels smartly together, swept his arm out and back across his stomach as he bowed with all the olde world charm at his command.

The matron laughed merrily and Benny wished it could be Christmas all year round if this is how it affected people. "It is my pleasure dear sir," she told the lieutenant as she returned his bow with a truly grand old fashioned curtsey. Or at least, as much of one that her prim and proper uniform would allow.

Benny raised his glass and called for a toast. If the matron and lieutenant could let their hair down so could he and cried, "My lords, ladies and gentlemen, a toast to all those gallant gentlemen of the 'ferret-forces' and all those who assist them, wherever they may be. And to all those kind and wonderful, caring, understanding angels of mercy who nurse them, and us, through illness and injury ... the 'ospital staff and all who sail in her." He added the bit on the end in an effort to make it sound nautical though why he should wish to do that, heaven alone knew,

"To the 'ferret-forces' and angels of mercy!" he cried clinking his glass with that held by Sergeant Riley. He placed the glass to his lips and drank deep. It was nothing more than lemonade. Benny was one of the unfortunate ones not allowed alcohol.

The guardsmen were still not permitted to leave. This time it was Sister Plant who detained them. She took hold of Benny's left hand and Sergeant Riley's right hand and shouted gleefully, "Come along all of you, all grab hands for Auld Lang Syne."

When she deemed them ready the sister began the singing and everyone joined in. Benny glanced past her and winked at his friend the sergeant. The sergeant grinned back at him as they sang away. Bert was singing at the top of his voice and since his voice matched his size he could be heard above all the others. He too grinned back at Benny. The whole atmosphere was wonderful. Benny was pleased the patients who may well have been disturbed by all this merrymaking had previously been taken to a smaller ward.

Like all good things, it had to end. And once his friends had gone Benny felt very depressed, even though he fought against it. The remainder of the day was spent eating nuts, dreaming of home and listening to carols and messages of goodwill broadcast over the radio. Now all the excitement had gone most of the patients realised how much it had taken out of them. Still, it was worth a whole cartload of pills and medicines.

On Boxing Day, a message was received from the naval authorities. It came in response to enquiries made by the hospital administrators who had requested the whereabouts of H.M.S. Consort, and where she was likely to be in the near future. It had been explained that her crew member was now almost fit and well enough to rejoin her.

The naval authorities expressed regret but for all the obvious reasons of security it was not naval policy to divulge the movements or whereabouts of H.M. ships. However, should they wish to discharge this rating at any time they were to get in touch with the drafting officer at H.M.S. Sultan who would then arrange for an escort to collect the rating and see him safely on his way.

H.M.S. Sultan was the big naval shore base on Singapore Island. It was named Sultan, or so Benny believed, because it had at one time actually been the palace of the Sultan of Johore. How true this all was Benny could not be sure but ever the incurable romantic he liked to believe it so.

There was no delaying things now. Benny was given a thorough check and pronounced fit to travel but told that on no account was he to take up any duties until all the relative paperwork had been carefully studied by the medics at Sultan. They would provide him with some brief explanatory notes to take with him which should suffice until the formal documents arrived.

There was nothing more they could do for him now but inform the

239

naval authorities. This was duly done and Benny suddenly realised his trip ashore was soon to be over. How was he to know what lay ahead. He was sorry in a way for he had made a great many friends and yet, he knew it was unavoidable. On the other hand, he would be back with his old shipmates and that couldn't be bad. He had little dreamed when he first volunteered for this trip ashore that so much would happen to him. He had wanted a taste ashore with the other services and by thunder he had had a good bellyful instead.

The New Year came and went and a week later Benny was no longer the only matelot in the ward. There were three of them. His armed escort had arrived.

Their journey from the naval base to Kuala Lumpur had been a long, hot and tedious one which had taken almost a whole day. They had travelled during the day as a safety measure. To travel at night on an illuminated train would simply be to ask for trouble, making them easy targets for snipers.

The hospital staff had arranged food and shelter for this escort when they arrived. Transport had also been laid on to pick them up from the railway station and bring them to the hospital. It was only to be expected that Benny would sleep uneasily that night. His head was filled with mixed emotions as he lay there knowing this was to be his last night at the hospital. Tomorrow he would be away with the escort. He kept thinking about Nurse Bourne.

Pity he couldn't take her with him. He would much rather have her for company than the naval escort. His imagination began to run riot as he pictured the fun and games they could get up to on the journey to Singapore. A saucy smile spread over his face and at last he fell asleep.

CHAPTER FOURTEEN

Next morning Benny stood beside his escort waiting for their transport. His pallid complexion was emphasised by their deep tans and as he waited the thought crossed his mind that it may appear to casual observers that his was a prisoner's escort, not one provided to ensure his safe passage.

His nursing friends had worked wonders to turn him out looking immaculate. Nurse Bourne had given his shoes a rare old whitewash, the blanco gleamed white and even. His white socks, shorts, shirt and even the white cover of his cap, had been laundered and pressed. Sister Plant had organised all of this.

These two were with him now as the army truck pulled up outside the ward. Benny remarked on how baggy his uniform felt. He had to talk about something to ease the emotions he felt within. Sister told him not to worry, he would soon regain the weight loss now he was almost fit again.

"I'm glad I'm not too late," cried the night-sister hurrying up to them. She had left her bed for the sole purpose of wishing her young patient goodbye. Not to be denied she gave him a hug and handed him a small bag of mixed fruit. "I thought you might be glad of those on the journey," she told him.

"You lot are making it hard for me to leave," he said forcing a smile. "I can't ever remember being looked after so well."

Benny treated himself to hugs and kisses all round now and climbed aboard the truck. Reg and some of the other patients had come out to wish him well and a safe journey. He waved back and shouted a mixture of advice and thanks and reminded Reg not to forget to look him up when he got home. Finally, Nurse Bourne ran forward to reach up and throw her arms around Benny's neck. She forced his head down and kissed him full in the mouth before letting him go as the truck pulled away. Benny? He was speechless but he blew her a kiss and waved.

He had sensed the warmth of her firm, delightfully moulded breasts as she pressed up to him and the memory was to stay with him.

"She was bloody gorgeous weren't she?" gasped an escort wishing she had grabbed him like that.

The truck drove through the hospital grounds at a respectable speed and Benny caught sight of the matron waving from the doorway of another ward. "Bye!" she called. "Take care of yourself sailor!"

Benny was still waving to the friends waving back when the truck went out through the hospital gates and on out of sight.

"Well, that's that then," sighed Benny sitting round in his seat properly. He gazed across at the escort who had introduced himself last night as Stan Grainger. He was in charge of the escort, and Benny, and he was a leading stoker mechanic. Brian Hodges, the other half, was a telegraphist.

After a few moments of travelling in silence he remarked, "I'm surprised to see you two as escorts, I always imagined seaman ratings doing it."

"They send anybody on these sort of trips, as long as they are duty watch of course," said Stan "I enjoy it, makes a pleasant change."

Brian wanted to know if Benny had been in hospital for long. "Five or six weeks," Benny told him. "Mind you, it seemed like bloody years at times."

They chatted away as they watched the scenery flashing past and they were soon pulling into the forecourt of Kuala Lumpur's station. They were in no hurry to get out from the truck and the driver called out to them, meaning to spur them on. "Come on you lot, this is where you get off!"

Benny gazed at the milling crowd as they threaded their way forward. He sensed they stared back at him pointedly, not that they really did so. "They think I've been arrested, don't they?"

"It's because we're wearing belts and gaiters and carrying guns," grinned Brian. He gave a laugh. "It's your own silly fault for looking so guilty Chef," he said.

"Bollocks!" retorted Benny but chuckling as he said it.

"It's through on the other platform," Stan told them, still studying the paperwork. "We've got a good fifteen minutes to wait."

They decided to have a drink and made their way out of the station and found a likely looking hotel a few yards away. They quenched their thirsts and Brian and Stan questioned Benny about life in the hospital and Nurse Bourne, refusing to believe he never got his 'wicked way' with her.

"Honest," Benny insisted "I never got the chance, I only wish I 'ad."

The train was five minutes late. "First bloody time I've travelled on a Malayan train an' the soddin' thing's late," said Benny. "What are they like anyway?" he asked his escort.

"They're okay," said the leading stoker. "The only thing really is the terrorist problem, other than that ..." he shrugged his shoulders and left it to Benny to draw his own conclusions.

They clambered aboard quickly, eager to find seats. There was no problem, their tickets were for the better class of seat and there were a few spare seats dotted about the carriage they were on.

There was the minimum of delay before the powerful steam engine let out a commanding whistle and with a series of metallic grunts and groans and loud hissings of steam it started off on the journey to Singapore.

Benny was content to reminisce over the last weeks as he watched the landscape flash past the windows. He saw numerous rubber plantations with their long, neat and orderly rows of tall, slender trees. They also passed tin mines, each one almost identical to the last. His thoughts would go back to those he and the 'ferret-force' had searched. He wondered if they too had been searched, if they had the same smells and the same conditions.

The train stopped briefly at Kajang before they continued the journey south. They crossed the Selangor State line and travelled on into the State of Negri Sembilan. Stan, keeping an eye on his maps, told them the next scheduled stop would be Seremban, some thirty miles south of Kajang, the capital of Negri Sembilan.

As the white-coated attendant passed along the corridor serving drinks, Benny contemplated the truly cosmopolitan crowd of fellow passengers. He mused over how attractive the Eurasian girls looked. Stan spotted him eyeing them up and down and he nudged Brian, drawing his attention to it. He was admiring a real beauty when Stan spoke. "She'd soon have you back on your feet Benny mate," he said grinning suggestively.

"Come on," said Benny. He really was admiring the girl's dress. "Just look at it, you don't see dresses back 'ome like it, it's bloody gorgeous." His eyes reflected his admiration of it, and the girl wearing it.

Stan and Brian did look at the dress and they were forced to admit it was beautiful and it suited its wearer perfectly. Be that as it may, they still fancied the wearer rather than the worn. They ogled the pale tanned thigh protruding most seductively and provocatively through the long slit at the side of the dress.

The girl crossed her legs and even more of her silk stockinged thigh eased itself enticingly into view.

"Ooooh you bastard, just look at that," cried Brian in a strangely dry and strangulated whisper.

Even though this type of dress was common in this part of the world, it was nevertheless an accentuated style, leaving nothing to the imagination.

"If you ask me," said Benny thoughtfully, "she's on the game." Assuming this to be so he turned his attention to the passing scenery. His casual remark caused the other two to look at each other and then back at the girl seated up the compartment. They then looked at each other, shrugged their shoulders and, like Benny, found other means to occupy their time. It seemed obvious now he had pointed out the probability that she was a member of the world's oldest profession. Benny? He had no intention of paying for it.

Over to the left now, Benny saw quite biggish hills in the distance, he guessed they were almost mountain size. "'Ey up Stan, what 'ills would they be over there?" he chose to ask Stan since it was he who had the maps.

Stan was no help at all. "Buggered if I know Chef," he said with feigned indifference, although he added, "You'll be able to see them much better from the other side of Seremban."

They arrived at Seremban shortly and this time the train was in the station fully fifteen minutes before pulling out again. It steamed off south, past the range of hills looming up in the near distance now. Once they reached the end of this range the train cut inland, making for the rail junction of Gemas. Stan proved correct. Benny had a very good view of the hills just before they turned inland.

They travelled through the British settlement of Malacca, continuing in a southerly direction until finally cutting inlandand returning to Negri Sembilan State. The scenery on all sides was both colourful and interesting. With surprising regularity they passed little clusters of primitive huts, dotted about in small clearings close to the railway line.

Yet in spite of all this, Benny found his eyes straying back to the Eurasian girl. She would be, oh, eighteen, twenty perhaps. Long, jet black hair but then, they all had long jet black hair. He could not see too well the size or shape of her breasts. Again, tiny breasts were the norm out here. Mind you, that Sakai woman had been beautifully endowed. Boy! She was something else again. This young lady looked the sort to inspire artists and poets, he felt. Again his thoughts strayed to the Sakai woman. Now there was someone who would inspire even the dullest person. He knew he could write an epic of a poem for her. Yes, that was it. In her sweet memory, he would write a poem to beat all poems. And why not? He set his mind to it that very instant.

They arrived at Gemas and the only words Benny had put together were, 'When first I saw her', and he could get no further. They were such brilliant words he failed to find a single word more to match them.

The railways from North and Central Malaya ran to this junction town of Gemas and the train was compelled to wait twenty minutes for a train from the north to connect. While they waited, several passengers got out to stretch their legs, including Brian and Stan. Benny was content to remain where he was. At last, the train from the north arrived and once its passengers had been transferred they were off, this time making for Batu Anam. They still needed to travel across country but once they reached Batu Anam, just inside the state of Johore, their journey became fairly straight-forward as they travelled down country once more.

The next stop was Segamat, a journey of only fourteen miles. Wonder of wonders, Benny's Ode to a Sakai Sweetheart now boasted a second line. Added to 'When first I saw her' he now had, 'then saw I', the only trouble was, he could not decide just what he saw. Benny was not unduly concerned. All brilliant poets struggled in their day.

However, Benny the poet was still struggling and suffering when the train jerked to a standstill at Labis, twenty miles beyond Segamat. Inspiration hit him on the run from Labis to Kluang, the next stopping place. He almost cried out aloud in delight. He glanced at his escort but they both dozed. "That's it!" he said to himself. "That is what I saw ... I saw the light of day. Yes sir, the light of bloody day. Takes the touch of a genius to think up words like that, the light of day, brilliant."

In spite of being fully occupied trying to compose his 'Ode to a Sakai Sweetheart' Benny still found time to attempt an acquaintance with the young Eurasian girl. He raised his bottle of lemonade, offering her some by sign language but she immediately looked away.

He turned to gaze out at the scenery. Beginning to weary of the journey he was pleased to learn from Stan that their destination, Johore Bahru, would be the next stop. This was the capital of Johore State, forty miles from Kluang, here naval transport would meet them and take them across the long, narrow bridge spanning the Strait and on to the barracks on Singapore Island.

Soon after leaving Kluang, Benny realised the Eurasian girl was watching him. He took the bull by the horns and smiled his most friendly smile, this time she did not look away. Encouraged, he winked and could scarce believe his luck when she smiled.

The seat beside her was vacant and with a quick glance to make sure Stan and Brian were still dozing, he moved fast. Parking himself in the empty seat he smiled and said, "'Ello miss," and introduced himself. "My name's Benny, Benny Stretton of the Royal Navy, at your service ma' am." He bowed where he sat, his hand extended, hopeful of shaking hands with her.

"Pleased to meet you Mister Stretton," she smiled sweetly, her voice music to his ears. She took his hand in her cool slender one, fleeting. "I am Linda, Linda Guiterrez."

"That's more like it Linda," Benny said smiling happily, "but we should 'ave introduced ourselves much earlier, right at the start of the journey, not near the end." He placed a hand over his heart and with mock pathos said, "And I've been so terribly lonely too."

"Lonely?" She seemed surprised. "But you have your friends." She indicated his companions.

"Huh! Weary Willie and Tired Tim you mean?" he said pulling a face. She gave a little laugh. "That's better," smiled Benny, warming up to this flirting, only he was not flirting, somehow he sensed he might mean it. "You're a pretty young lady ordinarily but when you smile and laugh. Wow! You'd fetch the ducks off the water."

She laughed that soft gentle laugh again. "It is rather nice to meet someone who is able to show happiness," she said, a trace of sadness in her tone.

Benny poured on the charm. "'Ow can anyone be anything else but 'appy in your wonderful company?" he asked.

She returned the compliment with a comely smile then changed the subject. "Am I correct in assuming that you have only recently arrived in Malaya, Mister Stretton?"

"No love, sorry to disappoint you but you are not correct. Anyway, since we are getting along so well, why not call me Benny? Please."

"Alright then Benny, Benny it is. Now tell me, how long have you been out here?"

"My God Linda!" Benny thought. "You could 'ave your wicked way with me anytime, do me the world of good." What he actually said was, "Just over eighteen months now, mind you, it seems an awful lot longer at times."

"Oh? Really?" she was surprised at this."You will forgive me I know but you look so pale Benny. I imagined you had only recently arrived out here because of that, I'm sorry."

"That's alright Linda, don't worry about it." He liked the sound of her name as it rolled off his tongue.

She had stolen a glance at Stan and Brian and seen their gaiters, and guns. "Oh Benny, you have not been in prison have you?" She laughed as she made this remark, obviously thinking it immensely funny.

"No I 'aven't, you cheeky madam," he laughed with her. "Don't tell me I look like a criminal, please."

"No, of course not silly. I was only teasing you." Her girlish delight captivated him.

"Thank goodness for that," he patted the region of his heart and blew out air letting her see what a shock she had given him. "The truth is, Linda, I've only been released today, from 'ospital, not prison," they both laughed. "I'm on my way to rejoin my ship. I guess I must 'ave lost what little bit of tan I 'ad," he nodded towards his escort. "They're my escort, they've come along to see I make the trip safely."

"Oh I see, they were not in hospital with you then?"

"God no!" he gasped. He saw that Stan or Brian were both now wide awake, staring in disbelief at the way he and Linda were getting along. "No," he went on, "they travelled up from Singapore yesterday, just to keep their beady eyes on me."

"Were you in the hospital for very long Benny?" she asked and Benny, knowing to his cost that all women need to know everything, told her everything. He added a few trimmings here and glossed it up there.

When he concluded his tale Linda gazed at him rather sympathetically. "You must be finding this journey very tiring then Benny?"

He could not resist more flattery, besides, he played it up for their benefit as much as for her's. "Linda," he scolded her with an admonishing smile. "'Ow could any journey be tiring with a wonderful person like you around?" He thought about it. "Mind you, to tell the truth, I do feel jaded, still, I suppose it's only to be expected isn't it? My very first day out an about so to speak." He was after more of her sympathy now.

"Is that why you seemed so pensive back there Benny?" she asked. He loved the way she spoke his name, as if she adored him. Well, that is the way it sounded to him. "You seemed to be miles away, turning things over in your mind, were you?"

"I don't rem... Ah yes, now I remember." He remembered the poem he had been struggling to compose. What harm in a little white lie? "As a matter of fact Linda, and I swear it's the truth, I was 'aving a go at composing a little poem for a very charming young lady. A lady I did not know but who made such an impression on me I felt I just 'ad to do something to honour 'er memory. I wonder, can you understand that Linda?"

She took the bait at once, thinking Benny referred to her. He had hoped and intended, she should. "Oh Benny, how very sweet, and of course I understand." She fished for more. "Her name wouldn't be Linda by any chance?"

Benny proved he was no fool. "That would be telling now wouldn't it?" he said. There was no telling where he might end up by letting her think she had been his inspiration. He might even end up sharing her bed if he played his cards right. Besides, she was inspiring in her way, her delicate perfume roused his feelings something shocking.

The longer he sat chatting to her and she to him, the better he liked the situation. He was elated with his progress.

"How far have you progressed?" her question knocked him for six.

"What do you mean, 'ow far 'ave I progressed?" he asked.

She gave him an odd look, perplexed. "How far have you progressed, with the poem, what else?"

"Oh, of course the poem," he felt an utter idiot as he offered up a prayer of thanks that it was not the progress he had imagined. "I 'aven't progressed beyond the first verse I'm afraid and I've only managed two lines of that."

She smiled at him askance. "Well, it isn't easy, it has to be very special, she's a very special lady." He hoped she would not ask what the two lines were but knew she would. She did. He felt awkward about it all. She was going to laugh at him and consider the lines 'soppy' or something. Even so, as he recited the words he put all the sincerity into it he could muster.

He waited for her response, it was not the one he feared. Tenderly she placed her hand upon his arm and, with a dreamy look in her eyes, said: "Oh Benny, that was so beautiful, it really was, if the rest of it turns out as good it will be absolutely wonderful, really, oh Benny, do hurry up and finish the words for me," she cried all starry eyed.

Stan could no longer restrain himself. "Watch her Benny mate," he called. "She's after your money." Benny, out of sight of Linda, put two fingers up from down by the side of his seat. Stan saw them. "Yes, and you, you randy sod."

The two carried on as if he did not exist. Benny was sure she pulled his leg. "You're poking fun at me now, aren't you young lady?"

"No, of course I'm not, oh Benny, how could you think that? I meant every single word," her pained look told him she did.

By the time they reached Johore Bahru they had got to know each other quite well. Linda turned out to be an even bigger chatter-box than Benny and that took some doing.

The train was slowing down as it approached the station when Stan and Brian sorted themselves out and came over to the couple. "You'll have to excuse us miss but we've got to take Romeo away from you now, I know it's going to break your heart but ... well," a big grin spread itself over Stan's face.

"What the hell is 'e goin' on about?" thought Benny and felt it only proper to make the introductions. It made not the slightest bit of difference now. It was too late for them to louse things up for him.

"Miss Guiterrez, I would like you to meet Stan Grainger, and Brian Hodges, my escort." Acknowledgements were made all round and they then prepared to depart the train.

Benny hated to think this was the end of this new friendship but what could he do? His heart leapt when she took his arm and led him gently to one side. "Benny, is there any reason why we cannot see each other again, sometime?"

He could not believe his good fortune. He looked down into the eyes that pleaded with him. "No my little darlin', no reason at all. I would give anythin' to see you again you know that." He tenderly caressed a wisp of hair back off her forehead. "You're such a lovely person to be with."

"My, but you are a big flatterer Benny," she said adding before he could protest. "I must see you again. I want to know how that poem sounds when you've finished it."

He let it pass. "The trouble is, 'ow do we keep in touch? I've got no idea at all where my ship is, or where she's goin'." They were walking along the platform now. He had no suggestions to offer.

Linda had. "It isn't a problem, not if you really want to keep in touch and see me again Benny?" again the sweet pleading tone, that look of desire. "It's simple, I just give you my address."

Benny wanted to kick himself for being so stupid. "Oh no! Why the 'ell didn't I think of that? I must be goin' senile."

"Well, I thought of it so there is no harm done is there?" She fumbled in her large handbag. Benny had been mildly surprised that she carried no luggage.

"Come on Romeo," Stan called waiting at the ticket barrier for him.

"Shan't be a sec'," Benny told him watching Linda scribble on a page she tore from a notebook. She passed the paper over to him.

"That is my home address Benny, you will write?" she pleaded and he nodded. "Promise!" she insisted before he could utter a word.

"I give you my solemn promise I shall write to you, honest." He was anxious to catch up with Stan, who had his travel warrant. "Goodbye my little darlin' take good care of yourself," and he kissed her hurriedly on the cheek. She made as if to hug him but he had moved away. As he hurried towards the exit she called after him.

"Benny! What is the name of your ship?"

"Consort," he shouted over his shoulder, noticing that she remained on the platform.

The trio of matelots were walking off to the harbour-master's office. As they strode along Benny found himself wondering about Linda. He had put the bit of paper with her address in a pocket without even looking at it. He had made it a quicker parting than was decent out of embarrassment, nothing else. Why did she have no luggage? Why had she remained on the platform? Where was she going? Where did she come from? God! He could not get her off his mind.

They reached the harbour-master's office and in spite of being busy, he came over to them as soon as he saw them.

"You three from Kuala, escort and party of one?" he asked pleasantly. Before they could answer he continued. "Good, you're to wait here until your transport arrives. I'll go and give them a ring to let them know you've arrived, they won't be long."

Stan sat down on a nearby bench. "Aw, Jesus, I shall be glad to get these pissing boots off," he groaned, the pain of aching feet showing in his face.

The harbour-master returned. "They're on their way chaps. Did you have a good journey then?" he asked.

"This randy bastard had a good journey," sneered Brian jerking a thumb Bennywards and they related the story of Benny and the lovely Linda.

"Good luck to you, that's what I say, grab it while you can," said the harbour-master. "I'll have to leave you now I'm afraid, your transport won't be long," and off he went. Benny? Benny was too busy thinking of Linda.

All three of them sat on the bench now, gazing out at the tiny harbour. The fresh breeze, blowing across the strait, was exhilarating after the hot train journey. Benny stood up. He went through the motions of stretching arms and legs than strode off around the harbour. He looked to see if any warships were tied up to the buoys lying in the strait but his vision was limited by the cluster of trees. Neither Brian or Stan could tell him where Consort was. As far as they were aware, she was still out on patrol somewhere.

The news did not please Benny at all. It meant he would have to be billeted at the shore establishment with all its pomp and red-tape. All its discipline too.

The dark blue transport from H.M.S. Sultan arrived. With the minimum of delay they climbed aboard. The journey to barracks was short and they had soon crossed the long, narrow bridge connecting Singapore Island to the mainland and Benny was fascinated by the loud, crazy cacophony which every single person seemed intent on taking part in.

He saw only a few of the traditional rickshaws. They had been replaced by the tri-shaw, three-wheeled cycles which now plied madly to and fro, bells ringing incessantly, owners yelling and screeching loudly. Taxis fought them for room to progress, horns blaring out in competition with the rest of the din. Street vendors screamed out and the entire populace appeared hell bent on being heard, one way or the other, above everyone else.

At the end of the bridge the truck turned left and in a few minutes turned left again and up the drive to the gates of Sultan. The driver paused at these gates whilst the duty guard checked credentials against his list, as if he really had need to, checked the passengers and their reason for being in the vehicle and so on. Benny knew from experience he could never be truly at ease in this type of establishment.

Guard satisfied, they were permitted to travel on up the drive to the buildings that housed the various offices, workshops, the N.A.A.F.I., accommodation and recreational rooms. There was too, of course, the sick-bay to which Benny must report.

He was duly accepted as a temporary member of H.M.S. Sultan's ship's company, assigned to a billet and taken to it. He had handed the sealed papers given to him at the hospital to the doctor in the sick-bay.

The matelot showing him around, introduced him to several of the men with whom he would spend as much time as it took before

252

rejoining Consort.

Benny found himself a vacant bed and flopped wearily on it. It had been a long, hot day, but he found he was able to relax for only ten minutes however for then it was time for tea. He realised now how he longed for a good cup of tea.

It was during the meal that Benny heard the disquieting news that his ship was patrolling the east coast of Malaya and she had only been gone two days. This meant that she would be away for some weeks. "Wouldn't it make you bleedin' sick!" he growled. He had never taken to the discipline and routine in such large naval establishments. He much preferred to be aboard his own ship, whichever ship that happened to be at the time. After all, he joined the navy to sail the seas and this is where he felt he rightly belonged.

Surprise, surprise though. After a grand old time up in the N.A.A.F.I. bar that night he began to have second thoughts. Most of the lads off duty had assembled there and seemed determined to show the world at large that the Royal Navy knew how to live life to the full.

Next morning began the usual, boring routine, a routine carried out each time a naval person joined or left a ship or barracks. From office to department, from department to stores, from stores to another office and then perhaps the sick-bay and then another department. Signing for this, signing for that, getting a stamp on this, producing your paybook for that. At the outset he was given the usual 'station-card' and this went with him to be stamped or signed by all departments. The position would be reversed when he departed.

He saw the dentist, the doctor, the drafting officer, the divisional officer and numerous other officials until at last it was all over. Not only that, he was free for the rest of the day. The doctor had put him on light duties until his medical documents came through which meant he did virtually nothing in fact.

After lunch he went for a swim in the adequate pool at the far end of the base. He later basked in the glorious sunshine and felt on top of the world. He had been instructed to report to the galley next day and so relaxed while he may.

He had collected his big kit-bag and hammock from the baggage stores, they had been deposited there by his ship's officers in case he did not return to Consort. They'd been there since he had first been unable to rejoin her.

That evening, he sorted out his white cook's uniform ready for the next day and hung it on the clothes-line outside the billet. It had a stale musty smell clinging to it and needed a good airing.

Next morning, feeling strangely out of touch, he reported to the chief cook and got a pleasant surprise. In spite of having been placed on light duties, he did not expect this to carry any weight.

What a pleasure it was to discover this was not to be so. Instead, he found himself placed in charge of a duty watch which consisted of half a dozen Chinese and Malay cooks. All he was expected to do was to keep his eye on them and to see they did their job correctly. It did not end there. This particular watch had commenced its turn of duty the previous day and so it went off duty at lunch time. He had only four hours to worry about this day. He was soon out there by the pool once more.

After tea, Benny wrote to his mother. He reasoned it was long past due. He had waited until he was able to write truthfully that he was well and fit and had no wish to worry his dear mother before by writing and he had no wish to worry her now by not writing. She was bound to worry regardless, all mothers do.

Having completed the letter, he considered now was as good a time as any to write to his Eurasian miss. What had he got to lose? In the letter, he explained that he would be stuck at Sultan for a good few days at least but for security reasons was unable to say why. Then, he added what he had thus far written of the poem. This being the sum total to date: 'When first I saw her, then saw I the light of day, and all the heartaches and the tears of bygone years, were swept away.'

He read it over to himself, softly, poetically, dramatically. It pleased him. He liked what he had done. It did not really matter what others may think, he felt it was good. He hoped Linda liked it though, even if it had not been truly composed for her.

He sealed the envelopes and getting to his feet, stretched leisurely, then took a steady stroll to the pillar-box. Popping the letters in, he checked the time and continued his stroll, this time in the direction of the Fleet Canteen where many thirsty matelots were already warming up for another memorable session.

Two days had passed without incident when Benny was informed someone wished to see him at the main gate. Completely at a loss, he felt it only right to clean himself up a little, after all, it may be some-one of importance. He had just finished his watch at three-thirty, now it was almost four as he rushed about tidying himself up. He had a most uneasy feeling as he hurried down the drive towards the gate a little later.

Approaching the gate, he automatically went towards the sentry intent on asking who it was wished to see him and where were they? He stopped dead in his tracks when a sweet voice he knew called his name.

He whipped round and there, getting out of a huge American car, was Linda. He cried her name, struggling to grasp what was happen-ing, as she came to him, laughing that soft gentle laugh at the aston-ished surprise written all over him.

"Don't tell me you're sorry I came Benny," she teased. Oblivious of the ogling sentries she reached up and kissed him on the cheek. Benny stood there open eyed, open mouthed, rooted to the spot.

"I received your delightful letter yesterday and knew how desper-ately lonely you must be so, I decided to do something about it and here I am." She smiled so prettily and impishly he wanted to take her in his arms. "Besides Benny dear, I'm lonely too, and I've missed you."

At last he found his tongue. "I don't believe it, I just don't believe it," he said and his countenance reflected his words.

She pouted like a child but she smiled with her eyes, toying with him. "But it's true Benny, really. You would never believe how much I have missed you."

"No, I didn't mean I didn't believe you," to hell with it, he thought. He took her by the shoulders and kissed her. "I meant I didn't believe you were really here in the flesh, you." He had embarrassed her slightly by this sudden show of affection and he stood back to admire her. "I just don't know what to say. You look nice enough to eat, I know that, I expect I shall wake up in a minute and find it's all a flip-pin' dream."

"Do I look like a dream then?" she asked, a twinkle in her eye.

"My God yes, I'll say you do," he glanced uneasily at the matelots on the gate wondering what they were thinking. As he spoke he tried to reason things out. The big car was by far too luxurious and stately to be a taxi. And then there was the liveried chauffeur.

He realised Linda was saying something to him. "I said are you really pleased to see me?"

"Yes, of course I am," he smiled a fond smile. "It's just that you took me completely by surprise, I was having nightmares wondering who wanted to see me and what was wrong. You were the last person I expected."

"Is it possible for you to get away Benny?" she asked placing a hand on his arm and staring up at him with that demure, pleading look.

"Well, yes I can as a matter of fact, I've just finished my duty-watch and I'm off till tomorrow mornin' now, why?"

"Oh, that's wonderful," she cried with excitement. "Come along then, let's not waste a minute," she took his arm and made to lead him towards the car.

"Whoa! 'old on." He resisted and spread his hands indicating his clothes. "I can't go anywhere dressed like this." He had another, very sound reason indeed, for holding back. There was the inescapable question of finance. Benny hadn't a clue where she might intend they should go or what it was she meant for them to do but one thing was for sure. He did not have the kind of funds to support her apparent lifestyle.

"I shall give you thirty minutes then, no more," she wagged a finger under his nose. "And if you are not here by then, I shall come in and fetch you."

Heaving a sigh, Benny shook his head. "But you don't understand." He could hardly confess most of his pay, small as it was, had gone to swell the profits of the Fleet Canteen. Besides, if she knew he was almost a pauper she would probably make a swift exit from his life and that he did not want. She read his thoughts.

"But Benny, please, it is my treat," there she was, pleading with those lovely dark eyes again. "I am asking you to come out, you are not asking me. I shall take care of everything, I want to, please, for me?"

"But Linda ..." he felt trapped.

"No buts Benny," she interrupted.

"It just doesn't seem right, that's all."

She opened her handbag and took out a large purse. From this she withdrew a roll of Malayan dollars and the embarrassed Benny stole a quick glance at the matelots on the gate. What was she playing at? She had obviously come prepared for this.

"Benny, would you sell me something if you had something I wanted to buy?" she asked replacing the purse and closing the handbag, the dollars still in her hand.

"It all depends on what it was you wanted to buy," he told her, determined not to implicate himself. That was not to say he minded the idea of being paid to make love, especially to someone who so disturbed him anyway.

"I am sure you will sell me what I want Benny so please, take this money now and I will tell you what it is later when we are in the car." She went to thrust the roll of notes into his hand but he moved it away.

He stared at her, bewildered. "Don't be silly Linda, what kind of a fool do you take me for? What in 'eaven's name could I possibly 'ave to sell that is worth that kind of money?"

She shook her head. "You are not making things easy for me are you Benny? Why don't you trust me?" She softened again and pleaded once more with those dark sapient eyes. "What I want is worth this money, more even, honestly, and I certainly don't think you are a fool." She saw the look of disbelief still. "For goodness sake Benny, believe me, what must I do to convince you?" He stared back at her, unsure. "Money is no problem to me, especially a little amount like this. Oh come on Benny, we're wasting so much precious time, trust me."

"Alright, I'll be back in twenty minutes," and off he went, not at all certain that what he was about was the correct thing to do. Trouble was, she was so damned alluring, what with that perfume and her body-clinging dress and figure.

"I'll be waiting," she called after him, watching him up the drive. He had not taken the money and she retained it in her hand for him as she made her way to the car and got in, her every move studied by the matelots on duty at the gate and not for reasons of security.

That was not the only shock in store for Benny that evening. As he reclined in the plush luxury of the magnificent automobile, Linda informed him what she had in mind for them to do.

Her father, she explained, was an extremely wealthy man, his fortune in the millions, he was part-Chinese, part-Portuguese, her paternal grandfather being full blooded Portuguese. Her mother, like Linda herself, had been a Eurasian beauty. Her grandfather had left his only son a string of business ventures which the son continued to build upon until now he owned businesses in Kuala Lumpur, Singapore, Hong Kong, Formosa and Borneo, including a thriving import-export concern. He also 'dabbled' most successfully, in the stock-market and shipping world. Linda had actually been to Kuala Lumpur on business for her father when Benny met her.

As the car cruised along, she told him what she proposed to do. She wished to buy him suits and clothes and various trimmings for him to wear and to give him sufficient money, plus a little extra, to pay all the bills incurred whilst they were out together. All this of course for a price.

Benny sat there in a trance as she put her ideas to him. His jumbled brain getting more jumbled by the second. What, he waited to hear, was the price he was expected to pay?

The price was simply his companionship. In return for the financial side of things, he was to be her escort and friend, nothing more. He knew there had to be a catch. There was. The relationship must remain purely platonic. Benny knew it! Just when he thought he had it made, she dropped this damned bombshell.

Her father had fixed her up with an 'arranged' marriage with one of her father's business associates. She could refuse of course but that simply meant being disowned and disinherited but in any case, it was simply not done. Parents' wishes were really orders, and parents were always obeyed. Benny failed to understand all this.

Linda explained what she asked was all plain and straight forward. She confessed that she had been impressed by his frank and open manner, not at all to be compared with that of those supercilious clots she was normally compelled to socialise with. Her father's wishes also.

"It's all quite simple really Benny," she told him but he did not see it simple at all. "I like you a very great deal, you know that, but we can never be more than good friends." Where had Benny heard that before?

She went on, trying to be honest, both with herself and him. "You could never afford to keep me in the luxury I am used to and I know I would never settle down to being an ordinary, everyday, housewife. I have been waited-on all my life."

"Yes, I'm sure you 'ave," said Benny, his sarcasm striking home,

"Oh Benny, please don't take it like that. You know what I say is true. I'm not denying I have been spoilt if you like," she was pleading again but now her eyes were sad, she was in earnest as she twisted round in her seat to gaze at him. "I just would not know how to cope with such things as dirty dishes and laundry and housework."

He saw the logic of what she said. "I'm sorry Linda, I guess you're right," he said with a smile that did not come from within.

"You know I'm right Benny, but that does not mean we can't be very dear friends, does it?"

"So that's what you want to buy from me is it, my companionship and my friendship?"

"No! Please don't put it like that," she had turned to face him and was sitting on her knees in her seat, sideways on.

"Linda," he looked at her, aching to take her in his arms as always but fighting back the desire. "My friendship is not, and never has been for sale. I 'ave never believed you can buy friendship. Friendship is something offered and taken freely. What kind of friend would I be if I was only a friend as long as the money kept coming? That's not friendship for goodness sake."

"But I don't wish to buy your friendship Benny, I just want you, as my dear kind friend, to share some of the good things in life with me. I want to buy you fine clothes and take you to see shows, eat in the best restaurants, travel in style with me, all as presents, gifts ... oh!" She sat round in her seat properly as if giving up. "I like you so much, you know that." She sat facing him again. "I just want to look after you, that's all."

"Why didn't you say so in the first place?" he grinned, giving up the fight he had no doubt intended to give up in the first place.

"Oh you!" She threw her arms around his neck and kissed him. "You will carry the money for me as my ... oh what is the word?"

"What word are you looking for?"

"You know, the one who holds the purse strings." She nestled her head on his chest.

"Purser?" he suggested.

She sat up to look at him, her face alight. "Yes, that's it. You shall be my purser." With that, she dropped the roll of notes in his lap and sat round properly in her seat. Mission accomplished!

Benny had other ideas. "Not so fast young lady," he said, picking the money up to drop it in her lap. "I thought we agreed, my friendship is not for sale."

"But this is not for your friendship silly, I told you, I want to buy something from you," she picked up the money and went to return it to his lap but he caught her wrist, stopping her.

"I'm not takin' the money till I know what it's for, an' I might not take it then," he said holding her wrist well away from his lap.

She laughed. "My goodness me, you are different aren't you? Any other man I know would have taken it without a second thought."

"Very well then, if you insist, I want to buy that poem from you."

"You want what?" he could not believe it. This girl was so full of damned surprises. After the initial shock, Benny burst out laughing.

"Don't you dare to laugh at me Benny Stretton," she laughed back, making a grab at his hair intending to pull it hard.

"You must 'ave more flippin' money than sense," he told her, always remembering to hold his language in check. What would she say if she knew who had inspired the poem? He played her along. "'Ow can I take financial reward for something that springs from the heart?" That at least, he consoled himself, was the truth. "You can 'ave it for free, with my love an' best wishes," he told her chuckling.

"But I do not want you to give it to me," she persisted. "And what if I do have more money than sense? It is my money so I can do what I like with it."

"Now you just listen to me Linda," he was being totally dominant. "I 'ave no intention of takin' the money so you can forget the idea, alright? If, and it's a big if, I do manage to finish the poem, nothin' would give me greater pleasure than for you to 'ave it as a token of our friendship. My gift to a very beautiful friend."

"Benny Stretton, you great big flatterer you," she cried hugging him. Whether he was flattering or not, Benny did not say.

He did spend the next few hours enjoying her bubbling personality and being wined and dined by her before returning to the mundane world of Sultan.

CHAPTER FIFTEEN

After this, they went almost everywhere together whenever Benny had time off. They visited the cinema, the racetrack, went on picnics, sightseeing trips, boating, cycling, hiking, swimming. They were even to be seen wining and dining at the renowned Raffles Hotel in Singapore, she in her exclusive gowns, he in one of the immaculate suits she had bought for him.

Sometimes she would take him to her home. A very grand house on the outskirts of Singapore. It was situated in a most secluded and delightful spot, resting on the slopes of a tree-covered hill, surrounded by lovely and beautifully planned gardens.

Here, Benny would take a hot bath followed by a cool shower and would then dress in the clothes which a manservant had carefully laid out for him. He was living like a lord.

It didn't last. Just two weeks after his arrival at H.M.S. Sultan word came that he was to fly up the coast in a naval helicopter to rejoin Consort. The news devastated both of them.

The news was that Haggis had met with a nasty accident and the ship's captain had sent out an urgent call for his other cook. Benny was to take only the minimum of kit and was to report to the drafting office forthwith.

He had phoned Linda with the news and now sat waiting outside the regulating office for the transport that was to take him to the airfield. He had not really had time for it to sink in, it had all happened so quickly. No doubt about it now, he would soon be back aboard with his shipmates. The strident tones of a phone ringing reached out through the open windows of the office to startle Benny just when he felt himself dozing off.

It turned out to be the sick-bay, demanding that Benny Stretton report at once. "Now what the bloody 'ell's gone wrong?" he cursed.

He was in for a shock for when he got there he found the medical officer in a foul mood to say the least. It transpired that he had been trying to get hold of Benny all morning. While Benny had been getting a clearance stamp in one part of the sick-bay, the officer had been trying to contact him by phone in another.

For some reason, the medical history sheets appertaining to Benny's case had been delayed and had arrived at Sultan that very morning.

Having scanned through them, the M.O. immediately began arrangements for Benny to see a psychiatrist at the military hospital in Singapore. Until he had been thoroughly examined, the doctor flatly refused permission for Benny to perform any duties whatsoever. As for returning to Consort, this was "absolutely out of the question!"

So it was that some other member of the cookery branch of the Royal Navy found themselves being airlifted to the destroyer.

Benny decided to wait until after his appointment before telling Linda the news. The authorities wasted no time and he saw the psychiatrist the very next day. He was bombarded with questions, some of which, on the face of things, had no bearing on his case at all. There were questions like, "Do you still have the violent headaches?" and "Are you still studying hard in the hope of matriculating?" Benny had long since completely forgotten about all this as it happened. He was asked what sort of life he had as a child. How did he feel about life now? Did he get depressed easily? How many brothers and sisters did he have? What the hell would they be asking next?

At the end of it all, the specialist informed him that in view of the reports he had studied, the conclusions he had reached during the examination and the fact that the headaches had occurred several times since, he was recommending to the medics at Sultan that Benny be allowed to remain at the shore base for at least six months in order that he may build himself up, physically and mentally. He was also quite concerned over the headaches and wanted to see if anything developed from these.

"I wonder young man," he said to Benny, "if you realise how ill you were? I'm going to recommend that you perform only nominal duties, at least for the time being and you are to cease all studying at once. Have you got that?"

Benny said that he had indeed. The specialist suggested that he get all the outdoor activity and exercise he could. "Swimming, football, badminton, things like that, and of course plenty of sunshine." That then, was that. The ship's cook could not believe what was happening. Not that he minded, naturally. It was just that he did not feel all that ill.

Back at Sultan it was readily agreed that his duties were only nominal. He knew that if he did any less he would be doing absolutely nothing. It now appeared, Linda willing, that he would be continuing to live the high life.

He now needed to make regular visits to the sick-bay for his vitamin pills and tablets and get his medical and weight checks. Otherwise, it was precisely the same as before.

There was, of course, the inclusion of healthy activity to be added. He found himself thoroughly enjoying, football, cricket and hockey. He also joined a very enthusiastic weight-lifting club. There were only four members and they had some grand moments. Two of them entered the 'Mr Bodybuilder of Singapore' contest and when the day arrived, Linda joined them, bringing along some of her female friends to support and cheer them on.

It was held at the 'Happy World', one of several amusement centres in Singapore. These complexes included dance areas, coffee bars, Chinese theatres, boxing arenas, arenas for wrestling and stalls offering all sorts of items and opportunities.

Quite a cheer went up from the assembled servicemen when the girls taking part in the 'Miss Singapore' contest paraded in bikinis up and down the stage. All in good fun of course.

Benny considered most of these girls had reasonable features, some being quite pretty, some very attractive, some classical beauties but, in the main, they had no bust. Legs left something to be desired too. There were thin, spindly legs, bow legs and some gave the impression of having been the victim of childhood rickets.

Linda and Benny had a wager between themselves. He fancied a little miss from Malaya to win but Linda selected a Chinese maiden as her winner. They were both wrong. The winner was a Eurasian.

The man elected 'Mr Bodybuilder' was of Portuguese extraction.

His win was most pleasing to Linda and put her in such high good spirits that she immediately insisted on treating them all to a slap-up do at the Cathay building. When one of Benny's mates was elected runner-up she promptly added a magnum of champagne to the promised bill of fare.

They wined and dined and danced until the early hours. Alone with Linda in the car later, Benny was so happy and content from the mixture of wine and having such a grand time, that he took her in his arms and kissed her tenderly.

She accepted this kiss and even returned it but when Benny began to get that little bit too passionate she pushed him away from her.

"No Benny, don't, please," she cried.

"Why the 'ell not for goodness sake?" he asked. "Surely to God Linda, you must 'ave some warm blood in you?"

"Please don't get angry, you know I have warm blood, and feelings," she was as much afraid of herself as she was of him.

Benny was exasperated. He sat back, arms folded, stared at the roof of the car and hissed, "This is bloody ridiculous, it really is. 'Ow in God's name can you expect to keep turnin' me on all the damned while and yet sit 'ere like a cold bloody potato. I've grown that fond of you and my piggin' body aches for you like nobody's business. What am I supposed to do when you're sittin' right beside me, all warm an' invitin' an' your bloody perfume gettin' up my soddin' nose drivin' me silly for you?"

He spoke to the car roof, grim and determined. "Not only that, it doesn't 'elp when you're blood's hotted up wi' all that blasted wine." He did turn to stare at her now. "What the 'ell's wrong with you for Christ's sake? Ain't you got any sex in your system? You're not a bleedin' lesbian are you? Or nothin' else but a prick teaser?"

That did it! She swung her hand round and slapped him full across the mouth. He never flinched. She glared, her eyes spitting fire. "How dare you swear at me like that!" She reached across him and swung open the car door. "Get out!" she ordered. "Go on, get out!"

"I'm bloodywell goin' don't worry, I've taken all I can from you. All the strain of sittin' by you, achin' for you, desirin' you. You must think I'm made of bleedin' marble. I'm made of bloody flesh and bone an' I can't take any more of this strugglin' to keep myself in check an' mindin' my manners, I've 'ad it up to 'ere Miss Guiterrez, good soddin' night!" and with that Benny made his exit.

The car was parked on a road overlooking the moonlit sea and he stomped off in the general direction of the barracks. The wine had left him fuzzy headed but he was determined not to let either that or the girl get the better of him.

As he strode resolutely on, he listened for the car engine to start up but it didn't. "Oh well," he decided, "that's up to 'er." He had been pounding along some four or five minutes, not quite so determined now as at the outset. He was beginning to cool off for one thing and he did not have the energy for another.

Linda too had cooled down. She told her chauffeur to start the car and follow behind Benny slowly. She could just make him out up ahead. After a short spell of this she instructed the chauffeur to drive slowly past the now plodding Benny.

The cook set his jaw and pretended the car did not exist. The rage had left him now but he was still determined he had had enough of this cold, unfeeling female.

Linda was feeling sorry now. She was not used to this sort of behaviour but she cared so much for the poor fool stupidly walking when he should be riding with her. They travelled side by side for several hundred yards. Suddenly the car shot forward to stop up in front of the ship's cook. Linda stepped out onto the make shift pavement and stood there, her arms akimbo, determined to bar his way.

He made to walk around her but each time he changed direction she stepped in front of him, both neither speaking or caring to look at one another.

Then, without a word, Benny reached out and grabbed her and placed her to one side out of his way, ignoring the struggles and kicks. "You great big obstinate oaf you!" She yelled. A growl of frustration came from her and she ran after him, catching him up, she was just as determined as he.

She walked awkwardly beside him, the uneven ground causing her to stumble and trip as she strove to keep up. After only a few yards Benny stopped and turned to face her.

"Just what sort of game do you think you are playing?" he growled, fighting the urge to pull her to him.

"Since I am responsible for you being so far away from your barracks I feel obliged to offer you a lift back, that's all, you obstinate fool!" Her tone was one of defiance. "I suppose you realise it is at least eight miles away?"

"That's my problem, not your bugger!" Damn! He had not meant to swear again. He was hoping she was softening up and would tell him she was sorry.

"It is my problem," she certainly did not appear to be softening, her voice told him she would never give in. "I can be just as pig-headed as you and if you do not get in the car I shall walk all the way back with you!"

"That's up to you!" he snapped back. Just who did she think she was? He stomped off leaving her to it.

She came after him, finding it hard to keep up with his long strides. His shoes were far better suited to the going than her's. She cried out in pain as she stubbed her toe and all but fell headlong.

Benny stopped. "Why the 'ell don't you give up for Christ's sake. You ain't got a cat in 'ell's chance of keepin' up with me, especially in those damned shoes. All you're doin' is makin' a bloody fool of yourself." He turned and strode off angrily. Yet hell! He did so want her.

"My shoes are no problem," she called after him. To prove the point she snatched them off and tossed them through the car window. The man at the wheel did not even blink. He merely hugged the kerb, keeping a short but discreet distance behind the argumentative pair.

Barefoot now, Linda ran off after Benny yet again, even more determined. There were tears of anger in her eyes, she was used to having her own way but this was not the real reason she was so persistent. She had got so involved with this sailor she feared to lose him.

Benny waited for her to catch up. "You're a stubborn bitch," he began when she caught him with an almighty slap across the mouth for the second time.

"Well?" he said coldly. "Feel any better now?"

"Yes!" she yelled, eyes blazing.

Without warning he reached out and opened the car door. Before she realised what he was up to he had grabbed hold of her, lifting her up and had unceremoniously tossed her inside and slammed the door shut. He could have sworn he saw the flicker of a smile on the face of the chauffeur.

He had walked no more than half a dozen yards when he heard the car door open and slam shut. Damn the woman, she was walking beside him again.

"I have told you Benny Stretton," she fumed. "I shall walk every step of the way with you."

He lengthened his stride and was soon pulling ahead. "Alright then," she yelled after him. She beckoned her driver to her and called to him through the open window. "Kim, keep up with that fool and don't you dare to let him out of your sight," she ordered.

"Kim will stay with you, you ... you mulish moron you!" She waved her fist at his back. "Don't you worry, I shall keep walking, I'm not afraid to be on my own, it will serve you right if someone murders me. You will have to live with the thought for the rest of your life, I won't care."

"If that ain't typical of a blasted woman," Benny thought. "Make a man feel a louse and he is bound to weaken."

He stopped and turned round to see where she was. Poor Linda was quite some way behind. Should he walk towards her? No! Let her walk to him. He waited.

"You really mean to walk all the way don't you?" he said icily.

"You know I do Benny," she told him fighting back the tears. Seeing her disconsolate state, he could resist no longer.

"Aw what the 'ell," he sighed opening the car door. "For God's sake get in before I change my mind." He held the door for her and then went around to get in the opposite side.

Neither spoke on the journey to Sultan but both of them longed to. At the gates Benny let himself out and without a word closed the car door and made his way up the drive without looking back. Not until he heard the car pulling away did he succumb to temptation and turn and cursed himself for the idiot he was.

Over the next few days Linda did her best to contact Benny but he deliberately avoided her. He did not reply to letters. He read them and dearly wanted to see her again but deep down he knew it was futile and took the hard way out to make it easier in the long run. His mates told her over the phone that he was on duty or had gone away or whatever other excuse sprang to mind.

On the fifth day after the quarrel, Benny was summoned before his divisional officer.

"What have you been up to Stretton?" asked the officer when Benny stood before him. Try as he might, he could think of nothing he had done for as far back as he could remember, that warranted this meeting.

"Well Stretton? I'm waiting," the officer's words jolted him out of his efforts at recalling. "It so happens Stretton, that I have here a letter from a gentleman named Guiterrez ..." Benny's heart dropped into his feet and the blood drained from him, "... concerning you."

"Me sir?" Benny struggled to find his voice. He had never seen Linda's father, not once in all the time he had known her. Was something wrong with her? He was vaguely aware of the officer talking to him.

"What was that sir?" he asked with a strangled sound.

"Hmmm!" The D.O. continued. "It would appear you are a friend of this gentleman's daughter and he desires to make your acquaintance, Stretton. Insists that you call at his residence in point of fact."

"Excuse me sir, I don't know why 'e should write to you an' not to me sir."

"From the context of this letter Stretton," the D.O. waggled the letter, "it appears Mister Guiterrez has been trying to get in touch with you but for some odd reason ..." he looked at Benny suspiciously "... seems his daughter is, well, ill. Haven't been getting into mischief have we Stretton, is that why her father is unable to get hold of you?"

"No sir, I give you my word that nothing has gone on between Miss Guiterrez and me."

"You are quite sure now?" the divisional officer knew what these young matelots were like. "Quite sure you have not 'rung her bell'?"

Benny coloured up at this. Did this nosy damned officer know something? If Linda was in the club, it certainly wasn't his child she was having. "I'm positive sir," he told the officer. "We 'ave never been together in that way sir, ever."

"Well, be that as it may, his car will be waiting for you at six-forty five this evening, alright? You're not on watch, I've already checked that. Whatever happens now is up to you Stretton but don't you dare let the Service down." The D.O. held the letter for Benny to take. "You had better take this."

"Thank you sir," said Benny. He replaced his cap, saluted, smartly about-turned and made his exit.

He thought six-forty five would never come. His nerves were on edge as he waited at the gate for the car to arrive and he turned up early too. The car arrived and he sat beside the chauffeur for a change. Benny tried to engage him in conversation but, despite speaking excellent English, Kim declined to talk about Linda.

When they arrived, Benny was ushered into the library and asked to wait. The old Chinaman who led him into the library had said, "They will not keep you waiting long sir."

Maybe not, but to the anxious and agitated Benny it seemed long. He glanced at the rows of books lining all four walls. "Bloody 'ell," thought the ship's cook. "There's more books 'ere than in Nuneaton library."

He had his back to the door, studying a row of encyclopedias and did not see or hear it open. "Hello Benny dear, I'm so glad you have come."

He swung round to see Linda standing there. He stood staring at her, not believing she was really so close at last. He had to clear his throat before he dared to speak but it still came out wrong. "Your father sent for me. What does 'e want me for? And don't tell me you don't know." My God, she looked ravishing.

She stood just inside the door, looking down at her feet she told him her father was in Hong Kong. She dare not look up.

"But 'e can't be, 'e wrote a letter to the barracks... I've got it 'ere, the D.O. had me on the carpet about it..." he fumbled to find the letter.

"I wrote the letter Benny, not my father," she still dare not trust herself to look up.

"You wrote it? But why?" he really should have guessed.

Without looking up she came across the room to stand just in front of him. She was much too close for his liking. "I had to see you Benny, I've been so miserable, so lonely not seeing you, being with you. Writing that letter was the only way I knew of getting to you."

"Oh my God!" thought Benny. His knees trembled, a powerful current coursed through him. He looked down at her and said simply, "I've been lonely myself but I thought you were ill otherwise I wouldn't 'ave come."

"If you came because you thought me ill it shows you care for me," she said, fishing for more.

"You know I care for you," he told her quietly struggling to keep a grip on his emotions. "I don't think you realise just 'ow much."

"I think I do dear," she said.

"You can't bloody well know," he insisted, kicking himself for swearing.

"Please don't swear, it cuts me like a knife when you do, it really does."

"You're enough to make an angel swear with all your tantalisin' an' teasin' an' ..." he tried to find the word. He gave up, "...everythin'."

"But if we both feel this way, why do we quarrel?" she looked at him, those dark brown eyes tugging at his feelings.

"Aw come off it. You know why we quarrel. It sticks out a mile that we love each other yet just because your old man say's he'll stop your money you won't marry me, instead you're goin' to marry some ponce you ain' even seen yet. But the real trouble stems from the fact that I'm supposed to behave like a cold blooded celibate. Well for your information Linda I'm not cold blooded an' I ain't celibate either nor am I a gentleman I suppose, I get far too many ideas about you and me."

She stood away from him and without looking at him said quietly. "Do you need sex so badly Benny?"

Her words caught him off guard. "I didn't say anythin' about needin' sex," he wore a hurt expression. "What I need is you. I want to make love, yes, but only to you. Physical love, sex if you like, should be the fulfilment of spiritual love, the two go 'and in 'and."

"Benny please, answer me a plain yes or no," she looked at the floor with embarrassment. "Do you want sex?"

Where was all this leading? "Ah well," he thought, "in for a penny, in for a pound," and so he said bluntly, "Yes, of course I do."

"I see," she said very quietly. "I have a friend Benny, a very dear friend. Her husband is an invalid, has been for some years," her voice was toneless, as if she read from a book, fearing to hear the words come out. "He is quite incapable of making love to her, we ... we had a long talk about it and I know she would let you make love to her Benny. I could arrange a meeting for you. I don't mind ..." She saw the look on his face and stopped.

He stood there aghast. "I'm not sure I'm 'earin' right am I?"

She blushed deeply, acutely aware of the embarrassing situation she had created for herself. "But don't you see?" she cried. It would mean you and I could go on seeing each other, just like we did before, only now you could, well, you ..." she had difficulty putting it into words. "... you could visit my friend whenever you felt the need to ... relieve yourself ... I mean your feelings ... your urge to make love to me would be cooled then and there would be no problem when we were together." Her voice had trailed off almost to a whisper.

Benny stood there, staring back at her, his face a picture of confusion and utter disbelief at what he was hearing. "You're mad!" he hissed. "Right out of your tiny little mind." Disgusted at what she suggested, he glared at her. "Just what sort of a bloke do you think I am eh? What the 'ell do you take me for, for God's sake? Jesus wept woman, if you don't take the bloody biscuit I don't know who does."

He stormed towards the door but before he reached it she ran past and with her back to it barred the way. "Please Benny!" She was pleading with those damned dark eyes. "I'm sorry, truly I am. Please don't go."

He sighed. "For God's sake Linda. The most important thing to me is the way I feel about you. Sure I want sex as you put it. But only with you, can't you understand that for 'eaven's sake? I'm in love with you dammit, not your lovesick mate, let 'er get some other mug, I'm not the least bit interested. You're the one I want. I would marry you like a shot an' be 'appy to spend the rest of my days with you."

He paused. "Besides, if I merely wanted sex I'm quite capable of gettin' my own women thank you." He groped for the right word, "You can stuff your mate an' any other female you might be got in mind."

"I said I was sorry," she told him, tears trickling down her cheeks. "I want you too, Benny but I'm to be married."

"But you don't even know the damned bloke, you've never met 'im, what sort of a stupid marriage is that? Nothin' more than a marriage of bloody old fashioned convenience."

"It goes on all the time Benny, even in your country. People all over the world get married for all kinds of reasons other than love." She still had her back to the door, leaning on it, one knee raised so that the sole of her foot rested on a door panel.

He ached to crush her to him, every part of him cried out for her but he hung on. "I just don't understand why we can't share the love we 'ave, even if you are marrying this geezer. Why shouldn't you 'ave some love in your life? 'Ow are you to know, you may never ever get another chance of love."

Somebody had to make her see sense. Why should she throw herself away like this without ever knowing the fulfilment of love? "And that's another thing. Have you stopped to think 'ow many women this client must 'ave 'ad in 'is life? I'll lay you odds 'e 'asn't gone short. Huh! 'E's probably got some woman in bed with 'im right this minute for all you know."

"How can you be so cruel Benny?" all the fight had long since gone. Nothing seemed to matter anymore.

"It's the truth an' you know it, besides, it's life that's cruel, not me, all I know is you're a long time dead so why bury yourself before your time?" He spoke in earnest tones now, trying to get Linda to see the sense of what he said. "You've got no right to throw your life away on some old fuddy-duddy."

"He won't be an old fuddy-duddy," she said quietly, staring at the carpet.

"Of course 'e will, bound to be." He paused trying to catch her eyes by bending slightly and turning his head to look up at her. She turned away. "The old bugger might even be older than your own dad. Fancy buryin' yourself away wi' somebody who might be ready for a wheel-chair." He sensed she was weakening and changed his tone. "Linda love, you know 'ow we feel about each other, why shouldn't we 'ave our love? It ain' as if I don't want to marry you, I do but you say I can't. Oh darlin', why can't we at least share our love while we 'ave the chance?"

"Because I'm scared to, can't you see that?" she blurted out, staring at him angrily. "I'm scared that we'll fall so much in love we won't be able to part when the time comes."

"Good! Then maybe we can get married instead of you an' that geezer your old man 'as picked for you."

"My father would never allow it Benny, I've told you, you don't know him."

"Huh! If 'e's as bad as 'e sounds, I don't want to know 'im either." He thought of another angle. "Besides, if you've missed me so much over these last few days, you must love me a lot now anyway, so what's the odds?"

She was staring down at her feet as she said, "I do love you, I love you so much it hurts."

"Well, there you are then, we've got nothing to lose by sharing our love fully." She still hesitated. God! If she felt as he did there would be no problem, he yearned to take her warm sensuous body in his arms and to expend all the pent up passion she created within him. To shower her with kisses, to show her the love he had known for so long but had been forbidden to display.

Unable to resist her another moment he reached out to take her in his arms but instantly her hands were on his chest warding him off.

"Jesus Christ woman, what the 'ell do you think I am?" he reached for the door handle meaning to get away from her. "You're drivin' me up the bloody wall with wantin' you an' I can't take any more."

They struggled with each other as he sought to open the door, she to see it remained closed. Benny's inflamed desires almost took control as her body and his made contact and he had to stand away from her.

"Benny," she spoke his name with disarming tenderness and she gazed into his eyes in a way that drove him wild and he had to look away. She reached out gently to turn his head, forcing him to look at her. "Does it really mean so much to you ... our making love?"

"'Ow many more times must I spell it out for you for God's sake?" His heart thumped, his pulses raced and his throat was dry as he spoke to her.

"For pity's sake Linda, please try to understand what you're doin' to me. I just can't go on pretending any longer, the constant strain of being with you but not being able to love you is sheer bloody murder. You get me so hot and bothered I don't know what damned day it is, honest, I get so worked up I don't know 'ow I've managed to stop myself ... you're such a desirable woman, dammit!"

"So you think I'm desirable do you Benny?" she asked softly.

"You know damned well you are," he growled.

"Thank you," she said and then taking his hand in hers she added, "come with me my darling."

Benny's expression reflected the confusion he felt within. She had never called him 'my darling' before and as though in a trance he let her lead him out into the impressive hall and up the wide, banistered stairway.

She ushered him into a luxurious bedroom and closed the door behind them, an impish smile on her face. Once inside she moved up close to him, they each felt the other's warm body, bodies that both trembled with anticipated passions. She placed her hands on his shoulders and gazed up into his eyes, her own reflecting the love she felt for him. Benny did not dare to move.

"Well?" she said inviting action.

He cleared his throat and nodded to the bed. "Do you mean ...?" he asked, his voice betraying his feelings.

She placed a finger over his lips. Her words were full of warmth and softly though she uttered them, there was no concealing the passion and love and need of him. She had that pleading appeal in her eyes as she told him, "I want you to love me my darling, please."

Benny, uneasy, hesitated. "But what about the servants, aren't you scared about what they'll think? And suppose they tell your old man?"

"Benny darling, you are a silly, I've given them the night off and I told Kim he could go when he had brought you," she smiled that impish again. "You and I are all alone. We have the house to ourselves."

"'Ey ...You must ...'"

She placed a finger across his lips again. "Darling, don't you see? I planned it this way. I arranged everything so that you and I could be all alone together like this."

"You planned it? I don't get it. What about your sex-starved friend, what would 'ave 'appened if I'd taken you up on your offer?"

She clasped her hands behind his neck and gazed up at him with a confident smile and kissed him lightly on the nose. "There was no friend. I made it all up to see what your reaction would be." She reached up on her toes now and kissed him firmly and passionately on the mouth, taunting him.

"You mean if I 'ad said, 'yes, you would 'ave said to yourself, 'aha, 'ow can 'e really love me when 'e's prepared to take someone else to bed," he marvelled at the workings of her mind. "Is that it?"

"Something like that. I felt sure in my heart that you loved me but I had to be certain, I have so much love to give you I had to know it was going to be returned."

Benny stood there shaking his head in disbelief. Small wonder her father was so successful if he schemed and plotted as she had just done.

274

She pressed her warm, vibrant body close to his. "You are a funny one," she told him, her eyes tormenting the life out of him as much as the nearness of her. "You quarrel with me because I won't let you make love to me and now I am offering myself to you, you stand there spurning me."

"Oh no, Linda, you couldn't be more wrong," he put his arms about her waist. "It's just that I can't believe what's 'appening, that's all, my God, who could ever spurn you love, so warm and wonderful?"

"Then why don't you take me my darling, take me before I change my mind," her voice vibrated with emotion, he could sense the passion within her, aching to be set free. Her lips were moist and inviting as she kissed him, forceful and demanding, her body moving against his. Benny melted. All his doubts, fears, inhibitions, resolutions, were swept away.

Neither of them had any fears or cares now. All reservations were cast aside as they allowed natural instinct to take control. He crushed her to him, returning her kiss with a hungry, greedy passion that had been restrained these past weeks. Linda responded to the full with complete and wonderful abandon.

"'Ow I've longed for this moment. I love you so much. I love you, I love you, I love you."

"And I love you too, my own handsome sailor," she gave a deep sigh of contentment.

"Linda my darlin'," he stood away from her to look down into her eyes. "Is this what you really want? Are you absolutely sure?" He was concerned she may regret later.

"Absolutely positive. I'm only sorry we've wasted so much precious time dearest," and she pulled him back into her arms, nestling her head on his chest, eyes closed.

Kissing the top of her head, he gently and lovingly lifted her up and carried her to the bed. "Be gentle with me darling," she pleaded softly. He answered by tenderly kissing her warm, dewy lips.

"Benny," something in her tone caused him to pause and look at her. "Please Benny, promise me, no baby," she begged.

"I promise you my sweet precious love, no baby."

They remained together in blissful contentment all night, each giving full vent to the love and passion that had for so long been denied.

When the time came for leaving, Linda got the car from the garage and drove him back to H.M.S. Sultan herself. They remained in the car, kissing and holding tight, long after they reached the gate, afraid to part.

With a final kiss, Benny got out of the car and stood waving to his love as she drove away.

Benny chose to completely ignore the inevitable remark of the matelot on duty at the gate. He strode off up the drive at a brisk pace, a man revitalised and rejuvenated. He wanted to shout out to the whole world about his love.

For two delightful, delectable months they loved each other dearly. At times their love would consume them with wild and passionate abandon, other times it was sweet and tender and sometimes they loved with a fierce, consuming intensity that saw their very souls soaring heavenwards. They were intoxicated by their love.

It had to end. They both knew this. Yet they never spoke of it ending. One evening, after a visit to the cinema, they dined at a seclusive little Chinese restaurant and it was towards the end of the meal that Linda dropped the bombshell. Benny had sensed something was wrong but never for one moment did he suspect the truth.

She told him in hushed tones that her father had arrived from Hong Kong and she would be unable to take Benny home with her that night as usual.

"Not to worry my darlin', there will always be other nights," he told her cheerfully. "I thought something was wrong but if that's all it is there's nothin' to worry about is there sweetheart? So stop all this worrying, I still love you as much as ever."

"Yes I know you love me darling and that's the trouble," so quietly he barely heard her words. She stared at her plate as she spoke, afraid to look at him.

"Trouble?" He tried not to let her sense his concern for the way things were going. "It's not a trouble being in love with the most wonderful woman in the world, it's a treasure beyond price to love you." He held her hand in both his across the table, he squeezed it gently but firmly trying to instil confidence and comfort and to cheer her up.

"Forgive me my darling, I didn't want to spoil tonight," she forced a smile she clearly did not feel and with her free hand, reached out and patted his.

"But you're not spoilin' tonight. Just being with you makes it a special night so let's hear no more of this nonsense." He was so falsely chirpy and carefree it rubbed off on Linda and she did cheer up slightly, if only on the outside. "That's more like it my little darlin', now come on, promise me, no more worryin'."

Shortly after this they travelled down a road that Benny did not recognise and it puzzled him. He asked, "Where the devil are you takin' me sweetheart?"

"We are going to a quiet spot that I used to visit with my parents before mummy died. I was only a child but it holds so many precious moments, so many happy memories that I have always longed to come back to it."

She fought back the tears as she spoke. "Tonight, being what it is, I felt I had to come back here, now, with you beside me my darling. I hope you understand." Her voice was charged with emotion.

Benny still sought to brighten up the situation, not daring to believe what he suspected. He put an arm around her shoulders and hugged her gently.

She drove slowly as if hanging on to every minute. She had given Kim a few hours off, after first obtaining his firm assurance that he would not breathe a word to her father. She had arranged for him to meet her at a specific rendezvous at midnight, he would then drive her home leaving her father believing he had been her chauffeur-cum-chaperon all the evening.

When Benny saw the spot Linda held dear, he understood why. It was a perfect haven, situated right on the coast with glorious views of the sea and beyond and gorgeous scenery on every side. In the dim distance he could see sampans and junks set against a backcloth of the Malayan mainland.

After the hustle and bustle of cosmopolitan Singapore, the acute silence of this spot cast its spell upon them both. It was as if nothing else existed. They were all alone in the world with their very special, very precious love.

That night they made love in the car. They made love with great tenderness and emotion. Linda, knowing it to be the last time they would make love, Benny somehow suspecting it. She put up a very brave front but her heart was breaking and she knew it was her own choice, yet what else could she do?

She had explained to Benny earlier that she must be home shortly after midnight since she had led her father to believe that she was at a dance with friends. Normally, young, single girls like herself, would always have a chaperone with them wherever they went, this being the custom but in Linda's case her father permitted more liberty and trusted Kim to keep his eye on her. She told Benny it would be courting disaster if she were to be late and arouse her father's suspicions.

Linda was unable to hold back the tears as they approached Sultan and when Benny went to speak she put her hand across his lips. "No my darling, not a word, please. I could not bear to have you plead with me. Just hold me tightly." The car was stationary and she clung to Benny, sobbing. "I love you sailor boy, I love you," she cried.

They remained embracing, not speaking, not daring to and not caring to and afraid to. At last Linda forced herself to break away. She reached into her handbag and took out a letter which she handed to him. He refused to take it. Shaking his head he said, "No Linda, whatever it is, I don't want it."

She persisted. "Please Benny, take it. It isn't money my darling, honestly. You should know that, it is just a letter that I've written. I want you to promise me you will not open it before tomorrow." She held it out but he did not take it. "Please Benny my darling, it will explain everything much better than I could ever explain now, please take it."

He could promise nothing, his emotions refused him speech. She threw herself into his arms and sobbed and sobbed. Benny stroked her hair with tenderness and suddenly she broke away only to instantly reach for him and to kiss him, a long, last, passionate kiss of farewell.

She broke away a second time, fearful she may yet change her mind. "Please go now my darling," she urged, dabbing her eyes with her handkerchief.

He took the handkerchief from her and dried her eyes. He kissed her on the forehead and forced himself to ask the question he feared he knew the answer to anyway. "What's all this about for 'eaven's sake? Anyone would think I was never goin' to see you again."

She made the excuse that it was long past the time she should have gone. "Benny please darling, I really must go. Read the letter tomor-

row, it will explain everything." She gave him a quick peck and started up the engine. He sensed it would be better to let her go. No point
in causing her further anguish by persisting in getting her to tell him
the truth. He opened the car door and got out.

Linda called softly to him. "Goodbye my precious and God bless
you for everything." She had difficultly finding her voice. "And
Benny darling, you must believe I love you with all my heart, I
always will." She blew him a hurried kiss and sped off leaving Benny
watching until the car was out of sight. She did not turn round or
wave.

Benny stood there many seconds after the car's departure, stunned
and dejected. There was something too in his grim expression which
warned the sentry that it would be wise to say nothing.

During a sleepless night he decided he simply must see his love
again. Damn her old man! What right had he got to ruin his daughter's life? He felt convinced he could persuade her to forsake the marriage of convenience and get her to marry him instead. Why not?

But it was already far too late for Benny to do anything. Even as he
lay there in mental torment Linda was on an aircraft travelling farther
away from him. She read and re-read the poem that he had given her,
tears misting up her eyes as she scanned the lines again and
again.She turned her head to stare out at the darkness beyond the
window of the aircraft, she studied the reflection of herself and recited the poem in her head, words she believed to have been inspired by
herself.

When first I saw her, then saw I the light of day
and all the heartache and the tears of bygone years,
were swept away.
When first I heard her, then heard I the angels sing
and soft sweet music and a love from heaven above,
made me a king.
When first I touched her, then touched I a treasure rare
and all life's blessings and content, so heaven sent.
were our's to share.

As her father slept beside her she prayed that she was doing the right
thing, that her love would understand, that her future would not be

so bleak, that God would look after her lost love, that things might have been so very different. But things were as they were. There was no turning back and she knew it.

She wondered what Benny would feel and what he might do when he opened her letter next day. How was she to know that the matelot had already opened the letter and was sitting on his bed, shattered and numb.

He had tossed and turned and finally, hoping to set his mind at rest, opened the letter. It now lay beside him on the bed. It read,

'Dearly beloved, Please, please forgive me for saying goodbye this way but my darling there is no other way I know of. My father will be waiting for me when I arrive home and we shall be going direct to the airport. My things have all been packed in readiness for the flight and so my dearest sailor boy I shall be in Hong Kong by the time you read this.

'I am to be married in one month's time in Macao. I shall never be able to repay you for all the wonderful, most heavenly times we shared together and I shall never ever stop loving you, no matter what. Thank you for our love. I shall cherish our memories forever and always my precious darling, no one can take these away from us. Please forgive and understand, I am not taking the easy way out, as you may believe, there is no easy way, it is breaking my heart. Goodbye my own true darling, your Linda. P.S. I shall treasure our love and our poem eternally.'

She had added several lines of kisses but Benny was impassive to it all. For several days he moved about in a state of shock. He had lost all desire for anything and everything, life had no meaning, he had no sense of what he was about or what time it was, or even what day it was. He was nothing more than an empty shell. Even the news concerning Consort seemed to fall on deaf ears. His mates were most concerned and covered up for him quite considerably. Sick-bay put it all down to his illness.

It was left to one of his weight-training colleagues to finally bring him out of it. He set his mind to work and got him thinking straight once more. His chum explained that if he did not snap out of it he would never be able to rejoin his ship and that surely to leave Sultan would be the best thing that could happen to him.

He worked on this idea until eventually his words got through and the cook joined him in a little weight-training. It worked wonders and in a few days Benny was on his way to the sick-bay to request permission to rejoin his ship. The M.O. was adamant. He explained that it was essential Benny should derive full benefit from a stay ashore of at least six months and these last few days of apparent depression bore this out. The M.O. did concede one point however. He arranged an appointment with the psychiatrist at Benny's request.

Even here he met with disappointment for the psychiatrist held the view that he would derive far greater benefit by remaining on shore rather than return to his ship. He remarked on how tired Benny looked but Benny swore it was nothing but total boredom. He swore to the specialist that he really was fit and well now and begged to be allowed the return to Consort. Against his better judgement the psychiatrist finally gave him clearance, extracting from him a promise that should he suspect an attack of maleria coming on, he would report it immediately to the shipís medical officer.

All of this happened on the day that H.M.S. Consort steamed down the Straits of Johore and into the Royal Naval Dockyard. Up before the M.O. at Sultan, Benny was told he must wait until his ship had completed a boiler clean and had been provisioned before he would be allowed to rejoin her, all in all, about a week.

The next bit of news came as a most wonderful surprise. He was informed that Consort was to sail from Singapore Island back to England! This was the final tonic he so badly needed. "That should mend my bleedin' 'eart," he told himself but he knew he would never forget her, he did not wish to for she was a cherished memory.

And so, the day dawned when Benny made his last farewells to his friends at Sultan and it was with palpitations that he sat in the launch Consort had sent to pick him up.

"My God Chef," the coxswain greeted him warmly. "I thought you were dead."

"Not me mate," grinned Benny, enjoying the wit. "Take more than what I've been through to kill me off."

"I'll tell you what, you've had the longest run ashore I've ever known." The coxswain gave orders to his crewmen to let go, then returned to Benny. "And I thought it was only going to be for a couple of days or so."

"Yeah, so did I Scouse, so did I," laughed the cook, alive with anticipation now. "I never dreamt I'd be gone all this while, seems like a bloody lifetime don' it?"

"There's one thing about it, you jammy bugger you, you've come back at the right time," the coxswain scanned the waters around them as he spoke. "I suppose you've heard we're off to Blighty first thing in the morning?"

"In the morning? Honest?" Benny's face lit up with delight.

"Honest. Set sail first thing. First stop, Trincomalee." The man at the helm waved to a fellow coxswain whose launch was passing on their port side. "That's the Cossack's launch," he told Benny. "They're all sick as pigs, they thought they'd be going as well but she's got to stop out here a bit longer, something to do with being flotilla leader."

But Benny never really heard. "Bloody 'ell," he gasped, thrilled and overjoyed at the news of starting for home in the morning. He shook his head and grinned fit to burst.

The coxswain shared his grin and pleasure. "Yeah, great ain' it?" he agreed leaning hard on the tiller with his thigh as he steered around a drifting piece of tree trunk.

"Here, what do you think about poor old Haggis then?" asked the coxswain suddenly remembering.

"'Aggis? What's the little Scots git been up to now?" He imagined his colleague had been up to more of his drunken escapades.

The coxswain was surprised that Benny seemed not to know of events. "Didn't you hear about his accident then?" he asked.

"What accident?" Benny no longer grinned, he was concerned for his shipmate.

"He went missing one day and everybody thought he must have fallen overboard but it was so calm and everything and nobody had heard or seen anything and ..."

"What time of the day was it?" interrupted Benny as if this may have some bearing on the matter.

"In the afternoon sometime, anyway, one of the duty-watch went up into the for'ard paint locker after some paint and found Haggis pissed out of his mind."

"I knew it'd 'ave to be somethin' to do with drink," said Benny.

"Yeah, but it weren't drink, it was Bluebell."

"Bluebell?" The ship's cook screwed up his face in disgust and shocked disbelief. Could the coxswain be pulling his leg? "Bluebell?

Metal polish? You're not tryin' to tell me 'e was drinkin' bloody metal polish for Christ's sake are you?"

"He bloodywell was mate," insisted the coxswain. "He downed at least three tins before they found him."

They were in sight of Consort now, lying out in the strait, tied to one of the many buoys.

"'E must 'ave been mental the dozy sod." Benny pulled a face at the thought of anyone trying to drink the vile liquid. "What 'appened when they found what 'e'd done?"

"They whipped the poor bastard off to hospital in Singapore and tried emptying his guts with stomach-pumps and all sorts but it was no good." The coxswain leaned on the tiller hard, having to go against the current.

"Bloody 'ell," gasped Benny. "What 'appened then?"

"He died," said the coxswain so casually. "We buried the poor bastard at sea."

"Bloody 'ell," gasped Benny yet again only this time there was a world of difference in the way he said it. "Poor old 'Aggis," he shook his head sadly. "What a way to go," sighed a saddened Benny.

He went over in his mind the many memories he had of his little Scots shipmate. They were almost alongside now, only yards separating them. He could clearly make out several of his old shipmates as they leaned on the guardrail or walked along the upper-deck.

He saw Chief standing in the galley doorway and they exchanged waves. He spotted Pedlar Palmer, and Smokey and grumpy old Scouse. His mind drifted from thoughts of Alex for the moment.

"Hi!" shouted Pedlar waving, his great voice booming out over the water. "Enjoy your 'oliday?"

"Not 'alf!" Benny wanted to shout back. He could not trust himself for that emotionally disturbed lump threatened to choke him again. Instead he gave his friendly adversary a hearty wave, his waves acknowledged and returned by the growing number of shipmates now lining the rails.

It had been a long trip ashore. He was smiling now as he thought of the tales he could relate to any grandchildren in his old age. And just wait till Pedlar heard about Linda. The thought of her had him looking back to the shore wondering where she was, what she was doing and for one fleeting moment his mind's eye pictured her there.

He glanced down to the large suitcase at his feet containing the expensive suits and clothes and mementoes she had insisted on buying him. He sighed, remembering.

With a gentle bump the launch came to a stop at the foot of the ladder hanging over the ship's side bringing an abrupt end to his reverie. He looked up at the happy faces welcoming him back and as a seaman handed up his case Benny reached for the ladder and began to climb.

"Come on 'ere yer little sod," grinned big Pedlar with one huge hand reaching out to haul his little shipmate aboard. "It's bloody great to 'ave yer back!" He buried Benny's hand in his own shaking it vigorously before rounding off the welcome with a warm hug. Others surged forward to add their own welcome for the ship's cook. He stood there, his eyes and expression reflecting the happy contentment within. His gaze drank in the beauty that was Consort and with tremendous pride he turned to big Pedlar, "Tell you what Ped! It's good to be back," he said, beaming.

Benny knew one thing was certain, it had been one run ashore he would never forget.